Field Guide

Wildflowers of the West Coast Hills

The Plants and Flowers
of the Darling Scarp and Range
in the Kalamunda Shire
The Backdrop to Perth,
Western Australia

by
Members of the
Darling Range Branch
Wildflower Society of Western Australia

Photography by
Brian Tullis

Illustrations by
Margaret Wilson

Published by QPA
Quality Publishing Australia
Revised 2002 Edition
Botanical names updated Aug 2001

ISBN 1-875737-24-3

Bickley Scarp

Gooseberry Hill
National Park

Lesmurdie Scarp

CONTENTS

| Chapter | Page |

1 Use of This Book 4

2 Trees and Tall to Medium Shrubs 9

3 Medium to Small Shrubs 43

4 Scramblers, Climbers and Perchers 97

5 Plants with Grasslike Leaves 109

6 Orchids 143

7 Herblike Plants and Annuals 163

8 Flowering Calendar 209

9 Interesting Snippets 221

10 Parks, Reserves and Walk Trails 229

11 Illustrated Glossary 241

Credits and Acknowledgements 244

Index 245

CHAPTER 1
Use of this Book

There are as many ways of getting to know the plants of an area as individual ingenuity allows. This book provides several avenues. Unquestionably, for the beginner, the technique of thumbing through the colour photographs is both valid and appealing. Accordingly, every effort has been made to feature, in the colour photographs, species which have much of the feel of the group to which they belong. The intention is that by thumbing through these, the reader will either find a photograph of the plant for which a name is sought or one which is recognisable as being related to that plant. From there, the reader can scan the list of related species, noting how their characteristics match the one in hand, till a correspondence in flower colour, time of flowering, and habitat is found.

Another ready means of identifying plants is to use Chapter 8, Flowering Calendar. There, species are listed, by colour of flower and by the months they are usually found flowering. This can narrow the choice considerably, especially outside the main flowering season months of September and October. Reference to the photographs and to the species descriptions will then usually result in an identification.

The main way plant identification has been designed for this book depends on their growth form. That is, whether the plant is a tree, a shrub, a climber, has grass-like leaves, is an orchid or is herb-like. These different kinds of plants are featured in Chapters 2 to 7.

The main distinction is between woody plants (trees and shrubs) and non-woody - that is herbaceous, pliable plants (those with grass-like leaves, orchids, herb-like plants and annuals). A small Chapter separates those plants which scramble over others, climb, grow perched, or even in other plants.

Trees ideally have single trunks or stems, shrubs, several - a useful distinction although exceptions occur. Tall shrubs, an adult looks up to, medium shrubs come between knee and chest height, small shrubs are below knee height. Trees and shrubs are split between Chapters 2 and

3. Should identification prove unsatisfactory in one, the other Chapter should be tried.

Grasslike plants have leaves or green stems coming from a crown near the ground. When their flowers have obvious coloured parts, these are usually in threes (i.e. three or six). Orchids (with one exception) spend the warmer months below ground; their above ground parts are renewed each year. Their flower parts can be in threes or appear as five or variously modified.

Herblike plants and annuals have non grass-like leaves (i.e. not long and strap-shaped or rounded with parallel veins). Their flower parts number two, four, five or more: not threes. Many are very small.

Technical terms have been kept to an absolute minimum. Where unfamiliar terms occur, an explanation of them may be found in Chapter 11, Glossary.

Use of the Plant Identification Chapters (2 to 7)

Each chapter has, after a brief introduction, a table of Groups and Sub-Groups for identifying plants. The main Groups separate species on the basis of whether the flowers are showy, have their petals regularly arranged, have some part other than petals as the showy part, have the flowers clustered into a tight head of flowers or have flowers which are inconspicuous. These Groups are further divided into Sub-Groups depending on how many obvious petals or petal-like parts there are (five, four or threes) and whether these are separate or joined to form a tube when the individual petals may just appear as lobes. The species are organised under each Sub-Group according to flowering months, and alphabetically under that.

Read ALL Alternative Group/Sub-Group descriptions before deciding where your plant belongs. Then go to the page number indicated alongside the Group/Sub-Group. A number of species are described which by comparison with your plant, will allow its identification. If the selection is quite large, a further division allows the alternatives to be narrowed down.

Each species description is laid out in the same way with key information summarised in a two-line heading. The information given is:

Scientific name	Flower colour	Flowering time
Common name	Habitat	How common it is

The scientific name is a latinised description of the plant in two words. The first the genus (plural, genera), the second the species. (See also the following section: The Naming of Plants). An asterisk denotes an introduced plant.

The common name is a name in English by which the plant is known. Because common names vary with region and in the absence of a long tradition of use, comparatively few of the wildflowers have common names, use of common names is of limited value.

Flower colour describes the predominant colour by which the flower is recognisable. (See also Chapter 8, Flowering Calendar).

Habitat describes where the species is usually found. Four general habitats are recognised for the Hills: forest and woodland: shrubland: rock outcrops: streamsides and damp places.

Flowering time indicates which months of the year the bulk of the plants of a species are in flower. Flowering times are taken from records for the Hills over many years. (See also Chapter 8, Flowering Calendar).

How common the species is. Species are ranked on their occurrence in the Hills according to one of five classes: very common, common, uncommon, rare and very rare.

Following the two-line heading, a further few lines describe any notable field characteristics of the species (e.g. for trees, their average height, bark, leaf and gumnut characteristics). Measurements are often given in this description.

The Naming of Plants
Kinds of plants are called species. These, in turn, are found to be more or less closely related. Closely related species are placed together in the next level of grouping called genus (plural: genera). In the scientific name of a plant, two words are given: the first is the genus (the generic name): the second is the name of the species. Often, the species name gives a clue to its identifying characteristic but as with the generic name it is latinised, making scientific names of plants off-putting on first encounter. These names are very advantageous, however, because they provide an identity which can be checked by botanists anywhere in the world.

Naming of plants is carried out by a group of botanists called taxonomists. Taxonomy is an activity which has been going on in its present form since Linnaeus devised the two-name (bi-nomial) system in the eighteenth century. As new techniques of study allow the relationships between plants to be re-examined, the need arises, from time to time, to revise plant groupings and rename plants. The names given in this book are the most up-to-date available.

Changes of name should, however, be expected as long as advances are being made in taxonomy. These, for the most part, reflect increasingly better understanding of the relationships between different kinds of plant.

Lesmurdie Scarp

Gooseberry Hill National Park

As with related species being grouped into genera, so these too are found to be more or less related. Those more closely related are grouped into the next major level, that of plant families. The characteristics used to identify Groups and Sub-Groups in the plant identification chapters are often those of plant families. Family names generally end in -aceae.

On Flowers (see Chapter 11 for illustrations)

What is technically a flower is very variable, with many "flowering" plants not obviously possessing any flower in the showy rose-and-carnation sense. Flowers of plants in this book vary. They may not exist, as in ferns and cycads, or be small and inconspicuous with "normal" flower parts (especially petals) reduced, as in grasses, sedges and rushes. They may be "normal flowers" or showy. While showy, however, they may be deceptive, being many flowers massed in heads as in, for example, daisy-like plants, Banksias and Dryandras. Or they may be showy, not because of petals but because another part of the flower is conspicuous (e.g. stamens in wattles, Callistemon and Calothamnus species; sepals in Thomasia). In many sedges and rushes, the brown, scaly heads often enclose many reduced flowers.

On leaves (see Chapter 11 for illustrations)

These are not always what you would imagine either. In the She-Oaks, which include two trees and two low-growing shrubs in this book, the green, needle-like parts are stems. The leaves are reduced to tiny, papery triangles at the "joints". The twine rushes are similarly deceptive with their leaves reduced to single brown scales at their joints.

A few of the wattles have divided leaves in the adult plant. The majority have entire, undivided 'leaves', which are not actually leaves but flattened leaf stalks, called phyllodes. Their origin can be observed in seedlings, where the divided leaves show a transition, with developing prominence of the leaf stalk, to the adult phyllodes.

Observing Plants

When identifying plants with the use of this book, the purchase of a simple, x10 magnification, hand-lens (magnifying glass) is strongly recommended. A hand-lens will also add greatly to your enjoyment as an introduction to a new world as well as an aid to identification. When viewed through a hand-lens, the most ordinary flower or leaf surface can change to something fascinating and exciting.

CHAPTER 2

Trees and Tall to Medium Shrubs

The distinction often made between a tree and a shrub is that trees have single stems or trunks and shrubs have several stems. This distinction, like many used to describe plants, can cause confusion.

In this guide, the main features separating trees and tall shrubs from other plants are their woodiness, as distinct from being herbaceous, and their stature, mature specimens exceeding the height of human beings. Trees are woody and at a maturity the tallest, largest elements in the vegetation. Trees grade into shrubs.

The distinction for the category of trees and tall shrubs is that the shrubs included are those which regularly exceed the height of adult human beings. Medium shrubs are tall for most two to four year olds.

GROUP 1
Flowers showy: petals NOT OBVIOUS instead, spiky flowers of prominent anthers or styles), Includes TREES. page 12

Sub-Group	Families	Genera
1A Flowers borne singly, loosely grouped page 12	Myrtaceae	Eucalyptus
1B Flowers apparently borne singly but actually many in yellow pom-pom or sausage-shaped heads or in drooping greeny-yellow heads page 13	Mimosaceae	Acacia Paraserianthes
1C Flowers clustered page 15	Myrtaceae Proteaceae	Beaufortia Callistemon Calothamnus Melaleuca Banksia

GROUP 2
Flowers showy: IRREGULAR arrangement of petals page 16

Sub-Group	Families	Genera
2A Petals five, separate PEA flowers page 16	Papilionaceae	Bossiaea Chamaecytisus Daviesia Gastrolobium Hovea Jacksonia Mirbelia Oxylobium Viminaria
2B 'Petals' four, joined to form more or less obvious tube. Petals often curled back; style often obviously protruding page 18	Proteaceae	Grevillea Hakea Lambertia
2C Petals four, separate page 21	Caesalpinaceae Sapindaceae	Labichea Diplopeltis
2D Petals five as unequal lobes with lowermost prominent as protruding 'lip' and joined to form distinct tube. page 21	Lamiaceae	Hemigenia

Trees and Tall to Medium Shrubs 11

GROUP 3
Flowers showy; REGULAR arrangement of petals.
Includes W.A. Christmas Tree page 22

Sub-Group	Families	Genera
3A Petals five or more page 22	Myrtaceae	Agonis
		Astartea
		Calytrix
		Kunzea
		Leptospermum
		Melaleuca
		Pericalymma
	Asclepiadaceae	Gomphocarpus
	Dilleniaceae	Hibbertia
	Loranthaceae	Nuytsia
	Pittosporaceae	Sollya
	Rosaceae	Rubus
	Sterculiaceae	Lasiopetalum
		Thomasia
3B Petals four, separate page 24	Caesalpiniaceae	Labichea [Grp2C]
	Sapindaceae	Diploleltis [Grp2C]
3C 'Petals' 4, joined to form a tube. Flowers sometimes in HEADS, individually indistinct page 24	Proteaceae	Isopogon
		Persoonia
		Petrophile
	Thymelaeaceae	Pimelea
3D Petals four, separate to base. Flowers in HEADS and individually indistinct page 26	Proteaceae	Dryandra

GROUP 4
Flowers individually inconspicuous sometimes
in massive heads or clusters which are conspicuous, or borne singly. Includes TREES page.27

Sub-Group	Families	Genera
4A Flowers crowded in massive spearlike or oval heads page 27	Xanthorrhoeaceae	Xanthorrhoea
	Zamiaceae	Macrozamia
4B Flowers on drumstick heads page 27	Dasypogonaceae	Kingia
4C Flowers in more or less showy clusters or tasssels page 28	Epacridaceae	Leucopogon
	Proteaceae	Conospermum
	Stirlingia	
	Rhamnaceae	Trymalium
	Santalaceae	Santalum
4D Flowers tiny, grouped on branchlets or borne singly page 29	Casuarinaceae	Allocasuarina
		Casuarina
	Euphorbiaceae	Beyeria
4E Flowers in heads surrounded by colourful bracts. page 29	Myrtaceae	Darwinia

GROUP 1
Flowers showy: petals NOT OBVIOUS
(instead, spiky flowers of prominent anthers or styles) Includes TREES

1A Flowers borne singly, loosely grouped
MYRTACEAE: *Eucalyptus*

EUCALYPTUS - Gum Trees
Much of the Hills are forested, in particular, the Darling Range to the east of the Scarp, and those slopes where there are deeper or more fertile soils, and the streamsides. Elsewhere, the trees are scattered or absent.

Eucalyptus patens Swan River Blackbutt	Creamy-white Broad drainage lines of wetter areas and uppermost ends of Scarp gullies	Feb-Mar Uncommon

    Tree to 30m. Bark grey, appearing partly like marri and jarrah. Leaves 15x2cm like those of jarrah but more blue-green. Habitat too damp for jarrah. Gumnuts similar to those of jarrah but smaller, 7mm across.

Eucalyptus calophylla Marri	Creamy-white Forests and woodlands	Feb-Apr Very common

    Tree to 30m. Bark grey, lower bark often charred, in 2x4cm blocks, fibrous. Red gum sometimes evident on trunks. Leaves rounded, about twice as long as broad, 7x3cm, with numerous, closely-spaced, parallel veins coming from the midrib at about 90° (calophylla = beautiful leaf). Gumnuts 3cm across, the 'honkey' nuts of children and the models for May Gibbs' 'Snugglepot and Cuddlepie'.   Page 38

Eucalyptus wandoo Wandoo	Creamy-white Open woodlands on slopes	Feb-Apr Common

    Tree to 25m. Bark silvery-white, smooth with occasional patches of rough bark and apricot blotching following shedding. Leaves much smaller 12x3cm and a lighter green than those of jarrah. Gumnuts 4mm across, in clusters. Often on darker-red, shallow but nutrient-richer soils indicating the presence of dolerite.   Page 38 & 37

Eucalyptus drummondii Drummond's Gum	Creamy-white Sparsely-treed slopes	Jun-Dec Rare

    Mallee (many-stemmed from underground woody base) to 6m. Bark silvery-grey, blotchy. Leaves like wandoo. Gumnuts rounded, 9mm across.

Eucalyptus rudis W.A. Flooded Gum	Creamy-white Streamsides	Aug Common

    Tree to 20m. Bark pale grey, blocky, 2x2cm, on trunk and main branches; upper branches smooth. Leaves 12x2.5cm like those of jarrah but distinctive blue-green. Gumnuts 5mm across.

Eucalyptus laeliae Darling Range Ghost Gum	Creamy-white Sparsely-treed slopes	Oct Rare

    Tree to 8m. Bark white, smooth. Leaves like wandoo. Gumnuts cylindrical, 5mm across.   Page 36

| Eucalyptus marginata | Creamy-white | Nov-Dec |
| Jarrah | Forests and woodlands | Very common |

Major forest tree to 30m in S W Western Australia. Bark grey, rarely charred, in strips 30x2cm. Leaves slightly curved, sickle-shaped, 8x1.5cm, with widely-spaced veins coming from the mid-rib at about 45° and with a distinct marginal vein near the thickened edge of the leaf (marginata). Gumnuts marble-sized, 1cm across.   Page 36

1B Flowers apparently borne singly but actually many in yellow pom-pom or sausage-shaped heads or in drooping greeny-yellow heads

MIMOSACEAE: *Acacia Paraserianthes*

ACACIA - Wattles (For fuller description see Chapter 9). Of the 21 wattles, 10 are described here and the other 11 in Medium to Small Shrubs page 70

Groupings for identification are:
- 1B-1 Phyllodes ('leaves') cylindrical, page 13
- 1B-2 Phyllodes ('leaves') flattened, page 13
- 1B-3 Leaves divided with many leaflets, page 14

■ **1B-1 Phyllodes ('leaves') cylindrical**

| Acacia sessilis | Deep yellow | Jun-Jul |
| Spiny wattle | Slope shrublands | Uncommon |

Shrub to 1.5m. Phyllodes needle-like, 1.5cm, sometimes projecting in all directions including backwards. Flower heads spherical, usually stalked, occasionally stalkless, borne singly at phyllode-stem junction.

| Acacia extensa | Yellow | Aug-Sep |
| Wiry wattle | Damp areas, often sandy | Uncommon |

Tall shrub 2-4m loose spreading habit. Phyllodes, angular, pliant, needle-like, 120x2mm. Flower heads spherical, stalked, four or more on side branchlets.

■ **1B-2 Phyllodes ('leaves') flattened**

| Acacia horridula | Pale yellow | May-Jul |
| Prickly wattle | Streamsides | Rare |

Shrub to 1m. Phyllodes 5x2.5mm, blunt triangular, viciously pointed, crowded. Flower heads spherical 4mm across on stalks 7mm long borne singly at phyllode stem junction.

| Acacia urophylla | White to cream | Jun |
| Net-leaved wattle | Slope woodlands | Uncommon |

Shrub to 2m. Phyllodes two to three nerved with prominent network of cross veins, broad, varying up to almost as wide as long, 5cm, and with two small prickles at phyllode junction with stem. Flower heads spherical, stalked, up to three at the junction of phyllode and stem. Hanging pods 120x3mm, twisted.   Page 40

| Acacia alata | Creamy-white to rich yellow | Jun-Aug |
| Winged wattle | Streamsides and damp areas | Common |

Shrubs to 2m, in groves, rarely singly in woodlands. Phyllode with single nerve extending as a prickle, broad, continuing as a wing (alata), 1cm wide, down the stem. Phyllode green or grey green, without hairs or densely hairy. Flower heads spherical, stalked, two arising where upper margin of phyllode joins stem.   Page 40

Acacia saligna	Orange-yellow	Aug-Sep
Orange wattle	Damp areas	Common

Straggling shrub to 2.5m. Phyllodes very variable, broad, 10x3cm to narrow, 10x1cm, with one lengthwise nerve. Flower heads spherical, stalked, six to eight along a stalk arising at the junction of phyllode and stem.

Acacia oncinophylla	Yellow	Sep
Hooked-leaf wattle	Granite outcrops	Common

Shrub to 2m. Phyllodes three-nerved, 100x4mm, hooked at end. Flower heads cylindrical, stalked, one or two arising at the junction of phyllode and stem.

Acacia dentifera	Yellow	Sep-Oct
Toothed wattle	Damp areas	Common

Shrub to 3m. Phyllodes single-nerved, 120x5mm, flattened with up to three small teeth at the end. Flower heads spherical, stalked, one or two occasionally four or more on stalk arising at junction of phyllode and stem.

Acacia divergens	Yellow	Sep-Oct
Sailboat wattle	Broad drainage lines	Uncommon

Shrub to 2m. Phyllode curiously shaped; one-nerved, short, 7mm, with little of the phyllode projecting beneath and a sail-like, upper part, the top of the sail being nearest the stem resulting in the phyllode being about as long as broad. Flower head spherical, 10mm across on 10mm stalk, yellow, arising singly at the junction of phyllode and stem.

■ 1B-3 Leaves divided with many leaflets

Paraserianthes lophantha	Yellow-green	Jul-Aug
Albizia	Streamsides	Common

Tree to 4m with distinctive branching, the branches coming off the trunk at about $90°$ and turning up at the ends. Leaves compound, divided into several leaflets, appearing fern-like, blue-grey green. Flowers, several in head 7x1cm, as hanging tufts of anthers. In fruit, as bunches of flattened, red-brown pods 7x1cm.

Acacia pulchella	Yellow	Jul-Oct
Prickly Moses	Woodlands and slopes	Very common

Shrub to 2m. Leaves, in pairs, once-pinnate with two to five pairs of leaflets on leaf stalk, each leaflet flat, 5x2.5mm; one or two prickles at junction with stem. Flower heads spherical 12mm across, on stalks, 15mm arising singly at leaf-stem junction. Regenerates strongly from seed after fire. Page 39

Trees and Tall to Medium Shrubs 15

1C Flowers clustered or in heads
MYRTACEAE: *Beaufortia Callistemon Calothamnus Melaleuca*
PROTEACEAE: *Banksia*

MYRTACEAE - Myrtles
This Family, with its leaves scented when crushed, is described more fully in Medium to Small Shrubs, page 43

Calothamnus sanguineus	Bright red	Mar-Jul
Pindak	Gravelly woodlands	Uncommon

Shrub 1x1.5m, twiggy. Leaves 15x1mm, crowded round stem, dark green, pine-like. Flowers 2.5cm, made up of four bundles of anthers, the upper two wider and longer than the lower two, grouped along 4cm of one side of the stem. Page 39

Calothamnus quadrifidus	Red	Sep-Nov
One-sided bottlebrush	Lower slope shrublands	Common

Shrub 1.5x2.5m. Leaves, sparsely hairy, 30x1mm, crowded, spreading, pine-like. Flowers clustered to one side of stem, each flower with anthers grouped into four bundles appearing petal-like, 3cm. Woody, rounded seed capsules, 7mm across, persistent on stems. Page 32

Calothamnus hirsutus	Red	Sep-Nov
One-sided bottlebrush	Slope shrublands	Rare

Smaller and denser than Calothamnus quadrifidus but otherwise similar except that the anthers are grouped into five bundles.

Beaufortia purpurea	Purple	Oct-Dec
Purple beaufortia	Slope shrublands	Rare

Shrub to 1m. Leaves 10x2mm. Flower heads 1cm across at ends of stems.

Callistemon phoeniceus	Bright Red	Oct-Dec
Lesser bottlebrush	Streamsides	Rare

Shrub to 3m. Leaves 70x7mm, blue-green, thickened. Flowers in bottlebrush head at ends of stems, 8x3cm. One of only two bottlebrush species native to south-west Western Australia.

Melaleuca rhaphiophylla	Creamy-white	Nov
Swamp paperbark	Streamsides	Common

Tree to 10m. Bark soft, papery. Leaves needle-like, 3cm. Flowers, clustered like a bottlebrush in heads of 4x1cm. Woody seed-capsules from previous flowerings persist, and can be found further down the stem. Page 31

Melaleuca preissiana	Creamy-white	Nov-Dec
Moonah	Swampy areas	Common

Tree to 10m. Bark white, papery. Leaves short, flattened, 10x1mm. Otherwise similar to Swamp paperbark. Page 32

PROTEACEAE - Banksia Family
(For fuller description see Chapter 9, Page 225)

Banksia littoralis   Orange-yellow   Sep
Swamp Banksia   Swampy places   Uncommon
    Tree to 6m. Bark similar to Bull banksia. Leaves 15x1cm, finely-toothed. Flower heads 6x20cm. Cones similar sized, somewhat irregularly-shaped.   Page 34

Banksia grandis   Greeny-yellow   Oct-Nov
Bull banksia   Forest   Common
    Tree to 6m. Bark brown, baubly-textured (1cm baubles). Leaves to 30x5cm, coarsely-toothed, radiating, pale pink velvet when emerging in January changing to delicate pale green, contrasting with the dark green of the older leaves in February. Flower heads 10x25cm. Cones similar size, hard woody, persistent, with new branches coming from beneath.   Page 33

GROUP 2
Flowers showy: IRREGULAR arrangement of petals

2A Petals five, separate, PEA flowers

PAPILIONACEAE: *Bossiaea Cytisus Daviesia Gastrolobium Hovea Jacksonia Mirbelia Oxylobium Viminaria*

PAPILIONACEAE - Peas (For fuller description see Chapter 9,)
    Groupings for identification are:
- 2A-1 Leaves alternate, longer than 1cm, flat, not divided, page 16
- 2A-2 Leaves alternate, shorter than 1cm, flat, not divided, page 17
- 2A-3 Leaves alternate, compound (i.e. with leaflets), page 17
- 2A-4 Leaves opposite and simple, page 17
- 2A-5 Leaves attached to the stem in whorls of three, page 17
- 2A-6 Leafless, page 18

■ **2A-1 Leaves alternate, longer than 1 cm, flat, not divided**

Hovea pungens   Purple   Jul-Aug
Devil's pins   Granite outcrops   Common
    Shrub to 1.5m. Leaves 18x3mm, rigid, very sharply-pointed, (pungent), spreading, 10x3mm. Flowers 1cm across, several at each leaf-stem junction, arresting. Pods light brown, almost round, 1cm across.   Page 40

Daviesia horrida   Bronze-orange   Aug-Sep
Prickly bitter-pea   Slope shrublands   Common
    (See Chapter 3, Medium to Small Shrubs, p 48)

Daviesia cordata   Yellow-brown   Sep-Oct
Book-leaf   Woodlands and slopes   Uncommon
    Shrub to 2m with upright slender stems. Leaves heart-shaped, 10x5cm, stem-clasping, lime-green when young. Flowers 10mm across in bunches at the ends of the stems. After flowering the triangular pods (characteristic shape for species of Daviesia) become enclosed in a pair of

rounded light brown bracts 2.5cm across, which have enlarged after fertilisation. These bracts are held together suggesting the common name of 'Book-leaf Daviesia'. Page 30

Oxylobium lineare   Yellow and red   Nov-Jan
Narrow leaved oxylobium   Streamsides   Rare
     Shrub to 3m. Leaves 10x1cm parallel-sided with edges curled under. Flowers 10mm across at the ends of stems.

■ **2A-2 Leaves alternate, shorter than 1cm, not divided**
Bossiaea spinescens   Yellow-brown   Jul-Aug
                                         Damp areas   Rare
     Shrub to 2m much-branched. Leaves 8x4mm lance-shaped at all angles on the branches intermingled with spines. Flowers 8mm across, single, stalks to 8mm in leaf axils.

Mirbelia spinosa   Red and yellow   Aug-Oct
                         Granite outcrops   Common
     Shrub to 1.5m. Leaves 6x2mm, lance-shaped clustered around base of spines. Flowers 1cm across, stalkless, in leaf axils.

■ **2A-3 Leaves alternate, compound (i.e. with leaflets)**
Chamaecytisus palmensis*   White   Aug
Tree Lucerne, Tagasaste   Forest edge, disturbed places   Common
     Tree to 6m, young shoots softly, hairy. Leaves pale green each with three leaflets, 3.5x1mm on 15mm stalk. Branches drooping. Flowers 15x12mm grouped in fives on short side branches. Introduced from the Mediterranean Region.

■ **2A-4 Leaves opposite and simple**
Bossiaea aquifolium   Orange-yellow   Aug-Sep
Water bush   Forest   Uncommon
     Shrub to 2.5m with slender branches. Leaves 10x15mm with spiny margin, broadly semi-circular, blue-green, in pairs. Flowers 22mm shortly stalked occurring singly at each leaf-stem junction, hence, also paired.   Page 36

Gastrolobium spinosum   Yellow-orange   Nov-Dec
Prickly poison   Slopes, sandy soils   Rare
     Shrub to 2.5m. Leaves 2.5x3cm, triangular, prickly-toothed, mid-green. Flowers 15mm across, few in loose clusters in leaf axils and at the ends of stems.

■ **2A-5 Leaves attached to the stem in whorls of three**
     Take care to distinguish this group from Clover-like trifoliate leaves, three leaflets attached to each other with a single stalk to the stem.

Gastrolobium bilobum   Orange   Sep-Oct
Heart leaf poison   Damp areas   Rare
     Shrub to 4m. Leaves 35x12mm, tip sometimes with notch, dark green upper surface. Flowers 8mm across, stalks 5mm, densely bunched at the ends of stems.

Aotus cordifolia	Lemon yellow	Oct-Nov
	Swamp margins	Rare

Shrub to 1.5m, straggling. Leaves 10x6mm heart-shaped, hairy, yellow-green with edges curled under. Flowers 6mm across, up to three in leaf axils.

Mirbelia dilatata	Pinky-purple	Nov-Dec
Holly-leaved mirbelia	Disturbed damp areas	Rare

Shrub to 2.5m. Leaves 2x2cm, three-lobed, pointed, scattered or in threes. Flowers 13mm across, stalks to 5mm, single in leaf axils.

■ 2A-6 Leafless

Jacksonia sternbergiana	Orange-yellow	All year
Stinkwood	Sparsely wooded slopes	Uncommon

Shrub to small tree to 4m with weeping branches. Branchlets green, pointed. Flowers 1cm across scattered along branchlets.

Jacksonia furcellata	Yellow	Sep-Nov
Grey stinkwood	Slope shrublands	Uncommon

Shrub to 2.5m, straggly. Branchlets grey-green, pointed. Flowers 1cm across, grouped on stalks along and at the ends of branchlets.

Viminaria juncea	Yellow	Oct-Dec
Swishbush or native Broom	Streamsides and damp areas	Common

Shrub to small tree to 4m with weeping branches. Branchlets wiry, shiny-green. Flowers 1cm across, several on hanging stalks.
Page 30

2B 'Petals' four, joined to form more or less obvious tube. Petals often curled back; style often obviously protruding

PROTEACEAE: *Grevillea Hakea Lambertia*

Groupings for identification are:
2B-1 Without persistent woody fruits. Grevillea. page 18
2B-2 With persistent woody fruits. Hakea. page 19
2B-3 Leaves in threes on stem, flowers yellow. Lambertia. page 21

■ 2B-1 Without persistent woody fruits

Of the twelve species of Grevillea, five are described here, the remainder in Chapter 3, Medium to Small Shrubs (page 43).

Grevillea diversifolia	Off white	Jun-Oct
Variable-leaved grevillea	Lower slopes	Uncommon

Shrub to 2.5m. Leaves variable, 5x1cm, simple or lobed. Flowers both along and at ends of stems, in clusters 2cm across.

Grevillea endlicheriana	Pinky-white	Jun-Nov
Spindly grevillea	Slopes near granite	Common

Shrub to 3m with slender upright flowering stems above a low, leafy, shrubby base. Leaves 7x1cm silky-hairy, silvery-green. Flowers 1cm across, shortly stalked, in clusters towards the end of stems.
Page 31

Trees and Tall to Medium Shrubs

Grevillea manglesii	White	Jun-Sep
Smooth grevillea	Open woodlands on slopes	Uncommon

Shrub to 1.5m. Leaves wedge-shaped, 3x1.5cm with three to five pointed lobes. Flowers both along and at ends of stems, in clusters 2cm across.   Page 32

Grevillea wilsonii	Scarlet	Jul-Jan
Native fuchsia	Gravelly open woodland	Common

Shrub to 1.5x3m, sprawling stems with up to half appearing dead. Leaves 4x4cm, much-divided, near-cylindrical lobes, crowded on stem as tangled wire-mesh-like covering. Flowers 2.5cm long, several loosely- clustered on stalk at ends of stems. Spectacular.   Page 38

▪ 2B-2 With persistent woody fruits
Illustrations of all the Hakea leaves and fruit see Chapter 11, page 243)

   Groupings for identification are:
   - ▪ 2B-2a Leaves prickly-edged, flat; cone stigma, page 19
   - ▪ 2B-2b Leaves smooth-edged, flat; cone stigma, page 19
   - ▪ 2B-2c Leaves cylindrical, divided, sharply-pointed; cone stigma, page 20
   - ▪ 2B-2d Leaves prickly-edged, flat; flat stigma, page 20
   - ▪ 2B-2e Leaves smooth-edged, flat; flat stigma, page 20
   - ▪ 2B-2f Leaves cylindrical, flat stigma, page 21

▪ 2B-2a Leaves prickly-edged, flat; cone stigma

Hakea varia	**White**	**Jul-Aug**
Variable-leaved hakea	Damp swampy areas	Rare

Shrub to 2m open with arching stems. Leaves variable (varia), from cylindrical to flat, simple to lobed, about 3cm long, blue-green. Flowers 1cm clustered at ends of short branches along stem. Nuts 2x1cm with knobbly surface.

Hakea undulata	**White**	**Late Aug-Sep**
Wavy-leaved hakea	Slopes and open woodland	Common

Erect shrub to 2m. Leaves 6x3cm, edges wavy (undulata) with sparse prickles and noticeable cross-veining. Flowers 1cm long in clusters in leaf axils towards ends of branches. Nuts 2x1cm cream with brown spots, in clusters.   Page 35

▪ 2B-2b Leaves smooth-edged, flat; cone stigma

Hakea petiolaris	**White and maroon**	**May-Aug**
Sea Urchin hakea	Below granite outcrops	Uncommon

Shrub to 3x3m sometimes tree-like. Leaves 7x4cm widening from stalk, rounded, blue-green. Flowers 2cm long clustered into ball 5cm across in leaf axils towards ends of branches. Nuts 3x1.5cm in near spherical bunches.   Page 36

■ 2B-2c Leaves cylindrical, divided, sharply-pointed; cone stigma

Hakea lissocarpha	White and pink	Jun-Aug
Honey bush	Slopes and open woodland	Common

Shrub to 1.5m. Leaves 4x3cm, much-branched cylindrical sections, wiry, prickly. Flowers 1cm long, on stalks 5mm, massed in loose clusters in leaf axils. Nut 2.5x1cm, pear-shaped, rough, few, often single. Noticeable honey smell. Page 42

■ 2B-2d Leaves prickly-edged, flat; flat stigma

Hakea cristata	Pinky-white	May-Jul
Snail hakea	Slopes	Uncommon

Shrub to 3x3m. Leaves 7x5cm widening from base, rounded with toothed edges, blue-green. Flowers 1.2cm long, on 5mm stalks in clusters in leaf axils. Nuts 4x3cm rounded with pointed end and two prominent, toothed crests (cristata). Page 39

Hakea amplexicaulis	White, cream or pinkish	Jul-Oct
Prickly hakea	Woodlands	Common

Shrub to 2m, sparse, straggly, few-stemmed. Leaves 15x3cm broader at stem-clasping (amplexicaulis) base, strap-shaped, edges sharply-toothed. Dead leaves remaining clasped to stem, swinging in the wind producing a characteristic rustling noise. Flowers 2cm long on 1cm stalks, clustered in axils of leaves near ends of branches. Nut 2.5x1cm, smooth, tapering to a point, usually borne singly. Page 41

Hakea prostrata	Pinky-white	Sep-Oct
Harsh hakea	Damp areas with sandy soils	Uncommon

Shrub or small tree to 3.5m, not ground-hugging as 'prostrata' suggests. Leaves 4x2.5cm tongue-shaped, slightly stem-clasping, broadest towards tip, edges prickly-toothed. Flowers 1.5cm across with 5mm stalks nestling in clusters in the axils of the leaves. Nuts 2.5x1.5cm, rough, tapering to a point, a few in each group. Page 34

■ 2B-2e Leaves smooth-edged, flat; flat stigma

Hakea ruscifolia	White	Jan-Feb
Candle hakea	Woodlands; upper-slope shrublands	Uncommon

Shrub to 2m, straggly. Leaves 20x7mm, flat, oval, entire with long point, spreading and densely packed on stems. Flowers 6mm long on 5mm stalks in the axils of leaves towards the stem tips, similarly crowded giving a candle-like appearance. Nuts 15x8mm, rounded at end, few borne singly. Page 32

Hakea cyclocarpa	White with dark red style	Aug-Sep
Ramshorn	Upper slopes	Uncommon

Shrub to 2m, open with a few straggling stems. Leaves 10x2cm widening from stalk, smooth-edged, strap-shaped ending in a short point. Flowers 2.5cm long, in loose clusters in axils of leaves towards ends of stems. Nuts 3.5x3cm, the pointed ends curled back like the horns of a ram, single or few.

■ 2B-2f Leaves cylindrical; flat stigma

Hakea erinacea	Cream	Jun-Sep
Hedgehog hakea	Slopes	Common

Dense shrub to 2x2m often in dense thickets. Leaves 3x3cm divided cylindrical sections, stiff with very hard, sharp points. Flowers 1.5cm on 5mm stalks, few in loose clusters in the leaf axils. Nuts 20x5mm tapering to a point.   Page 33

Hakea trifurcata	White	Jul-Oct
Two-leafed hakea	Woodlands	Common

Shrub to 3x6m with young stems red. Leaves two kinds: some, flat, 4x1cm, most, cylindrical leaves, simple up to three-pronged, 8cm. Flowers 1.5cm long on 3mm stalks, few in loose clusters in axils of the cylindrical leaves. Nuts 2cmx5mm flattened-cylindrical, resembling the flat leaves.   Page 37

■ 2B-3 Leaves in threes on stem, flowers yellow

Lambertia multiflora	Bright yellow	Jul-Nov
Many-flowered honeysuckle	Woodland; slope shrubland	Uncommon

Shrub to 2m often in groups. Leaves 4x1cm entire, pointed, often clasping the stem at the leaf-base, stiff. Flowers 2cm in heads of less than 10 spreading outwards at the ends of stems. Good for studying the flower details of members of the Proteaceae Family.   Page 39

2C Petals four, separate

CAESALPINIACEAE: *Labichea*

Labichea lanceolata	Yellow with red spots	Sep-Nov
Tall labichea	Streamsides	Uncommon

Shrub or small tree to 3m. Leaves in three parts, rigid, sharply pointed, the middle part the longest, 5cmx8mm. Flowers 2cm across on 1cm stalks, single at the leaf-stem junction.

SAPINDACEAE - *Diplopeltis*

Diplopeltis huegelii	Pale pink	Aug-Nov
	Slopes	Common
(See Chapter 3, Medium to Small Shrubs page 53)		Page 41

2D Petals five as unequal lobes with **lowermost prominent as protruding 'lip' and joined to form distinct tube**

LAMIACEAE: *Hemigenia*

Hemigenia incana	Pink-mauve	Jun-Nov
Silky hemigenia	Slopes and granite outcrops	Uncommon

Shrub to 2m. Leaves 3x1cm opposite, spreading with grey felty hairs. Flowers 1.5cm across single in leaf axils.

GROUP 3
Flowers showy: REGULAR arrangement of petals.
Includes WA Christmas Tree

3A Petals five or more (WA Christmas Tree), separate. If joined, then to form a cup, not a narrow tube

MYRTACEAE:	Agonis Astartea Calytrix Kunzea Leptospermum Melaleuca Pericalymma
ASCLEPIADACEAE:	Gomphocarpus
DILLENIACEAE:	Hibbertia
LORANTHACEAE:	Nuytsia
PITTOSPORACEAE:	Sollya
ROSACEAE:	Rubus
STERCULIACEAE:	Lasiopetalum Thomasia

Groupings for identification are:
- 3A-1 Flowers in heads or paired opposite, page 22
- 3A-2 Flowers clustered, page 23
- 3A-3 Flowers single, yellow, paired opposite, page 23
- 3A-4 Flowers single, not yellow, page 23

■ **3A-1 Flowers in heads or paired opposite**

MYRTACEAE - Teatrees

Agonis linearifolia	White	All year
Swamp peppermint	Streamsides and damp areas	Very common

Shrub to 3m often in dense thickets. Leaves 20x5mm, peppermint smell when crushed. Flowers in round heads, 1.5cm across, along stems on small branchlets. Woody capsules persistent. Page 38

Leptospermum erubescens	Pinky-white	Aug-Oct
Roadside teatree	Open woodlands	Uncommon

Shrub to 2m. Leaves 7x3mm, hairy when young. Flowers 1cm across along stems on short branchlets.

Kunzea recurva	Purply-pink	Aug-Nov
	Swampy areas	Uncommon

Shrub to 1.5m. Leaves spreading and recurved, 5x2.5mm. Flowers in rounded heads, 15mm across, at the ends of branches.

Leptospermum laevigatum*	White	Sep-Oct
Coast teatree	Disturbed areas	Uncommon

Shrub to 3m. Leaves 25x6mm, blue-green, broadest near tip. Flowers shortly stalked, 2.5cm across along stems. Introduced from eastern Australia.

Pericalymma ellipticum	Pinky-white	Sep-Oct
Swamp teatree	Swamps and damp areas	Common

Shrub to 1.5m. Leaves, 10x4mm. Flowers 1cm across at ends and along stems. Woody capsule cylindrical with pointed top.

Trees and Tall to Medium Shrubs 23

Melaleuca radula | Pinky-mauve | Sep-Nov
Graceful honeymyrtle | Slope shrublands | Common
    Shrub to 1.5m, straggly. Leaves 35x3mm, grey-green, opposite. Flowers in pairs, opposite, 2cm across with fringed, spreading petals. Woody capsules persistent lower on stems.

Calytrix acutifolia | Creamy-white | Oct-Nov
 | Slope shrublands | Uncommon
    Shrub to 1m. Leaves, pointed, 10x1mm, crowded round stem, yellowy-green. Flowers grouped around 6cm of stem near the end.

Astartea fascicularis | White | Oct-Feb
 | Streamsides | Uncommon
    Shrub to 1.5m. Leaves 10 x1mm, in clusters. Flowers 6mm across, stalked, two to four where leaf clusters join stem.

■ 3A-2 Flowers clustered
LORANTHACEAE - Christmas Tree

Nuytsia floribunda | Bright orange | Nov-Dec
Christmas Tree | Winter damp slopes and flats | Common
    Trees to 8m often in open groves. Trunk stout, often blackened. Leaves finger-shaped, dark blue-green, 8x1cm. Flowers in showy clusters 30x10cm, prolific after fires. One of the best known and loved trees in Western Australia for its spectacle near Christmas time. It is also one of the World's largest semi-parasitic plants obtaining its nutrients from other plants. Page 30

■ 3A-3 Flowers single, yellow
DILLENIACEAE - Guinea flowers or Buttercups

Hibbertia serrata | Yellow | Jun-Sep
Serrate leaved guinea flower | Woodlands and damp slopes | Uncommon
    Shrub to 1.5m, few erect stems. Leaves to 5x2cm, margins notched, with spreading hairs. Flowers 3cm across in the axils of leaves along and at the ends of the stems.

Hibbertia subvaginata | Yellow | Sep-Nov
 | Granite outcrops | Uncommon
    Shrub to 2m straggling. Leaves 30x8mm blue-green, slightly stem-clasping, oblong with squarish ends. Flowers 2cm across in leaf axils.   Page 35

■ 3A-4 Flowers single, not yellow
ASCLEPIADACEAE - Hoya family

Gomphocarpus fruticosus* | Creamy-white | Jan
Narrowleaf Cottonbush | Streamsides | Uncommon
    Small tree to 3m. Leaves entire, 80x7mm, exuding milky white sap when picked. Flowers 5mm across. The stalk of the fruit resembles the neck and beak of a swan; the fruit, the body. When ripe, numerous seeds with silky hairs are dispersed by wind. The food-plant of the Monarch Butterfly supporting its local population in the Hills. Introduced from South Africa.

PITTOSPORACEAE - The Pittosporum family

Sollya heterophylla	Sky blue	Oct-Feb
Australian bluebell	Forest and woodlands	Common

Shrub with twining stems, 2x1.5m with tendency to be a climber if support available. Leaves 35x8mm, hairless, smooth upper surface. Flowers 1cm across on slender stalks, 2cm, hanging downwards. Fruit pod-like, fleshy, cylindrical, 20x5mm.   Page 41

ROSALCEAE - Rose family

Rubus aff. selmeri*	White	Nov-Dec
Blackberry	Steamsides and roadsides	Uncommon

Shrub 1.5x3m with scrambling arching thorny stems. Leaves 10x6cm with three or five leaflets, shiny green upper surface, lower with prickles. Flowers 2.5cm across, petals rounded, in sparse groups on stalks along the stems. Fruit edible purple-black berries often failing to ripen, remaining pinky-green. Native to N.W. Europe.

STERCULIACEAE - Thomasia, Lasiopetalum

Lasiopetalum bracteatum	Pink	Aug-Nov
Helena velvet bush	Streamsides	Uncommon

Shrub to 1.5m. Leaves 4x2cm elongated heart-shaped densely hairy underneath. Flowers 7mm across scattered along 10cm ends of branches with an obvious, attractive, triangular pink bract at the base of each flower.   Page 35

Thomasia macrocarpa	Pinky-violet	Sep-Oct
Felt-leaved thomasia	Open woodlands on damp slopes	Uncommon

Shrub to 1.5m. Leaves maple-shaped, 6x4cm, densely white-hairy, stalked. Flowers 14mm across, few on stalks from the leaf-stem junction.

Thomasia pauciflora	Pink	Sep-Nov
Few flowered thomasia	Streamsides and damp areas	Uncommon

Shrub to 1.5m, straggly. Leaves 4x1cm, slightly crinkled, broad with lobes at base, covered with rusty hairs, stalked. Flowers 12mm across, up to three on stalks from leaf-stem junction.

3B Petals four, separate

CAESALPINACEAE: Labichea [Grp 2C] page 21
SAPINDACEAE: Diplopeltis [Grp.2C] page 21

(See Chapter 3, Medium to Small Shrubs page 53)

3C Petals four joined to form a tube.

Flowers sometimes in HEADS, individually indistinct
PROTEACEAE: Isopogon Persoonia Petrophile
THYMELAEACEAE: Pimelea

Trees and Tall to Medium Shrubs 25

Groupings for identification are:
- 3C-1 Flowers clustered on oval (egg-shaped) heads which remain after flowering page 25
- 3C-2 Flowers not in heads, yellow, often hidden amongst leaves page 25
- 3C-3 Flowers clustered in heads but not egg-shaped page 26

■ **3C-1 Flowers clustered on oval (egg-shaped) heads which remain after flowering**
ISOPOGON and PETROPHILE - Coneflowers

Isopogon sphaerocephalus	Creamy-yellow	Jul-Aug
Drumstick isopogon	Woodlands	Common

Shrub to 2m, exceptionally to 3m. Leaves entire, strap-shaped, 7x2.5cm, leathery. Flowers initially in flat-topped heads, 5cm. The outer flowers of the head flower first across upright stems. As flowering proceeds, the heads become round (sphaerocephalus). Growing solitary or in small groups: not in extensive groves. Page 31

Petrophile biloba	Pink and grey	Jul-Aug
Granite petrophile	Granite outcrops	Very common

Shrub to 2m, but exceptionally a small tree to 4m. Leaves, sharply pointed, variable but mainly two-lobed (biloba), 3x1cm, partly folded. Flowers 2cm velvety in heads 3cm across with short, silky hairs and contrasting yellow to orange stamens, the outer flowers of the head flowering first. Page 42

Isopogon dubius	Shocking pink	Jul-Oct
Rose coneflower	Slopes and gravelly woodland	Uncommon

Shrub to 1.5m. Leaves 6x4cm divided into flat segments, dark green. Flowers 2.5cm long in thistle-like cone heads 2.5cm across mainly at the ends of stems. Slender 'petals' with white tufted tips and contrasting protruding yellow styles. Page 35

Isopogon divergens	Grey-pink	Aug-Nov
Spreading coneflower	Lower slopes	Rare

Shrub to 1.5m. Leaves to 10cm as divided cylindrical segments. Flowers 2cm on cone-shaped head, 1.5cm across at tips of branches.

■ **3C-2 Flowers not in heads, yellow, often hidden amongst leaves**
PERSOONIA - Snottygobbles

(For fuller explanation see Chapter 9, Page 225)

Persoonia elliptica	Yellow	Dec-Jan
Spreading snottygobble	Forest	Uncommon

Robust tree to 6m with trunk 30cm across. Bark is hard and baubled like that of Banksia grandis. Leaves broad (elliptical) 5x2.5cm, almost apple-green, with the spherical canopy well-filled with leaves contrasting with the duller, grey-green of the forest. Flowers 1cm long, insignificant developing into pea-sized, lop-sided, stalked fruits. Page 38

Persoonia longifolia	Yellow	Jan
Snottygobble	Forest	Uncommon

Slender tree to 4m with trunk rarely more than 20cm across. Bark flaky-papery, rusty-grey outside, burnished copper-coloured inside. Leaves parallel-sided, 7x1cm, downward hanging giving the canopy a more graceful, willow-like appearance. Flowers and fruit similar to the previous species.

THYMELAEACEAE - Rice flowers

Pimelea argentea	Yellow	Sep-Nov
Silvery leaved pimelea	Wandoo woodland and lower slopes	Uncommon

Shrub to 2m, single-stemmed. Leaves 2x1cm tapering to a point, silvery with silky hairs. Flowers, 5mm long, shortly-stalked, in clusters in leaf axils. This is an exception amongst the Pimeleas in not having its flowers in heads at the ends of stems and with female and male flowers separate.

■ 3C-3 Flowers clustered in heads but not egg-shaped

THYMELAEACEAE - Rice flowers
Plants with flowers in heads appearing like fluffy rice.

Pimelea spectabilis	White	Sep-Nov
Bunjong	Woodland and near granite outcrops	Uncommon

Shrub to 1.5m, sparingly-branches. Leaves 30x4mm opposite, lance-shaped, smooth. Flowers 1x20mm, lower part with long silky hairs, grouped in heads 5cm across and cupped by four smooth, pointed bracts, 15x17mm at the ends of the erect stems. Page 37

3D Petals four, separate to base, in HEADS and individually indistinct

PROTEACEAE: Dryandra

Dryandra sessilis	Pale yellow	Mar-Nov
Parrot Bush	Open woodlands	Very common

Shrub or small tree to 3.5m. Leaves prickly, wedge-shaped, 4x4cm, blue-green. Flowers grouped in heads, 4cm across surrounded by leaves at the ends of branchlets. Often found in groves from ready regeneration from seed after fire. Page 40

Dryandra armata	Yellow	Jun-Aug
Prickly Dryandra	Gravelly open woodlands; slope shrublands	Very common

Shrub to 1.5x1.5m. Leaves very scratchy (armata = armed), 8x3cm, coarsely saw-toothed, dark green with yellowing margins. Flowers, yellow, grouped in heads, 7cm across, at the ends of branches. Page 33

Dryandra squarrosa	Pale yellow	Aug-Nov
Pingle	Woodlands	Uncommon

Shrub or small tree to 3m, slender stemmed. Leaves prickly, 6x1cm, shiny dark green. Flowers grouped in heads spaced down the stems at the junction of the leaves and stem. Page 41

Trees and Tall to Medium Shrubs 27

GROUP 4
Flowers individually inconspicuous: sometimes in massive heads or clusters which are conspicuous, or borne singly. Includes TREES (Sheoaks).

4A Flowers crowded in massive spearlike or oval heads

XANTHORRHOEACEAE:	*Xanthorrhoea*
ZAMIACEAE:	*Macrozamia*

XANTHORRHOEA -   Grass trees (For fuller description see Chapter 9 page 226)

Xanthorrhoea preissii	White	Jul-Nov
Balga	Woodlands; slope shrublands	Very common

Grass tree to 4m, single or multiple-headed, with trunk to 40cm across consisting of stem and leaf bases. Balgas have a stout trunk, green leaves without any silky hairs, and carry their white flowers aloft on a huge flower spike which may be, from top to base, 3m or more. Observations on Balga flowering spikes when the flowers are just coming out provide an excellent example of the effect of temperature on this process. The flowers come out first on the warmer, north side of the spike. They do not sprout from the base, but are often found in groves in the forest or are evenly scattered in the shrublands of the slopes.   Page 34

MACROZAMIA - *Zamia*
(For fuller description see Chapter 9, page 227)

Macrozamia riedlei	Green cones	Apr-Jun
Zamia	Forest and woodlands	Very common

Usually trunkless with crown of palm-like leaves less commonly with rounded base to 1m. Leaves 1-2m with opposite flattened leaflets, 8x1.5cm, on a central leaf stalk. At the base of these is light brown, woolly material, which keeps the complex-folded leaves separate before emerging.   Page 37

4B Flowers on drumstick heads

DASYPOGONACEAE: *Kingia*

Kingia australis	Cream	Nov-Mar
Grasstree	Forest; woodlands	Common

Slender grass tree to 6m with trunk to 25cm across, unbranched but often in groups because of suckering. Leaves silvery-tipped. The flowers are inconspicuous, usually inaccessible, and are hidden by the scaly bracts which make up the head of the persistent drumstick flowering stalk.   Page 33

With a growth rate of about 3cm a year, many of the taller Grasstrees are over 200 years old. In dating these, allowance has also to be made for the 10-14 years of growth before visible trunk-formation begins.

| 4C | Flowers in more or less **showy clusters or tassels** |

EPACRIDACEAE:	*Leucopogon*
PROTEACEAE:	*Conospermum Stirlingia*
RHAMNACEAE:	*Trymalium*
SANTALACEAE:	*Santalum*

EPACRIDACEAE - Heath

Leucopogon verticillatus	Pink	Sep-Oct
Tassel flower	Forest	Uncommon

Shrub to 1.5m, many stemmed. Leaves in whorls, 10x2.5cm, tapering to point, light green. Flowers individually small, 4mm, crowded on drooping, unbranched tassels to 6cm from the leaf bases along and at the ends of the stems. This is the least typical of the white (Leuco-) bearded (-pogon) heaths, most of which have short, pointed leaves 4-15mm long and white hairy lobes to their tubular flowers. Page 42

PROTEACEAE - Banksia family (For fuller description see Chapter 9)

Conospermum stoechadis	White	May-Jul
Common Smokebush	Woodland on sandy soils	Uncommon

Shrub to 1.5m consisting of slender flower stalks above a shrubby base. Leaves 150x1mm white-hairy. Flowers 6mm, white hairy with black centre, scattered along uppermost 30cm of densely white-hairy stalks. The traditional smokebush of the sandy Coastal Plain. Page 34

Stirlingia latifolia	Rusty yellow	Aug-Sep
Blueboy	Woodland on sandy soils	Uncommon

Shrub flower stalk extended above basal leaves to 1.5-2m usually occurring in extended patches. Leaves blue-green, erect, to 30cm, divided into two or three strap-shaped lobes, entire, flattened and leathery, each 2cm across. Flowers small, 5mm, in clusters, 20x10cm, at ends of flower stalk. Fruits have outwardly-projecting fringe of short grey hairs, the old flower-mass appearing grey.

RHAMNACEAE - Buckthorn Family

Trymalium floribundum	Cream	Aug-Sep
Karri hazel	Rock outcrops; streamsides	Uncommon

Shrub to 3m. Leaves 3x1.5cm, stalked, shiny green above, matted white-hairy below. Flowers 3mm across, massed in branching clusters, 10x20cm at the ends of branches. The sepals form the petal-like parts of the small creamy-white flowers with the petals, minute and cup shaped, enclosing the stamens.

SANTALACEAE - Sandalwood Family

Santalum acuminatum	Greeny-yellow	an
Quandong	Open woodlands; slope shrublands	Common

Small tree to 3m usually in groves sprouting from roots. Leaves yellowy-green, fleshy, 6x1.5cm. Flowers 3mm across, strongly-scented, in small clusters. It rarely sets fruit. Like the Christmas Tree, Sandalwood is also semi-parasitic. Page 36

4D Flowers tiny, grouped on branchlets or borne singly

CASUARINACEAE: *Allocasuarina*
EUPHORBIACEAE: *Beyeria*

CASUARINACEAE - Sheoaks (For fuller description see Chapter 9, Page 222)

Allocasuarina fraseriana	Male: orange-brown,	Jul-Aug
Sheoak	Female: dark red	Very common
	Forest	

Tree to 10m. Trunk to 30cm diameter. Bark pale grey-brown, flaky. Branchlets grey-green with about six scale leaves (teeth) at joints. Female trees distinctive by their cones as dark spots in the canopy and scattered on the ground beneath. Female flowers 5mm across as red clusters of stigma along the newly-forming wood. Male trees have no cones but when flowering the tips of their branches are pale orange where the anthers are clustered. A tap on a branch in this condition produces clouds of pollen.   Page 31

Allocasuarina huegeliana	Male: orange-brown,	Jul-Aug
Rock sheoak	Female: dark red	Common
	Granite outcrops	

Slender tree to 6m. Trunk to 15cm across. Bark grey, smooth with thin dark markings around trunk. Branchlets dark green with eight to fifteen scale leaves (teeth) at the joints.   Page 42

Allocasuarina humilis	Male: pale brown	Aug-Sep
Scrub sheoak	Female: dark red	Uncommon
	Open woodland;	
	slope shrublands	

Shrub 1.5x1.5m. Twiggy with grey-green branchlets, sometimes pink-tinged, with five scale leaves (teeth).   Page 30

EUPHORBIACEAE - Beyeria

Beyeria lechenaultii	White	Sep-Oct
Pale turpentine bush	Slope shrublands	Very rare

Shrub to 1.5m. Leaves 20x2mm, shiny and smooth above, white, matted-hairy below. Flowers 4mm across, white-hairy.

4E Flowers in heads surrounded by colorful bracts

MYRTACEAE - Darwinia

Darwinia citriodora	Red and cream	Jun-Nov
Lemon-scented darwinia	Rock outcrops	Common

Shrub to 1m but can be rock-hugging. Leaves 15x3mm, opposite, each successive pair at 90° to the preceding, blue to reddish green, strongly scented. Flowers 4mm, tubular, four to six surrounded by showy yellowy or reddish bracts 1cm in head to 7mm across.   Page 42

Daviesia cordata
Book-leaf

Nuytsia floribunda
Christmas Tree

Viminaria juncea
Swishbush

Allocasuarina humilis
Scrub sheoak

Allocasuarina humilis
Scrub sheoak

Trees and Tall to Medium Shrubs 31

Allocasuarina fraseriana
Sheoak

Isopogon sphaerocephalus
Drumstick isopogon

Grevillea endlicheriana
Spindly grevillea

Melaleuca rhaphiophylla
Swamp paperbark

Banksia littoralis
Swamp Banksia

Hakea ruscifolia
Candle hakea

Calothamnus quadrifidus
One-sided bottlebrush

Melaleuca preissiana
Moonah

Grevillea manglesii
Smooth Grevillea

Trees and Tall to Medium Shrubs 33

Banksia grandis
Bull banksia

Hakea erinacea
Hedgehog hakea

Kingia australis
Grasstree

Dryandra armata
Prickly Dryandra

Banksia littoralis
Swamp Banksia

Conospermum stoechadis
Common Smokebush

Xanthorrhoea preissii
Balga

Hakea prostrata
Harsh hakea

Trees and Tall to Medium Shrubs 35

Isopogon dubius
Rose coneflower

Hibbertia subvaginata

Hakea undulata
Wavy-leaved hakea

Lasiopetalum bracteatum
Helena velvet bush

Eucalyptus laeliae
Darling Range Ghost Gum

Hakea petiolaris
Sea Urchin hakea

Eucalyptus marginata
Jarrah

Santalum acuminatum
Quandong

Bossiaea aquifolium
Water bush

Trees and Tall to Medium Shrubs 37

Eucalyptus wandoo
Wandoo

Hakea trifurcata
Two-leafed hakea

Pimelea spectabilis
Bunjong

Macrozamia riedlei
Zamia

Agonis linearifolia
Swamp peppermint

Persoonia elliptica
Spreading snottygobble

Grevillea wilsonii
Native fuchsia

Eucalyptus wandoo
Wandoo

Eucalyptus calophylla
Marri

Trees and Tall to Medium Shrubs

Calothamnus sanguineus
Pindak

Acacia pulchella
Prickly Moses

Lambertia multiflora
Many-flowered honeysuckle

Hakea cristata
Snail hakea

Dryandra sessilis
Parrot Bush

Hovea pungens
Devil's pins

Acacia alata
Winged wattle

Acacia urophylla
Net-leaved wattle

Trees and Tall to Medium Shrubs 41

Dryandra squarrosa
Pingle

Solly heterophylla
Australian bluebell

Diplopeltis huegelii

Hakea amplexicaulis
Prickly hakea

Allocasuarina huegeliana
Rock sheoak

Leucopogon verticillatus
Tassel flower

Hakea lissocarpha
Honey bush

Petrophile biloba
Granite petrophile

Darwinia citriodora
Lemon-scented darwinia

CHAPTER 3

Medium to Small Shrubs

These are woody, single or multi-stemmed plants distinguished by size.

Medium shrubs are 0.75m to 1.5m tall; small shrubs 0.5m or less tall.

They dominate the slope shrublands of the scarp, but are to be found in all districts.

GROUP 1
Flowers showy: IRREGULAR arrangement of Petals page 46

Sub-Group	Families	Genera
1A Petals five - parts separate, PEA-flowers page 46	Papilionaceae	Aotus, Bossiaea, Chorizema, Daviesia, Dillwynia, Euchilopsis, Gastrolobium, Gompholobium, Hovea, Jacksonia, Mirbelia, Nemcia, Oxylobium, Pultenaea, Sphaerolobium, Templetonia
1B Petals five, appearing separate, unequal so that sometimes there appears to be only one obvious petal page 52	Goodeniaceae / Violaceae	Lechenaultia, Scaevola / Hybanthus
1C Petals five, as unequal lobes, not all the lower lobes protruding, lip-like, always obvious but are joined to form a TUBULAR flower page 52	Lamiaceae	Hemiandra, Hemigenia, Lavandula, Microcorys
1D Petals four, separate page 53	Sapindaceae / Caesalpiniaceae	Diplopeltis / Labichea
1E 'Petals' four, joined to form tube though sometimes short. 'Petals' often curled back with obvious protruding style. page 54	Proteaceae	Adenanthos, Conospermum, Grevillea, Hakea, Lambertia, Synaphea

GROUP 2
Flowers showy: REGULAR arrangement of petals; petals SEPARATE (or if joined, forming an open cup with joined bases, not a long narrow tube.) page 58

Sub-Group	Families	Genera
2A Petals five, yellow, rounded tips page 58	Dilleniaceae	Hibbertia
2B Petals five, white, pink. IF yellow, with pointed or fringed tips page 59	Myrtaceae	Baeckea, Calytrix, Hypocalymma, Rinzia, Verticordia
	Sterculiaceae	Lasiopetalum, Rulingia, Thomasia
	Euphorbiaceae	Ricinocarpus
	Tremandraceae	Tetratheca
	Boraginaceae	Halgania
	Rutaceae	Asterolasia, Eriostemon
2C Petal-like parts six page 64	Euphorbiaceae	Phyllanthus
2D Petals four page 64	Rutaceae	Boronia
	Proteaceae	Stirlingia
	Caesalpiniaceae	Labichea [Grp 1 a
	Sapindaceae	Diplopeltis [Grp

GROUP 3
Flowers showy: REGULAR arrangement of petals;
petals JOINED to form a TUBE. page 65

	Sub-Group	Families	Genera
3A	'Petals' four page 65 flowers in heads	Proteaceae	Banksia Isopogon Persoonia Petrophile
3B	Petals five page 67	Thymelaeaceae Epacridaceae (Heaths)	Pimelea Andersonia Astroloma Leucopogon Styphelia
3C	'Petals' five page 70	Rhamnaceae Asteraceae (Daisies)	Cryptandra Olearia

GROUP 4
Flowers showy: petals NOT OBVIOUS
(instead, spiky flowers of prominent anthers or styles, or finely-divided petals). page 70

	Sub-Group	Families	Genera
4A	Flowers yellow, pom-pom or sausage-shaped page 70	Mimosaceae	Acacia
4B	Flowers not yellow, or if yellow not pom-pom or sausage-shaped. page 73	Myrtaceae	Beaufortia Calothamnus Darwinia [Grp 5] Melaleuca Verticordia [Grp 2b]

GROUP 5
Flowers individually inconspicuous page 74

	Sub-Group	Families	Genera
		Casuarinaceae	Allocasuarina
		Euphorbiaceae	Monotaxis Stachystemon
		Haloragaceae	Gonocarpus
		Myrtaceae	Darwinia
		Proteaceae	Stirlingia [Grp2d]
		Rhamnaceae	Trymalium
		Santalaceae	Leptomeria
		Sapindaceae	Dodonaea

GROUP 6
Flowers clustered in tight HEADS Page 76 [MOST are referred to previous Groups]

	Sub-Group	Families	Genera
6A	Flower heads nodding page 76	Myrtaceae Rutaceae Thymelaeaceae	Darwinia [Grp 5] Diplolaena Pimelea [Grp 3a]
6B	Flower heads not nodding page 77	Asteraceae Mimosaceae Myrtaceae	Olearia [Grp 3c] Acacia [Grp 4a] Beaufortia [Grp 4b] Callistemon[Grp 4b] Calothamnus[Grp4b] Melaleuca [Grp 4b]
		Papilionaceae	Pultenaea [Grp 1a] Sphaerolobium [Grp 1a]
		Proteaceae	Conospermum [Grp 1e] Dryandra [Grp 3] Isopogon [Grp 3a] Petrophile [Grp 3a]

GROUP 1
Flowers showy: IRREGULAR arrangement of petals

1A Petals five, parts separate, PEA-flowers
PAPILIONACEAE: *Aotus Bossiaea Chorizema Daviesia Dillwynia Euchilopsis Gastrolobium Gompholobium Hovea Jacksonia Mirbelia Nemcia Oxylobium Pultenaea Sphaerolobium Templetonia*

PAPILIONACEAE - Peas (For fuller description see Chapter 9, Page 224)
Initial identification of species depends on the arrangement of leaves on the stem and then on leaf characteristics as indicated by the following sub-sub groupings. Here leaves refer both to true leaves and phyllodes.

Groupings for identification are:
- 1A-1 Leaves arranged alternately (not opposite) on the stem
  - 1a Leaves hard, almost cylindrical or vertically flattened, with pointed tips, page 46
  - 1b Leaves soft, more or less cylindrical, not pricking to the touch, page 47
  - 1c Leaves longer than 1cm, very flat in cross-section, and not branched. Very flat means the leaf is more than three times as broad as thick, page 47
  - 1d Leaves almost 1cm or shorter, flat in cross-section, and not branched, page 49
  - 1e Leaves branched, page 49
- 1A-2 Leaves not arranged alternately around the stem, page 49
  - 2a Leaves opposite, simple, page 49
  - 2b Leaves grouped in threes on stem, page 50
  - 2c Leaves compound with three leaflets on each leaf-stalk, clover-like, page 50
  - 2d Leaves compound with more than three leaflets either on a leaf stalk or as several finger-like leaflets from the leaf base, page 50
  - 2e Leafless, page 51
  - 2f Leaves mainly from the base of the plant, page 52

If the difference between 1A-1 or 1A-2 is unclear, use 1A-1. Sometimes leaves can be so close that 'alternate' or 'whorled' are hard to separate - e.g. Templetonia biloba.

- 1A-1 Leaves arranged alternately (not opposite) on the stem
- 1A-1a Leaves alternate, hard, almost cylindrical or slightly vertically flattened, with pointed tips

Daviesia angulata	Yellow, tinged red	May-Jun
	Woodland	Common

Shrub to 1m, spreading, many closely-spaced stems. Phyllodes 20x2mm cylindrical or slightly flattened, pointed, mid-green, never winged onto the stem. Flowers 6mm across in few-flowered clusters at phyllode axils.

Daviesia decurrens	Rusty red	Jun-Jul
Prickly bitter-pea	Woodlands	Common

Upright shrub to 70cm, inter-twined stems. Phyllodes ('leaves') projecting up to 4cm from flattened stems, triangular and continuing down the stem (decurrent) as a wing, whitey-blue-green or emerald green. Flowers 5mm across in few-flowered clusters at phyllode axils sometimes

Medium to Small Shrubs 47

hosts Pilostyles hamiltonii (see Chapter 4, Scramblers, Climbers and Perchers). Page 88

| Daviesia hakeoides | Brown | Jun-Aug |
| | Lower slope | Uncommon |

Shrub to 1x2m with knitted stems. Phyllodes 80x1mm needle-shaped, stem-like, scattered, giving plant leafless appearance. Flowers 6mm across clustered in phyllode axils enclosed by distinctive overlapping brown bracts up to 3mm across.

| Daviesia polyphylla | Pinkish-brown | Aug-Sep |
| | Lower slopes | Common |

Shrub to 40cm, many closely spaced stems. Phyllodes 10x2mm flattened vertically, pointed, crowded on stems. Flowers 5mm across few clustered in phyllode axils.

| Daviesia preissii | Yellow and red | Nov-Jan |
| | Damper woodland | Common |

Shrub to 50cm, many closely-spaced stems. Phyllodes length variable to 30x2mm, needle-like with lengthwise ridges, blue-green. Flowers 7mm across in few-flowered clusters at phyllode axils. Page 88

| Daviesia longifolia | Yellow-brown | Nov-Jan |
| | Open gravelly woodland | Uncommon |

Shrub 0.75x1m, many stemmed, spreading. Phyllodes 200x3mm flattened, ribbed, strap-shaped. Flowers 9mm across, unlike other Daviesias, flowering sparingly with flowers on branched stalks in phyllode axils.

- 1A-1b Leaves alternate, not hard, cylindrical or very narrow, without sharp tips

| Dillwynia species | Red-brown | Aug-Sep |
| | Shady woodland | Rare |

Erect shrub to 1m, slender stemmed with spiny ends. Leaves 10x0.5mm, cylindrical. Flowers 8mm across borne singly in the axils of the uppermost leaves. Page 92

| Pultenaea ericifolia | Red-brown | Aug-Oct |
| Woolly-heads | Slopes | Uncommon |

Erect shrub to 75cm, hairy. Leaves 10x0.5mm, cylindrical, channelled. Flowers 12mm across, several in dense hemispherical, white-hairy heads, 2cm across, at the ends of stems. Page 89

| Euchilopsis linearis | Yellow-red | Oct-Nov |
| Swamp pea | Sandy swamp flats | Rare |

Weakly ascending shrub to 50cm. Leaves 15x2mm, flattened, scattered along stem. Flowers 8mm across on slender stalks to 1cm, borne singly in the leaf axils.

- 1A-1c Leaves alternate, flat, unbranched and longer than 1cm

| Hovea chorizemifolia | Purple | May-Jul |
| Holly-leaved hovea | Woodlands | Common |

Shrub to 30cm, straggling. Leaves 5x2cm holly-like with prickly, toothed margins. Flowers 1cm across few in clusters in leaf axils. Page 85

Chorizema ilicifolium Red and yellow Jul-Aug
Holly flame pea Lower slopes and streamsides Uncommon
  Shrub to 75cm, weakly-stemmed and straggling. Leaves 4x2cm, holly-like with spiny, wavy margins. Flowers 14mm across on sparsely branching stalks at ends of stems and in leaf axils. The brightly coloured standard petals of the flowers on weak stalks appear as dancing hearts (Chorizema heart dancers).

Daviesia rhombifolia Dark brown-yellow Jul-Aug
  Damper woodland Uncommon
  Shrub to 0.6x1m, dense spreading shrub. Leaves 3x2.5cm off-square (rhomboid), pointed, grey-green. Flowers 5mm across, a few in clusters in the leaf axils. Sometimes hosts Pilostyles hamiltonii. Page 88

Hovea trisperma Purple Jul-Oct
Common hovea Woodlands Common
  Shrub to 40cm, straggling weak sometimes reddish stems. Leaves 5x1cm oblong, margins usually entire. Flowers 20mm across up to three in clusters in axils of upper leaves.

Daviesia horrida Bronze-orange Aug-Sep
  Slope shrublands Common
  Shrub to 1.2m. Branchlets rigid, numerous, pointed (horrida), leafless above phyllodes (flattened 'leaves') 10x1.5cm, blue-green. Flowers 8mm across, massed on branching flower stalks at the ends of branches. Page 88

Templetonia drummondii Yellow Aug-Sep
  Open woodland Rare
  Shrub with prostrate stems to 30cm. Leaves 20x5mm broadly lance-shaped, bluish green, pointed. Flowers 14mm across borne singly in leaf axils.

Nemcia reticulata Yellow-brown Aug-Oct
  Slopes Rare
  Shrub to 50cm. Leaves 30x4mm folded lengthwise and stiffly pointed, often not clearly in whorls or alternate or opposite. Flowers 12mm across in loose clusters at the ends of the stems and leaf axils. Pods 1cmx6mm rounded.

Bossiaea eriocarpa Yellow and red-brown Sep-Oct
Common brown pea Woodlands and slopes Uncommon
  Erect shrub to 1.5m. Leaves 2x0.5cm oblong, net-veined with glossy-green upper surface. Flowers 20mm across, solitary in the leaf axils.

Bossiaea ornata Yellow and red-brown Sep-Oct
Broad-leafed brown pea Woodlands Common
  Shrub to 50cm, upright, weakly-stemmed. Leaves 4x2cm, heart-shaped to oval, net-veined with glossy-green upper surface. Flowers 14mm across, solitary in the leaf axils. Page 86

Daviesia cordata Yellow-brown Sep-Oct
Book-leaf Woodlands and slopes Uncommon
(See Chapter 2, Trees and Tall to Medium Shrubs, page 16).

Medium to Small Shrubs 49

Oxylobium lineare　　　　　　　　　Yellow and red　　　　　　　　　　Nov-Jan
　　　　　　　　　　　　　　　　　　Streamsides　　　　　　　　　　　　Rare
　　(See Chapter 2, Trees and Tall to Medium Shrubs, page 17).

- **1A-1d Leaves alternate, flat, unbranched, about 1cm or less**

Templetonia biloba　　　　　　　　　Brown and yellow　　　　　　　　　May-Jul
Horn-leaved bossiaea　　　　　　　　Slopes　　　　　　　　　　　　　　Common
　　Upright shrub to 30cm. Leaves 10x4mm oblong with broader tip, notched, horn-like. Flower
　　15mm across, one or two in leaf axil.　　　　　　　　　　　　　　　Page 91

Bossiaea spinescens　　　　　　　　　Yellow-brown　　　　　　　　　　　Jul-Aug
　　　　　　　　　　　　　　　　　　Damp areas　　　　　　　　　　　　Rare
　　(See Chapter 2, Trees and Tall to Medium Shrubs, page 17).

Bossiaea pulchella　　　　　　　　　　Yellow-brown　　　　　　　　　　　Aug-Sep
　　　　　　　　　　　　　　　　　　Damp areas　　　　　　　　　　　　Rare
　　Shrub to 1m, much branched. Leaves 8x4mm heart-shaped in two neat rows along the
　　branchlets. Flowers 12mm across borne singly in the leaf axils.

Mirbelia spinosa　　　　　　　　　　Red and yellow　　　　　　　　　　Aug-Oct
　　　　　　　　　　　　　　　　　　Granite outcrops　　　　　　　　　　Common
　　(See Chapter 2, Trees and Tall to Medium Shrubs, page 17).

Chorizema dicksonii　　　　　　　　　Brick red　　　　　　　　　　　　　Aug-Nov
Yellow-eyed flame pea　　　　　　　　Slope shrublands　　　　　　　　　Uncommon
　　Shrub to 1m. Leaves 10x4mm pointed and curving backwards, triangular from base and folded
　　lengthwise. Flowers 14mm across, a few on simply branched stalks at the ends of the stems.
　　　　　　　　　　　　　　　　　　　　　　　　　　　　　　　　　　Page 82

- **1A-1e Leaves alternate, compound with three leaflets**

Mirbelia dilatata　　　　　　　　　　Pink　　　　　　　　　　　　　　　Nov-Dec
Prickly mirbelia　　　　　　　　　　 Disturbed damp areas　　　　　　　Rare
　　(See Chapter 2, Trees and Tall to Medium Shrubs, page 18).

■ **1A-2 Leaves not arranged alternately around the stem**
- **1A-2a Leaves opposite, simple**

Nemcia capitata　　　　　　　　　　 Yellow-brown　　　　　　　　　　　Jul-Sep
Bacon and eggs　　　　　　　　　　　Slopes; open woodlands　　　　　　Common
　　Shrub to 75cm, weak straggling stems. Leaves 5x1cm oblong lance-shaped, folded lengthwise,
　　dark-green with pointed tips bent down, well separated along stems. Flowers 12mm across, up
　　to five clustered in leaf axils. Calyx silky-hairy.

Bossiaea aquifolium　　　　　　　　　Orange-yellow　　　　　　　　　　Aug-Sep
Water bush　　　　　　　　　　　　　Forest　　　　　　　　　　　　　　Uncommon
　　(See Chapter 2, Trees and Tall to Medium Shrubs, page 17).

Nemcia spathulata — Yellow-orange — Sep-Oct
Poison Bush — Upper slopes — Uncommon
    Erect shrub to 0.5m. Leaves 20x8mm wider at the tip than the middle, spoon-shaped (spathulate), folded lengthwise, slightly notched at tip. Flowers 7mm across in clusters in leaf axils.

Gastrolobium spinosum — Yellow-orange — Nov-Dec
Prickly poison — Slopes, sandy soils — Rare
    (See Chapter 2, Trees and Tall to Medium Shrubs, page 17).

- **1A-2b Leaves grouped in threes on stem**

Take care to distinguish this group from Clover-like trifoliate leaves which have three leaflets attached to each other with a single stalk to the stem.

Nemcia acuta — Yellow-brown — Sep-Oct
 — Slopes near granite — Rare
    Upright shrub to 75cm. Leaves 10x4mm sharply lance-shaped, smooth stiff leaves folded lengthwise. Flowers 1cm across in clusters in leaf axils.

Aotus cordifolia — Lemon yellow — Oct-Nov
 — Swamp margins — Rare
    (See Chapter 2, Trees and Tall to Medium Shrubs, page 18).

Nemcia dilatata — Orange-brown — Aug-Oct
Wedge-leaved oxylobium — Wooded slopes — Rare
    Shrub to 75cm. Leaves 5x3cm wedge-shaped, dark green. Flowers 1cm across crowded on short branching stalks in leaf axils or at ends of short branchlets.

Gastrolobium bilobum — Orange — Sep-Oct
Heart leaf poison — Damp areas — Rare
    (See Chapter 2, Trees and Tall to Medium Shrubs, page 17).

- **1A-2c Leaves compound with three leaflets on each leaf-stalk, clover-like**

Gompholobium marginatum — Yellow — Aug-Oct
 — Woodlands — Common
    Shrub to 20cm. Each leaflet 10x6mm, stiff and with a small point and a noticeable mid-rib. Flowers 7mm across, few on short branched stalks in leaf axils. Page 85

- **1A-2d Leaves compound with more than three leaflets either on a leaf stalk or as several finger-like leaflets from the leaf base.** Apart from lupins which are introduced, this leaf type is characteristic of the Gompholobiums.

Gompholobium knightianum — Pinky-purple — Aug-Dec
 — Woodland — Common
    Shrub to 30cm, delicate with almost climbing stems. Leaves with five to eleven leaflets each 20x5mm, oval to oblong, dark green. Flowers 6mm across, few clustered on branched stalk at the ends of stems. Page 87

Gompholobium polymorphum — Yellow, orange or rust red — Sep-Dec
Variable Gompholobium — Woodlands; slopes — Common
    (See Chapter 4, Scramblers, Climbers and Perchers, page 102).

Medium to Small Shrubs

Gompholobium preissii Yellow Oct-Nov
 Woodland Uncommon
Shrub to 20cm, soft-hairy, herblike. Leaves with 11 to 15 leaflets, 15x2mm broadened towards tip, crowded on stem. Flowers 1cm few clustered at stem tips amongst leaves.

Gompholobium tomentosum Yellow Oct-Nov
 Open gravelly woodland Rare
Erect shrub to 75cm, shortly hairy. Leaves with five to nine leaflets 12x0.5mm, cylindrical. Flowers 11mm across few at the ends of stems. Hairy (tomentose) calyx remaining after petals have fallen, spreading, red-brown.

Gompholobium shuttleworthii Dark pink Oct-Dec
 Slopes Uncommon
Erect shrub to 50cm. Leaves with five to eleven leaflets 10x0.5mm, cylindrical. Flowers 1cm across on short branched stalks at the ends of the stems. Calyx black-hairy.

- **1A-2e Leafless**

Jacksonia sternbergiana Orange-yellow All year
 Sparsely wooded slopes Uncommon
(See Chapter 2, Trees and Tall to Medium Shrubs, page 18).

Jacksonia alata Orange Sep-Nov
Winged Jacksonia Granite outcrops; Common
 gravelly woodlands
Erect shrub to 20cm with flattened stems (alata = winged) 4mm wide and often crooked. Flowers 5mm across clustered at ends of stems.

Jacksonia furcellata Yellow Sep-Nov
 Slope shrublands Uncommon
(See Chapter 2, Trees and Tall to Medium Shrubs, page 18).

Jacksonia restioides Yellow-red Sep-Nov
Rush Jacksonia Slope shrublands Uncommon
Erect shrub to 30cm with silvery-grey, cylindrical, ribbed stems like a rush (restioides). Flower 14mm across, few sparse towards stem tips. Page 96

Mirbelia ramulosa Yellow-red Sep-Oct
 Granite outcrops Uncommon
Erect shrub to 30cm, much-branched spiny, divided, cylindrical stems. Leaves tiny triangular scales. Flowers 8mm across clustered at the ends of stems or along the stems. Reproduces prolifically from seed.

Sphaerolobium medium Yellow Sep-Oct
 Woodland; upper slopes Uncommon
Upright shrub to 50cm, with many erect stems. Leaves few, scattered, pressed to the stem, scarcely noticeable. Flowers 5mm across, forming a finger flower-head with successive whorls of flowers along the stem. Page 96

Sphaerolobium vimineum Pinkish yellow Oct-Nov
Leafless globe pea Lower slopes Uncommon
Similar to Sphaerolobium medium but with style having a small, fringing membrane beneath near its tip.

Viminaria juncea	Yellow	Oct-Dec
Swishbush or native Broom	Streamsides and damp areas	Common

(See Chapter 2, Trees and Tall to Medium Shrubs, page 18).

- **1A-2f Leaves mainly from base of plant**

Isotropis cuneifolia	Orange	Sep-Oct
Granny bonnets	Damp places	Common

Lamb poison (See Chapter 7, Herblike Plants and Annuals, page 179).

1B Petals five, appearing separate, unequal so that sometimes there appears to be only one obvious petal

GOODENIACEAE: *Lechenaultia Scaevola*
VIOLACEAE: *Hybanthus*

GOODENIACEAE - Lechenaultias

Lechenaultia biloba	Sky blue	Jul-Nov
Blue lechenaultia	Woodlands	Common

Shrub to 50cm straggling, with a few upright branches, often in groups. Leaves 8x1mm cylindrical grey-green, crowded on stems. Flowers 2cm across massed in clusters towards the ends of stems with colour forms varying from white to blue to grey. Blue Lechenaultia is the emblem of the Darling Range Branch of the Wildflower Society. Page 96

Goodenia fasciculata	White	Aug-Dec
Bristly scaevola	Slopes	Uncommon

Erect shrub to 1m. Leaves 7x0.5mm, cylindrical, several clustered at common points along stems, dense woolly-hairy at axils. Flowers 7mm across with dark spots in throat, stalkless, crowded towards ends of stems. Page 93

Scaevola platyphylla	Blue-purple	Sep-Jan
Broad-leaved fan flower	Woodlands	Uncommon

Erect shrub to 1m with few stout straggling stems. Leaves 4x2.5cm fleshy, shiny green, sparsely hairy, often stem clasping, rounded with notched margins. Flowers 4cm across, the petals spreading hand-like, single, stalkless towards the ends of stems in bract axils. Page 91 & 84

VIOLACEAE - Violets

The herbaceous violets of Eastern Australia and overseas are absent here. The Family is represented by a single woody species.

Hybanthus floribundus	Mauve-blue	May-Aug
Showy hybanthus	Woodlands and slope	Uncommon

Erect shrub to 30cm. Leaves 15x5mm oblong with pointed tips. Flowers 1cm with one prominent downward-projecting petal, clustered in leaf axils. Page 81

1C Petals five, as unequal lobes, not all always obvious, but with lower lobes protruding, lip-like joined to form a **TUBULAR** flower

LAMIACEAE: Hemiandra Hemigenia Lavandula Microcorys
LAMIACEAE - Mint bushes

Hemigenia ramosissima	Mauve	Jun-Oct
	Woodland	Uncommon

Shrub to 50cm, slender. Leaves 20x5mm stalkless, opposite, folded lengthwise, oblong, blunt, grey-green. Flowers 7mm on stalks 4mm single in the leaf axils. Calyx persistent, distinctive, two-lipped with upper lip 5x5mm, rounded, pale brown.

Hemigenia incana Silky hemigenia	Pink-mauve Slopes and granite outcrops	Jun-Nov Uncommon

(See Chapter 2, Trees and Tall to Medium Shrubs, page 21).

Hemigenia sericea Silky hemigenia	Mauve Open woodlands	Jul-Oct Uncommon

Shrub to 50cm spreading. Leaves 20x2mm oblong. Flowers 7mm with three-lobed lower lip, few, clustered in the leaf axils. Sepals five, narrow-pointed.
Page 80

Lavandula stoechas* French lavender	Purple Disturbed areas	Jul-Nov Rare

Shrub to 60cm aromatic. Leaves 10x2mm grey opposite or clustered on stems, strap-shaped with margins rolled under. Flowers 7mm long densely grouped into square-sided head with purple showy bracts. Native to the Mediterranean region.

Microcorys longifolia	Red Granite outcrop	Sep-Nov Rare

Shrub to 50cm, slender. Leaves 40x4mm stalkless, opposite, strap-shaped. Flowers 18mm long on stalks over 1cm borne singly in the leaf axils. At the southern extremity of its distribution: extends north to Wongan Hills.

Hemiandra pungens Snakebush	Pink or white Open gravelly woodland	Sep-Jan Uncommon

Prostrate shrub to 10cm, stiffly-hairy. Leaves 10x2mm very spiky, stalkless, triangular, the sharp tips curving over, stiffly-hairy. Flowers 2.5cm long, dark spots on throat, single in the leaf axils.
Page 79

| 1D | Petals four, separate |

SAPINDACEAE: *Diplopeltis*
CAESALPINIACEAE: *Labichea*

Diplopeltis huegelii	Pale pink Slopes	Aug-Nov Common

Shrub to 1m, slender-stemmed, straggly, open, weedy. Leaves 3x1cm variably lobed to divided. Flowers 2cm across on 5mm stalks loosely clustered on branching ends of stems giving the whole a misty pink appearance. Close examination of the apparently regular flower shows the four petals are not symmetrically arranged. There are five sepals, the eight stamens are twisted to one side, and the seed capsule is three-lobed.
Page 41

CAESALPINIACEAE - Senna family

Labichea punctata Lanced leaf labichea	Yellow (with red centre) Woodlands	Jul-Oct Common

Shrub to 50cm. Leaves 10x1cm, lance-shaped, net-veined, dark green. Flowers 2cm across, on short stalks scattered singly towards ends of stems.
Page 93

Labichea lanceolata	Yellow with red spots	Sep-Nov
Tall labichea	Streamsides	Uncommon

(See Chapter 2, Trees and Tall to Medium Shrubs, page 21).

1E Petals four, joined to form tube though sometimes short. Petals often curled back with obvious protruding style

PROTEACEAE: Adenanthos Conospermum Grevillea Hakea Lambertia Synaphea

PROTEACEAE - Banksia family *(For fuller description see Chapter 9, page 225)*

Groupings for identification are:
- 1E-1 Flowers not in tight heads, seed structure (woody nut) remains on plant (Hakea). Flowers clustered, white or pinky-purple in leaf axils or raspberry coloured at ends of stems (Hakea myrtoides), page 54.
- 1E-2 Flowers not in tight heads, seed capsules fall off. Flowers loosely clustered on stalks at leaf axils or at ends of stems (Grevillea and Lambertia), page 56
- 1E-3 Flowers single in leaf axils, red (Adenanthos), page 57
- 1E-4 Flowers blue, clustered in a head at the end of leafless stalk (Conospermum huegelii), page 57
- 1E-5 Flowers scattered along leafless stalks at ends of branches (Conospermum, Synaphea), page 57

- 1E-1 Flowers not in tight heads, seed structure (woody nut) remains on plant (Hakea). Flowers clustered, white in leaf axils or raspberry coloured at ends of stems (Hakea myrtoides)

Groupings for identification are:
- 1E-1a Leaves prickly-edged, flat; cone stigma, page 54
- 1E-1b Leaves smooth-edged, flat; cone stigma, page 54
- 1E-1c Leaves cylindrical, divided, sharply-pointed; cone stigma, page 55
- 1E-1d Leaves prickly-edged, flat; flat stigma, page 55
- 1E-1e Leaves smooth-edged, flat; flat stigma, page 55
- 1E-1f Leaves cylindrical; flat stigma, page 55

- 1E-1a Leaves prickly-edged, flat; cone stigma

Hakea varia	White	Jul-Aug
Variable leafed hakea	Damp swampy areas	Rare

(See Chapter 2, Trees and Tall to Medium Shrubs, page 19).

Hakea undulata	White	Aug-Sep
Wavy-leaved hakea	Slopes and open woodland	Common

(See Chapter 2, Trees and Tall to Medium Shrubs, page 19).

- 1E-1b Leaves smooth-edges, flat; cone stigma

Hakea petiolaris	White and maroon	May-Aug
Sea Urchin hakea	Below granite outcrops	Uncommon

(See Chapter 2, Trees and Tall to Medium Shrubs, page 19).

Hakea myrtoides	Raspberry-coloured	Jun-Aug
Myrtle hakea	Slope shrublands	Uncommon

Shrub to 75cm, spreading and semi-prostrate. Leaves 13x6mm, spreading and densely packed on arching stems, near oval, tapering to sharp point, pale green. Flowers 7mm long densely clustered in cylinder towards ends of stems, these cylinders of flowers being up to 10cm long. The top of the shrub commonly dies off.   Page 78 & 86

Medium to Small Shrubs 55

Hakea stenocarpa	White	Sep-Nov
Narrow fruited hakea	Woodlands	Common

Compact shrub 1x1m. Leaves 80x6mm strap-shaped and curled. Flowers 6mm clustered in the axils of upper leaves. Nut 25x6mm, tapering to long, narrow point (stenocarpa = narrow fruited).

- 1E-1c Leaves cylindrical, divided, sharply-pointed; cone stigma

Hakea lissocarpha	White and pink	Jun-Aug
Honey bush	Slopes and open woodland	Common

(See Chapter 2, Trees and Tall to Medium Shrubs, page 20).

- 1E-1d Leaves prickly-edged, flat; flat stigma

Hakea cristata	White	May-Jul
Snail hakea	Slopes	Uncommon

(See Chapter 2, Trees and Tall to Medium Shrubs, page 20).

Hakea amplexicaulis	White	Jul-Oct
Prickly hakea	Woodlands	Common

(See Chapter 2, Trees and Tall to Medium Shrubs, page 20).

Hakea auriculata	Pinky-purple or white	Sep-Oct
Hairbrush hakea	Slope shrublands	Uncommon

Compact shrub to 0.5x1m. Leaves 4x1cm stem-clasping, broadened at base, strap-shaped widening to tip, blue-green. Flowers 6mm long in clusters in axils of upper leaves. Page 90

Hakea prostrata	White	Sep-Oct
Harsh hakea	Damp areas with sandy soils	Uncommon

(See Chapter 2, Trees and Tall to Medium Shrubs, page 20).

- 1E-1e Leaves smooth-edged, flat; flat stigma

Hakea ruscifolia	White	Jan-Mar
Candle hakea	Woodlands and upper slope shrublands	Uncommon

(See Chapter 2, Trees and Tall to Medium Shrubs, page 20).

Hakea incrassata	White	Jun-Aug
Marble hakea	Slope shrublands	Uncommon

Compact shrub 1x1m, sturdy, rounded. Leaves 70x12mm broadly lance-shaped, widest beyond mid-point, stoutly pointed. Flowers 3mm long in clusters in axils of upper leaves. Nut 2.5cm across, round, marble-like.

Hakea cyclocarpa	White	Aug-Sep
Ramshorn hakea	Upper slopes	Uncommon

(See Chapter 2, Trees and Tall to Medium Shrubs, page 20).

- 1E-1f Leaves cylindrical; flat stigma

Hakea erinacea	Cream	Jun-Sep
Hedgehog hakea	Slopes	Common

(See Chapter 2, Trees and Tall to Medium Shrubs, page 21).

Hakea trifurcata	White	Jul-Oct
Two-leaved hakea	Woodlands	Common

(See Chapter 2, Trees and Tall to Medium Shrubs, page 21).

■ 1E-2 Flowers not in tight heads, seed capsules fall off. Flowers loosely clustered on stalks at leaf axils or at ends of stems (Grevillea and Lambertia). Of the nine species five are described in Chapter 2, Trees and Tall to Medium Shrubs.
   Groupings for identification are:
   • 1E-2a Leaves divided into lobes, stigma cone-shaped, page 56
   • 1E-2b Leaves entire, not lobed or divided, flowers white or yellow, page 56
   • 1E-2c Leaves oak-shaped with prickly edges, page 56
   • 1E-2d Leaves deeply divided, flowers red, page 57
   • 1E-2e Leaves mostly entire but a few with divided tips, flowers mixed brown, black and white, page 57

• 1E-2a Leaves divided into lobes, stigma cone-shaped

Grevillea synapheae	Creamy-white	Jun-Oct
Catkin grevillea	Forests; woodlands	Common

Shrub to 0.5m, sprawling. Leaves 8x4cm three-lobed, each further divided ending in a point. Flowers 6mm long, crowded on catkin-like, cylindrical heads, 3cm long, at the ends of stems.
Page 90

Grevillea manglesii	White	Jul-Oct
Smooth grevillea	Lower slopes; rock outcrops	Uncommon

(See Chapter 2, Trees and Tall to Medium Shrubs, page 19).

• 1E-2b Leaves entire, not lobed or divided, flowers white or yellow

Grevillea pilulifera	Creamy-white	May-Oct
Woolly flowered grevillea	Slope shrublands	Common

Upright shrub to 75cm. Leaves two to five, 50x6mm variable but often lance-shaped with shiny green upper surface, edges rolled under, woolly-white underneath. Flowers 1cm long, few clustered at the ends of stems and in the leaf axils, hairy and with yellow to orange stigma.
Page 95

Grevillea endlicheriana	Pinky-white	Jun-Nov
Spindly grevillea	Slope shrublands	Common

(See Chapter 2, Trees and Tall to Medium Shrubs, page 18).

Lambertia multiflora	Orange-yellow	Jul-Nov
Many flowered honeysuckle	Slope shrublands	Uncommon

(See Chapter 2, Trees and Tall to Medium Shrubs, page 21).

• 1E-2c Leaves oak-shaped with prickly edges

Grevillea quercifolia	Pinky-purple	Aug-Dec
Oak-leaved grevillea	Woodlands	Uncommon

Shrub to 0.5m, straggling, little-branched, weakly upright stems trailing to 1m. Leaves 10x3cm. Flowers 1cm long loosely clustered into cylindrical heads 8cm long at the ends of stems. Page 86

Medium to Small Shrubs   57

● 1E-2d Leaves deeply divided, flowers red

Grevillea bipinnatifida   Red to rusty   All Year
Fuchsia grevillea   Slope shrublands   Very common
    Shrub to 1x1m, spreading with arched branches. Leaves 12x6cm twice deeply divided (bipinnatifida), prickly. Flowers 25mm long, hairy, loosely clustered into one-sided spray and the ends of stems. One of the parents of the popular garden hybrid Robyn Gordon. Page 83

Grevillea wilsonii   Scarlet   Jul-Jan
Native fuchsia   Gravelly open woodland   Common
    (See Chapter 2, Trees and Tall to Medium Shrubs, page 19).   Page 82

● 1E-2e Leaves mostly entire but a few with divided tips, flowers mixed brown, black and white

Grevillea diversifolia   Off-white   Jun-Oct
Variable-leaved grevillea   Lower slopes   Uncommon
    (See Chapter 2, Trees and Tall to Medium Shrubs, age 18).

In addition to those listed, others known to occur nearby are Grevillea paniculata (1E-2a with leaves three-lobed and white flowers), G. drummondii (1E-2b with soft, hairy leaves and golden-orange flowers), and G. pulchella (1E-2d with deeply divided leaves and white flowers).

■ 1E-3 Flowers single in leaf axils, red (Adenanthos)

Adenanthos barbiger   Red   All Year
Hairy jugflower   Woodlands   Very common
    Erect shrub to 1x2m with several stems coming up from a patch of ground. Leaves 60x6mm lance-shaped. Flowers 2.5cm long, hairy, style curved back like a jug handle into the four petal-like sepals which remain together, not separating.   Page 90

■ 1E-4 Flowers blue, clustered in a head at the end of a leafless stalk

Conospermum huegelii   Blue-grey   Aug-Oct
Slender Smokebush   Granite outcrops   Common
    Shrub to 75cm with tuft of leaves at ground level and erect flower stalk. Leaves 170x2mm, wiry. Flowers 5mm long, two-lipped, crowded initially in domed head at end of flower stalk, becoming scattered with age as stalk lengthens.   Page 90

■ 1E-5 Flowers scattered along leafless stalks at ends of branches

Conospermum stoechadis   White   May-Jul
Common Smokebush   Woodland   Uncommon
    (See Chapter 2, Trees and Tall to Medium Shrubs, page 28).

Synaphea acutiloba   Yellow   Jun-Oct
Granite synaphea   Slopes and woodland   Uncommon
    Stemless to 60cm with tuft of leaves at ground level and erect flower stalk. Leaves 30cm including leaf stalk about 20cm and blade three-lobed, deeply divided with acute pointed ends. Flowers 3mm long scattered along uppermost 10cm of flower stalk.

Synaphea gracillimaYellowJun-Nov
SynapheaSlopes and woodlandCommon
   Similar to Synaphea acutiloba but with larger flowers and thick textured leaves, these with longer lobes and much less sharp tips. It is more widely distributed.Page 86 & 87

Synaphea pinnataYellowSep-Oct
Helena synapheaSlopesRare
   Shortly-stemmed, 10cm, shrub 50cm with a tuft of basal leaves at ground level, sometimes dome-shaped, with flower stalks scarcely extending beyond the leaves. Leaves to 30cm with stalk up to 20cm bearing three to nine leaflets, lance-shaped, 8x1cm. A gazetted rare and endangered species.Page 86

GROUP 2
Flowers showy: REGULAR arrangement of petals; petals separate (of if joined, forming an open cup with joined bases, not a long narrow tube)

2A | Petals five, yellow, rounded tips

DILLENIACEAE:**Hibbertia**
   Groupings for identification are:
   2A-1 Stamens all on one side of ovary, page 58
   2A-2 Stamens arranged evenly around ovary, page 59

■ **2A-1 Stamens all on one side of ovary**

Hibbertia hypericoidesBrilliant yellowMay-Oct
Yellow buttercupWoodlands and slopesVery common
   Shrub to 70cmx1m, domed, spreading, twiggy. Leaves 10x3mm, oblong shiny-green upper surface, edges curled under, short, matted, hairy underneath. Flowers 2.5cm across on stalks to 1cm, borne singly in leaf axils.Page 82

Hibbertia aureaGolden yellowJul-Oct
Golden hibbertiaGranite outcropsUncommon
   Erect shrub to 1m. Leaves 15x1mm, shiny-green above, pointed. Flowers 15mm across, stalkless, borne singly in leaf axils.

Hibbertia spicataBrilliant yellowAug-Nov
Slope shrublandsUncommon
   Shrub to 30cm, sprawling. Resembles Hibbertia hypericoides except five to six flowers 8mm across are borne on the end 5cm of the stems and all face the same way.Page 84

Hibbertia acerosaBrilliant yellowSep-Dec
Needle-leaved guinea flowerWoodlandsVery common
   Shrub to 30cm, domed, spreading often ground-hugging and mat-forming. Leaves 1cmx1mm pointed with glossy-green upper surfaces. Flowers 8mm across on stalks to 15mm borne singly in leaf axils. Also occurs as a completely prostrate, flat-leaved form.

Medium to Small Shrubs   59

■ **2A-2 Stamens arranged evenly around ovary**

| Hibbertia serrata | Yellow | Jun-Sep |
| Serrate leaved guinea flower | Woodlands and damp slopes | Uncommon |

(See Chapter 2, Trees and Tall to Medium Shrubs, page 23).

Hibbertia commutata   Lemon yellow   Jun-Oct
                      Woodlands   Common
    Erect shrub to 30cm. Leaves 25x6mm, variable in size, oval, hairy, dark green. Flowers 15mm across, stalkless, single in leaf axils or at the ends of stems. Sepals silky-hairy surrounded by papery, brown bracts 4mm across. Stamens arrranged in three tufts.   Page 83

Hibbertia ovata   Lemon yellow   Jun-Oct
                      Gravelly woodlands   Uncommon
    Erect shrub to 30cm. Very similar to Hibbertia commutata but has more stamens - up to 50 - arranged evenly and the sepals and ovaries are much less hairy.

Hibbertia amplexicaulis   Yellow   Aug-Nov
                          Woodlands   Uncommon
    Shrub to 30cm, with weakly upright stems. Leaves 60x15mm, blue-green, fleshy, stem-clasping (amplexicaulis), triangular. Flowers 3cm across on stalks to 3cm, single in leaf axils. Page 93

Hibbertia glomerata   Yellow   Aug-Dec
                      Gravelly woodland areas   Uncommon
    Shrub to 30cm, twiggy, hairless. Leaves 12x3mm, oblong, blunt, distinctive pale green. Flowers 2cm across, stalkless, single in leaf axils.

Hibbertia lasiopus   Yellow   Sep
Large flowered hibbertia   Forest   Uncommon
    Shrubs to 10cm, straggling. Leaves, near oval, 25x17mm, softly hairy. Flowers up to 65mm across, stalkless to shortly stalked. Sepals 20mm to pointed tip, hairy outside, smooth pink inside. Papery brown rounded bracts, 15mm across.

Hibbertia subvaginata   Yellow   Sep-Nov
                        Granite outcrops   Uncommon

(See Chapter 2, Trees and Tall to Medium Shrubs, page 23).

Hibbertia pachyrrhiza   Lemon-yellow   Sep-Jan
                        Woodlands   Uncommon
    Erect shrub to 30cm, weak-stemmed, hairy. Leaves 20x3mm, oblong, edges curled under, somewhat cylindrical, hairy, grey-green. Flowers 20mm across, stalkless, single in leaf axils. Prominent pointed sepals.   Page 85 & 92

2B Petals five, white, pink or blue. If yellow, with pointed or fringed tips
BORAGINACEAE: Halgania
EUPHORBIACEAE: Ricinocarpus
MYRTACEAE: Baeckea Calytrix Hypocalymma Rinzia Verticordia
RUTACEAE: Asterolasia Philotheca

STERCULIACEAE: *Lasiopetalum Rulingia Thomasia*
TREMANDRACEAE: *Tetratheca*
MYRTACEAE - Myrtles

A good test for this family is to crush some leaves and smell. The leaves contain oil glands, often visible to the naked eye, containing a variety of aromatic oils.
    Groupings for identification are:
- 2B-1 Flowers with rounded petals and sepals, page 60
  - 2B-1a Leaves opposite, stamens 10-20, flowers small, about 1cm or less across, page 60
  - 2B-1b Leaves opposite, stamens about 30, flowers large, more than 1cm across, page 60
- 2B-2 Sepals each with hair-like extension, page 60
- 2B-3 Petals much-divided giving the flower a feathery appearance, page 61

- 2B-1 Flowers with rounded petals and sepals
- 2B-1a Leaves opposite, stamens 10-20, flowers small about 1cm or less across

| Rinzia crassifolia | Pure white | Jul-Nov |
| | Slope shrublands | Rare |

Shrub to 20cm, domed. Leaves 8x1mm, oblong. Flowers 1cm across on stalks to 5mm, borne singly in leaf axils but crowded because of closely spaced leaves. Stamens about 10. Southerly occurrence of a species which is distributed to Watheroo.

| Baeckea camphorosmae | Pink | Nov-May |
| Camphor myrtle | Woodlands; slope shrublands | Very common |

Shrub to 75cm, spreading. Leaves 5x0.5mm clustered on short branchlets. Flowers 10mm across, on stalks to 2mm and up to four in the leaf axils. Flowers crowded along the stem. Each flower has ten stamens grouped in pairs. The crushed leaves smell of camphor. Page 81

| Baeckea species | Pink | Nov-May |
| | Gravelly woodland | Uncommon |

Very similar to Baeckea camphorosmae, but has about 20 stamens evenly distributed around the flower and the flowers are scattered along the stem.

- 2B-1b Leaves opposite, stamens about 30, flowers large, more than 1cm across

| Hypocalymma angustifolium | White or pink-tinged | Jul-Oct |
| White myrtle | Damp areas on lower slopes | Common |

Erect shrub to 75cm, many-stemmed. Leaves 25x1mm, cylindrical. Flowers 6mm across, stalkless, up to two in leaf axils. Page 80

| Hypocalymma robustum | Deep pink | Aug-Oct |
| Swan River myrtle | Woodlands | Common |

Erect shrub to 1m, slender-stems red-brown. Leaves 20x2mm, cylindrical, spreading curving over at tip. Flowers 12mm across, stalkless, up to four in leaf axils. Page 94

- 2B-2 Sepals with long hair-like (thrix, a thread) extensions

CALYTRIX - starflowers.

    The five, star-shaped, pointed sepals with hair-like tips remain after the petals have fallen giving the name to species in this genus.

Medium to Small Shrubs   61

Calytrix glutinosa   Light pink   Sep-Oct
Sticky calytrix   Slope shrublands;   Uncommon
                                     gravelly woodlands
   Erect shrub to 1m. Leaves 1cmx1mm, crowded on stem. Flowers 2cm across borne singly in
   leaf axils clustered a short distance back from the stem tips and accompanied by sticky
   (glutinose) bracts. Sepals 1.5cm.   Page 84

Calytrix angulata   Yellow   Sep-Dec
Yellow calytrix   Sandy woodland   Rare
   Erect shrub to 1m. Leaves 5x1mm, three angled, spreading. Flowers 1.5cm across, sepals 1.2cm.

Calytrix aurea   Yellow   Oct-Nov
                                     Sandy woodland   Rare
   Erect shrub to 1m. Leaves 8x3mm overlapping, oval. Flowers 1.2cm across borne singly in leaf
   axils clustered over 3cm of the stem tip. Sepals 1.5cm.

Calytrix variabilis   Claret red/purple   Oct-Nov
                                     Woodland   Common
   Erect shrub to 50cm. Leaves 8x0.5mm, cylindrical, delicate, crowded on stem. Flowers 1.5cm
   across borne singly in leaf axils clustered over 4cm of stem at or near the stem tip. Sepals 1cm
                                                                          Page 85

Calytrix depressa   Creamy yellow   Oct-Dec
                                     Rock outcrops   Rare
   Erect shrub to 1m. Leaves 8x1mm, three angled, spreading. Flowers 1.5mm across, petals
   rounded. Sepals 1cm.

■ 2B-3 Petals much divided, feathery
VERTICORDIA - featherflowers.
The 'feathers' are divided petals and sepals often with extra hairs at the base of the sepals.
Verticordia acerosa   Yellow turning brown   Aug-Nov
                                     Slope shrublands;   Common
                                     rock outcrops
   Erect shrub to 75cm. Leaves 10x0.5mm, cylindrical, variable, crowded on stem, shiny green.
   Flowers 8mm across loosely clustered in showy head at the end of the stem.

Verticordia huegelii   White ageing to pink   Sep-Nov
Variegated featherflower   Slope shrublands;   Common
                                     rock outcrops
   Erect shrub to 30cm. Leaves 7x0.5mm, cylindrical, crowded on short branchlets, blue green.
   Flowers 15mm across loosely clustered in showy head at end of the stem.   Page 78

Verticordia insignis   Pink   Sep-Nov
                                     Sandy open woodland   Very rare
   Erect shrub to 75cm. Leaves 10x3mm flat and lance-shaped, crowded on stem. Flowers 12mm
   across clustered in sprays along the stems.

Verticordia pennigera	Pink	Sep-Dec
	Slopes and granite outcrops	Uncommon

Erect shrub to 30cm with weak, arching branches. Leaves 5x0.5mm, cylindrical, crowded on short branchlets. Flowers 10mm across forming a spray along end 10cm of stem. The flowers have a ring of hairs where they join the stalk, a character absent in the next two pink-flowered species. Page 94

Verticordia plumosa	Pink	Sep-Dec
Granite featherflower	Rock outcrops	Uncommon

Erect shrub to 75cm. Leaves 12x0.5mm, cylindrical, crowded on short branchlets, blue-green Flowers 8mm across clustered in compact domed head at the ends of the stems. Page 94

Verticordia densiflora	Dull Pink	Sep-Dec
Compacted featherflower	Sandy open woodland	Rare

Erect shrub to 1m, straggling and open. Leaves 10x0.5mm, cylindrical, crowded on short branchlets. Flowers 5mm across with dark protruding style noticeable, clustered in several small heads at the ends of the stems and upper branchlets.

EUPHORBIACEAE - Spurges (For fuller description see Chapter 9,)

Ricinocarpos glaucus	White	Aug-Oct
Wedding Bush	Slopes	Rare

Shrub to 50cm, spreading. Leaves 25x2mm, oblong with edges rolled under, hairy beneath, shiny dark green above. Female and male flowers similar, 1cm across, on branching stalks, 3cm, few per stalk in the leaf axils. Page 79

STERCULIACEAE - Lasiopetalum Rulingia Thomasia

Thomasia foliosa	Off-white to pink-tinged	May-Aug
	Wandoo woodland	Common

Shrub to 1m with many stems. Leaves 3x2cm on 8mm stalks, roundly-lobed, broadest at the base. Flowers 4mm across clustered in sprays of up to 10 flowers on branching stalks opposite leaves. Page 89

Lasiopetalum glabratum	Pinky-purple	Jun-Sep
	Open woodland	Rare

Shrub to 40cm with many weak stems, often in groups. Leaves 2x1cm heart-shaped on 4mm stalk. Flowers 5mm across, three to six on branching flower stalks to 3cm at the ends of stems. A species at the northern limit of its distribution in the Kalamunda Hills.

Lasiopetalum bracteatum	Pink	Aug-Nov
Helena velvet bush	Streamsides	Uncommon

(See Chapter 2, Trees and Tall to Medium Shrubs, page 24.)

Thomasia macrocarpa	Pinky-violet	Sep-Oct
Felt-leaved thomasia	Open woodlands on damp slopes	Uncommon

(See Chapter 2, Trees and Tall to Medium Shrubs, page 24).

Thomasia pauciflora	Pink	Sep-Nov
Few flowered thomasia	Streamsides and damp areas	Uncommon

(See Chapter 2, Trees and Tall to Medium Shrubs, page 24).

Medium to Small Shrubs 63

Thomasia grandiflora	Dull purple	Sep-Nov
Potato flowered thomasia	Woodland and slope	Uncommon

Shrub to 1m with many stems. Leaves 4x1.5cm on stalks to 1cm with two large leafy lobes at the leaf axils. Leaves oblong with base broader. Flowers 14mm across, one to five scattered at the ends of the stems. Page 95

Rulingia cygnorum	Bright white	Sep-Dec
	Granite outcrops	Rare

Shrub to 1m with many weak stems. Leaves 3x1cm oak-shaped on 6mm stalk. Flowers 1.4cm across clustered in sprays 5cm across opposite leaves. The petals clasp the stamens and have long 10mm white extensions projecting between the sepal points in contrast with the minute petals of Thomasia. Page 87

Thomasia glutinosa	Bright pink	Sep-Dec
Sticky thomasia	Slopes and granite outcrops	Uncommon

Shrub to 75cm with many stems. Leaves 3.5x2cm on stalk 8mm broadest at base with two lobes, narrowing towards the tip. Flowers 1cm across clustered in sprays of up to 10 flowers along the flower stalk at the ends of the stems. Flower sprays very sticky (glutinose).Page 94

TREMANDRACEAE - *Tetratheca*

Nodding, stalked, pink flowers, with five rather crumpled petals surrounding a black centre suggesting one of the common names - 'Black-eyed Susan'.

Tetratheca hirsuta	Pink	May-Dec
Black-eyed Susan	Woodland and slopes	Very common

Shrub to 50cm, weak erect stems. Leaves hairy (hirsute) very variable from 5x3mm to 2.5x1cm becoming smaller up the stem, often grouped in threes but also in twos and alternate. Flowers 1.5cm across, nodding on stalks to 2cm borne singly in the leaf axils appearing as showy sprays of bell-shaped to spreading flowers with dark centres visible when turned over. Page 87

Tetratheca nuda	Light pink	Oct-Dec
Grass tetratheca	Woodland and slopes	Rare

Mostly leafless shrub to 30 cm, wiry stemmed. Leaves 5x0.5mm scattered, often absent. Flowers 1.2cm across, nodding on stalks to 7mm, scattered along the stems.

BORAGINACEAE - Borage Family

Halgania corymbosa	Deep blue	Aug-Nov
	Damp areas	Rare

Erect shrub to 50cm, hairy. Leaves 3.5x1cm oblong, hairy, toothed. Flowers 2cm across, up to 10 clustered loosely on branching stalk at the ends of stems. More common in the wheatbelt.

RUTACEAE - Citrus and Boronia Family (For fuller description see Chapter 9, Page 226)

Asterolasia pallida	White	Jul-Sep
	Shady gullies	Rare

Shrub to 1m, straggling. Leaves 1.8cmx8mm broadest at middle. Flowers 1.5cm across, on stalks to 1cm, up to five loosely clustered in heads. The undersides of the petals and the leaves are covered with small star-shaped brown hairs. Page 88.

Philotheca spicata Pink to lilac Jun-Nov
Pepper and salt Woodlands Very common
    Shrub to 60cm, slender erect stems. Leaves 18x2mm strap-shaped grey-green. Flowers 8mm across on stalks 7mm crowded along upper ends of stems, spike-like, to 15cm long. Page 95

Boronia cymosa. Often has five rather than the four petals characteristic of Boronias (see 2D, below).

2C Petal-like parts six

EUPHORBIACEAE: *Phyllanthus*

Phyllanthus calycinus Cream Jul-Oct
False boronia Slopes Very common
    Shrub to 75cm, spreading, twiggy. Leaves 15x4mm oblong, alternate, scattered along stem on short leaf stalks. Female flowers 1cm across nodding on stalks to 1cm borne singly in the leaf axils. Male flowers 4mm across on stalks to 6mm, up to three in the leaf axils. Page 92

2D Petals four

RUTACEAE: *Boronia*
PROTEACEAE: *Stirlingia*
CAESALPINIACEAE: *Labichea [Grp 1d]*
SAPINDACEAE: *Diplopeltis [Grp 1d]*

    Groupings for identification are:
    ■ 2D-1 Leaves simple or (less commonly) divided and flattened, page 64
    ■ 2D-2 Leaves much-branded, cylindrical tangled segments, page 65

■ 2D-1 Leaves simple or (less commonly) divided and flattened

RUTACEAE - Boronias (For fuller description see Chapter 9, Page 226)

Boronia crenulata Pink Apr-Aug
Aniseed boronia Streamsides Uncommon
    Shrub to 75cm, weak, slender stems, open habit, often straggling through other shrubs. Leaves 20x2mm strap-shaped or broadening towards tip, margins sometimes with small, rounded teeth (crenulate), opposite and scattered along the stem. Flowers 1cm across on stalks 4mm borne singly to a few in leaf axils and at the ends of stems, scattered.

Boronia cymosa Pink Jun-Nov
Granite boronia Rock outcrops Common
    Shrub to 50cm, sparingly branched stems. Leaves 25x2.5mm near cylindrical, somewhat stem-hugging and spiralling up the stem. Flowers 1cm across, four or five petalled clustered on branching stalks at the end of the stems often in loose, dome-shaped heads. In area of Bickley Reservoir, five petalled plants found August 1988, also scarp, West Terrace, August 1989. Page 79

Boronia ramosa Pale blue Jul-Sep
  Rock outcrops Uncommon
    Shrub to 25cm, scrambling and weakly-stemmed. Leaves with three leaflets 15x2mm, strap-shaped. Flowers 8mm across on stalks to 3mm, borne singly in the leaf axils.

Boronia tenuis · Blue · Jul-Nov
Blue boronia · Slope shrublands · Rare
  Shrub to 50cm, slender, weak stems, often straggling through other shrubs. Leaves 18x0.5mm, cylindrical, opposite on stem. Flowers 1cm across on stalks 1cm borne singly in the leaf axils.
  Page 81

Boronia ovata · Pink · Aug-Nov
Heart-leaved boronia · Woodlands · Common
  Shrub to 30cm, straggling weakly-stemmed. Leaves 14x8mm, heart-shaped, opposite, blue green. Flowers 1.5cm across up to four loosely clustered on branching stalks about 5cm at the ends of stems.
  Page 80

■ 2D-2 Leaves much-branched, cylindrical tangled segments
Stirlingia simplex · Yellow · Oct-Nov
 · Lower slopes · Rare
  Stemless shrub with leaves from ground level and flower stalk to 30cm. Leaves 20cm a lacework of grey-green segments on a stalk to 10cm. Flowers 4mm across, clustered on uppermost 10cm of branching flower stalk. More common inland.
  Page 84

GROUP 3
Flowers showy: REGULAR arrangement of petals; petals JOINED to form a TUBE

| 3A | Petals four, flowers in HEADS

PROTEACEAE: · *Banksia Isopogon Petrophile Persoonia*
THYMELAEACEAE: · *Pimelea*

  Groupings for identification are:
  ■ 3A-1 Flowers in compact heads, flowering progressing from the lower or outer to the upper or centre, persistent cones, page 65
  ■ 3A-2 Flowers in compact heads, the entire head of flowers in flower mostly at once with any progression from outer to inner quite rapid, no persistent cone, page 66
  ■ 3A-3 Flowers single in the leaf axils, page 67

■ 3A-1 Flowers in compact heads, flowering progressing from the lower or outer to the upper or centre, persistent cones

PROTEACEAE - Banksia family (For fuller description see Chapter 9) - page 225
Isopogons and Petrophiles are very similar in appearance with somewhat egg-shaped (less commonly flat), erect cones persisting.

Isopogon asper · Pink-grey · Jul-Sep
Flat-topped coneflower · Slope shrublands · Uncommon
  Shrub to 75cm, sturdy, upright. Leaves, divided and simple. Divided leaves 2.5x1cm, stem-clasping; simple leaves 15x2mm in the axils of the divided leaves. Flowers 13mm long much of which hidden in flat head 3cm becoming an attractive red button topping the stems after flowering.
  Page 78

Petrophile biloba · Pinkish-grey · Jul-Sep
Granite petrophile · Granite outcrops · Common
  (See Chapter 2, Trees and Tall to Medium Shrubs, page 25).

Isopogon dubius	Shocking pink	Jul-Oct
Rose coneflower	Slopes and gravelly woodland	Uncommon

(See Chapter 2, Trees and Tall to Medium Shrubs, page 25).

Isopogon sphaerocephalus	Creamy-yellow	Jul-Oct
Drumstick isopogon	Woodlands	Common

(See Chapter 2, Trees and Tall to Medium Shrubs, age 25).

Isopogon divergens	Grey-pink	Aug-Nov
Spreading coneflower	Lower slopes	Rare

(See Chapter 2, Trees and Tall to Medium Shrubs, page 25).

Petrophile seminuda	Yellow	Aug-Nov
	Lower slopes	Uncommon

Shrub to 50cm, upright. Leaves 5x2cm divided into two or three lobes, each further divided ending in pointed, cylindrical segments. Flowers 1cm long densely clustered on cone 13mm across. Page 91

Banksia littoralis	Orange-yellow	Sep
Swamp Banksia	Swampy places	Uncommon

(See Chapter 2, Trees and Tall to Medium Shrubs, page 16).

Petrophile striata	Pale yellow	Sep-Nov
	Woodlands	Common

Shrub to 75cm, upright. Leaves 3x2.5cm divided into three lobes themselves further divided into pointed, strap-shaped segments, harsh. Flowers 1.5cm long, hairy, densely clustered on cone 13mm across. Page 91

Banksia grandis	Greeny-yellow	Oct-Nov
Bull banksia	Forest	Common

(See Chapter 2, Trees and Tall to Medium Shrubs, page 16).

■ **3A-2** Flowers in compact heads, the entire head of flowers in flower mostly at once with any progression from outer to inner quite rapid, no persistent cone

THYMELAEACEAE - Rice flowers

Plants with flowers in heads appearing like fluffy rice.

Pimelea suaveolens	Yellow	Jun-Oct
Scented banjine	Woodlands	Common

Erect shrub to 50cm, single-stemmed. Leaves 25x4mm broadly spear-shaped, pale green. Flowers 12mm long with spreading hairs, many grouped in nodding heads 3cm across surrounded by broad bracts, 2cmx8mm. Page 93

Pimelea brevistyla	White	Sep-Nov
	Wooded slopes	Rare

Shrub to 1m, single stem at base. Leaves 25x3mm with 1mm stalk, lance-shaped, spreading, slightly cupped. Flowers 1cm long, hairy, style not extending beyond tube (brevistyla), many grouped in erect heads 2cm across surrounded by two or four bracts 15x8mm.

Medium to Small Shrubs 67

Pimelea lehmanniana	White-pink	Sep-Nov
	Wooded slopes	Rare

Shrub to 40cm, single stem at base. Leaves 23x5mm with 1mm stalk, lance-shaped, spreading. Flowers 8mm long, hairy, many grouped in head 1.5cm across sometimes tilted, surrounded by four or six bracts 16x8mm.

Pimelea preissii	White-pink	Sep-Nov
	Drier woodlands	Rare

Shrub to 30cm, few stems often growing through other plants. Leaves 15x4mm, lance-shaped. Flowers 8mm long, hairy, many grouped in erect heads 1.5cm across surrounded by four bracts 1cmx5mm.

Pimelea spectabilis	White	Sep-Nov
Bunjong	Woodlands; rock outcrops	Uncommon

(See Chapter 2, Trees and Tall to Medium Shrubs, page 26).

Pimelea ciliata	White	Sep-Dec
White banjine	Woodlands and slopes	Uncommon

Erect shrub to 1m with many upright, little-branched stems. Leaves 17x5mm, spreading, oblong with pointed tip curved downwards. Flowers 8mm long with spreading hairs on lower part of tube, many grouped in erect to slightly tilted heads 3cm across surrounded by broad bracts, 1cmx5mm.
Page 89

Pimelea imbricata	White	Sep-Dec
	Slope shrublands;	Common
	rock outcrops	

Shrub to 50cm, single stem at base. Leaves 12x3mm, oblong, soft, hairy, alternate. Flowers 11mm long, few hairs along length of the tube outside, hairy inside, many grouped in erect head 3cm across, surrounded by leaf-like bracts, similarly narrow, not broad.

■ **3A-3 Flowers single in the leaf axils**

Pimelea argentea	Yellow	Sep-Nov
Silvery leaved pimelea	Wandoo woodland and	Uncommon
	lower slopes	

(See Chapter 2, Trees and Tall to Medium Shrubs, page 26).

Persoonia angustiflora	Yellow	Nov-Jan
Shrub persoonia	Woodlands; slope shrublands	Uncommon

Shrub to 30cm with straggling stems. Leaves 100x1mm flattened cylindrical with lengthwise ribs. Flowers 7mm across, single to few in the axils of leaves.
Page 83

| 3B | Petals five |

EPACRIDACEAE (Heaths): Andersonia Astroloma Leucopogon Styphelia
RHAMNACEAE: *Cryptandra*

Groupings for identification are:
- ■ 3B-1 Tubes of joined petals: sepals and bracts visible outside, page 68
  - • 3B-1a Tips of petal lobes without tuft of hairs, tubes long (>1.5cm) or not white flowered, page 68

- 3B-1b Tips of petal lobes with tuft of hairs, lobes spreading, tubes short (1cm or less), page 69
- 3B-2 Tubes of joined sepals: petals as small hoods over the anthers, page 70

■ 3B-1 Tubes of joined petals: sepals and bracts visible outside

EPACRIDACEAE - Heaths

• 3B-1a **Tips of petal lobes without tuft of hairs, tubes long (>1.5cm) or not white flowered**

| Astroloma pallidum | White | Mar-Nov |
| Kick bush | Slopes | Common |

Cushion shrub to 20cm, domed. Leaves 15x3mm oblong parallel-veined tapering to sharp point, blue-green. Flowers 1.5cm long and 4mm in diameter, borne singly in leaf axils, mostly hidden.   Page 90

| Styphelia tenuiflora | Brilliant white | Apr-Jun |
| Common pin-heath | Woodlands | Common |

Shrub to 75cm. Leaves 18x5mm lance-shaped, sharply-pointed with shiny dark green upper surface. Flowers 2.8cm long, 2mm in diameter, borne singly in leaf axils of the upper stems. Lobes rolled back, hairy inside, with anthers and style protruding.   Page 87

Andersonia lehmanniana	Pink with blue	Apr-Oct
	Gravelly woodlands;	Common
	slope shrublands	

Shrub to 30cm with weak twisting stems. Leaves 7x3mm, stem-clasping, twisted and curled over, tapering to blunt point. Flowers 9mm long, the sepals longer than the pink tube, 4mm across, in clusters of about 10 on the upper portion of the stem.   Page 79

| Astroloma ciliatum | Scarlet, purple-black | May-Jul |
| Moss-leaved heath | Woodlands and slopes | Common |

Mat-like shrub to 5cm, ground-hugging. Leaves 8x1mm, lance-shaped, spreading, sharply pointed, blue green. Flowers 2.5cm long borne singly in leaf axils and largely hidden amongst the leaves. Tips appearing as bright red stars dotted over the cushion.   Page 85

| Astroloma foliosum | Scarlet, black and green | May-Jul |
| Candle cranberry | Slopes and woodlands | Rare |

Erect shrub to 1m, little-branched, miniature pine-like. Leaves 8x0.5mm, lance-shaped, spreading, finely-pointed, bright green. Flowers 2.5cm long borne singly in leaf axils along much of the upper stems. Striking appearance with black and green tip giving the illusion of a lit candle. Restricted to the Kalamunda area and killed by fire.   Page 83

Andersonia aristata	White	Sep-Nov
Rice flower	Slope shrublands;	Uncommon
	rock outcrops	

Shrub to 25cm, single-stemmed. Leaves 6x1mm flattened, needle-like. Flowers 1cm long, in clusters of about 10 crowded at the ends of the stems. As flower develops, the tube, anthers and style enlarge to eventually be longer than the sepals. Lobes hairy, curved back. Page 78

Medium to Small Shrubs   69

- 3B-1b Tips of petal lobes with tuft hairs lobes spreading, tubes short (1cm or less)

LEUCOPOGON - Bearded Heaths

Separation of the eight Leucopogon species [white (leuco)-bearded (pogon) heaths] is difficult. Differences in size, leaf size and shape, how the flowers are borne and habitat help to separate the species.

| Leucopogon propinquus | White | Mar-May |
| Common forest heath | Forests | Common |

Shrub to 1m. Leaves 20x2mm, pointed, blue-green. Flowers 6mm long, scattered along branches, pink tinge to bud tips.

| Leucopogon nutans | White | May-Jun |
| Drooping heath | Forests | Uncommon |

Shrub to 1m. Leaves 12x2mm, pointed, spreading or bent back on stems. Flowers 1cm long, hanging in rows from stems.

| Leucopogon oxycedrus | White | May-Jun |
| | Forest | Uncommon |

Shrub to 1m. Leaves 10x2mm, pointed, spreading in all directions on the stems. Flowers 1cm long, sometimes hanging but not in neat rows.

| Leucopogon pulchellus | White | Jun-Sep |
| Beard-heath | Slopes | Common |

Shrub to 50cm, dainty with hairy branchlets. Leaves 8x1mm, lance-shaped, keeled, pointed. Flowers 5mm across with short tube, in clusters of up to eight flowers in the axils of upper leaves or at the ends of stems and branchlets.   Page 78

| Leucopogon sprengelioides | White | Jul-Sep |
| | Slopes and granite outcrops | Uncommon |

Shrub to 50cm, dainty. Leaves 3x3mm, stem-clasping, heart-shaped, ribbed lengthwise, blunt. Flowers 4mm long in clusters of up to eight at the ends of the stem and branchlets.

| Leucopogon capitellatus | White | Jul-Oct |
| Clustered heath | Forests | Common |

Shrub to 1m. Leaves 10x2mm, pointed. Flowers 4mm long, about five, clustered at branch tips, buds pink tinged.   Page 79

| Leucopogon cymbiformis | White | Nov-Feb |
| | Slopes | Uncommon |

Shrub to 30cm. Leaves 5x2mm erect, triangular, sharply-pointed. Flowers 4mm long borne in twos and threes in leaf axils or at the ends of stems.

| Leucopogon tenuis | White | Nov-Feb |
| | Damp areas on slopes | Uncommon |

Shrub to 50cm. Leaves 12x3mm tapering to stem and blunt tip. Flowers 4mm long clustered on upper ends of stems in flowering spike to 3cm.

■ 3B-2 Tubes of joined sepals: petals as small hoods over the anthers

RHAMNACEAE

Cryptandra glabriflora	White	Jun-Aug
Lesser waxflower	Woodlands; slope shrublands; rock outcrops	Uncommon

Shrub to 30cm, very twiggy. Leaves 6x2mm edges curled under so as to appear cylindrical, bunched on stems. Flowers 2x2mm, lobes spreading, stalkless in loose clusters on short branchlets.

Cryptandra arbutiflora	Waxy-white	Jun-Sep
Waxy cryptandra	Slope shrublands	Uncommon

Shrub to 75cm, twiggy. Leaves 7x1.5mm oblong with edges curled under. Flowers 4x2mm stalkless, massed on spikes at the ends of stems and branchlets. Page 95

3C 'Petals' (Daisies)

ASTERACEAE: *Olearia*
ASTERACEAE - Daisies (For fuller description see Chapter 9)

Olearia paucidentata	White and pale blue	Apr-Jul
Autumn scrub daisy	Woodlands	Uncommon

Shrub to 1m, few stems. Leaves 25x7mm widening from base, toothed, shiny green upper surface. Flower heads 1.2cm across with 10 or more edge flowers (ray florets) giving spreading petal-like appearance to flower head. Tubular flowers in the centre of the flower head (disc florets) a handsome violet. Page 81

GROUP 4
Flowers showy: petals NOT OBVIOUS (instead, spiky flowers of prominent anthers or styles, or finely-divided petals)

4A Flowers yellow, pom-pom or sausage-shaped

MIMOSACEAE: Acacia
MIMOSACEAE - Wattles (For fuller description see Chapter 9)
    Groupings for identification are:
      ■ 4A-1 Leaves divided with many leaflets, page 70
      ■ 4A-2 Phyllodes ('leaves') winged along stems, page 71.
      ■ 4A-3 Leafless. A few divided juvenile leaves may be present, page 71
      ■ 4A-4 Phyllodes ('leaves') near-cylindrical, page 71
      ■ 4A-5 Phyllodes ('leaves') flat, width more than three times the thickness, page 72

■ 4A-1 Leaves divided with many leaflets

Acacia drummondii	Yellow	Jul-Oct
Drummond's wattle	Woodlands; slope shrublands	Uncommon

Shrub to 75cm, erect. Leaves twice-divided, leaflets up to five pairs, variable, 10x3mm, almost cylindrical to flat. Flower heads cylindrical 25x5mm on stalks to 2cm, single in the leaf axils.

Acacia pulchella	Yellow	Jul-Oct
Prickly Moses	Woodlands; slope shrublands	Very common

(See Chapter 2, Trees and Tall to Medium Shrubs, page 14).

Medium to Small Shrubs 71

Acacia varia   Cream   Sep-Oct
                                      Damp areas   Rare
   Shrub to 30cm, erect. Leaves twice divided, leaflets 5x2mm, sometimes curved back at tips,
   grey-green, three paired. Flower heads 15x5mm on stalks 12mm, single in the leaf axils.

■ 4A-2 Phyllodes ('leaves') winged along stems

Acacia stenoptera   Cream   Apr-May
Narrow winged wattle   Damp sandy flats   Rare
   Shrub to 40cm, straggly and weak-stemmed, flattened to 5mm. Phyllodes 30x6mm curving
   away from the winged part on the stem, hooked and pointed. Flower heads spherical 8mm
   across on stalks 7mm up to two in the phyllode axils.

Acacia alata   Cream or yellow   Jun-Aug
Winged wattle   Streamsides and damp areas   Common
   (See Chapter 2, Trees and Tall to Medium Shrubs, page 13).

Acacia willdenowiana   Yellow   Jul-Oct
Grass wattle   Woodlands   Uncommon
   Shrub to 25cm, weakly-stemmed, flattened to 5mm across. Phyllode ending as curved, pointed
   triangle 5mm across, separating from the wing of the stem. Flower heads spherical 6mm across
   on stalks 12mm up to two in the phyllode axils.

Acacia anomala   Yellow   Aug-Sep
Grass-wattle   Slopes   Very rare
   Shrub to 40cm, weakly-stemmed, sparingly branched and slightly flattened, rush-like. Phyllode
   60x4mm, few to absent, strap-shaped and pointed. Flower heads cylindrical 20x7mm on stalks
   3mm, borne singly, scattered towards the upper ends of the stems. A gazetted rare and
   endangered species.   Page 92

Acacia barbinervis   Yellow   Dec-Feb
                                      Woodlands; slope shrublands   Common
   Shrub to 25cm, many erect branching stems, flattened, 3mm across. Phyllodes 1.7cmx3mm with
   prominent midrib, stiffly-hairy, curved back to sharp pointed tips, pinched at the axils. Flower
   heads spherical 6mm across on stalks 5mm borne singly in the phyllode axils. Style protrudes
   shortly beyond stamens.

■ 4A-3 Leafless
Acacia aphylla   Yellow   Jul-Sep
Leafless rock wattle   Rock outcrops   Very rare
   Shrub to 1m, with branching, somewhat tangled, cylindrical, smooth, blue-green, stems ending
   in a point. Flower heads spherical 6mm across on stalks 1cm borne singly scattered on upper
   part of stem. A gazetted rare and endangered species.

■ 4A-4 Phyllodes ('leaves') stalked, near-cylindrical
Acacia horridula   Pale yellow   May-Jul
Prickly wattle   Streamsides   Rare
   (See Chapter 2, Trees and Tall to Medium Shrubs, page 13).

Acacia teretifolia — Yellow — Woodlands — May-Jul — Common
Shrub to 35cm, erect, stems blue green. Phyllodes 25x1mm cylindrical, lying along the stem, sharply pointed, blue green with two small thorns in axils. Flower heads spherical 5mm across on stalks 5mm borne singly in phyllode axils. Pods 100x3mm chestnut brown. Page 84

Acacia sessilis — Deep yellow — Jun-Jul
Spiny wattle — Slope shrublands — Uncommon
(See Chapter 2, Trees and Tall to Medium Shrubs, page 13).

Acacia extensa — Yellow — Aug-Sep
Wiry wattle — Damp areas, often sandy — Uncommon
(See Chapter 2, Trees and Tall to Medium Shrubs, page 13).

Acacia oncinophylla — Yellow — Sep
Hooked-leaf wattle — Rock outcrops — Common
(See Chapter 2, Trees and Tall to Medium Shrubs, page 14).

■ 4A-5 Phyllodes ('leaves') flat, width more than three times the thickness

Acacia obovata — Creamy-white — Apr-Jun
Wavy-leaved wattle — Woodlands; slope shrublands — Common
Shrub to 0.5x1m, spreading. Phyllodes 3x1.8cm rounded with prominent midrib, edges wavy, grey-green. Flower heads spherical 6mm across on stalks 12mm up to three in the phyllode axils. Pod 100x7mm flattened, twisted, dark brown.

Acacia urophylla — White to cream — June
Net-leaved wattle — Woodlands — Uncommon
(See Chapter 2, Trees and Tall to Medium Shrubs, page 13).

Acacia incrassata — Yellow — Jun-Aug
— Slope shrublands — Rare
Shrub to 25cm, erect inticately branched, often amongst other shrubs. Phyllodes 12x8mm rounded-triangular with long sharp point, dark green. Flower heads spherical 8mm across on stalks 5mm borne singly in the phyllode axils.

Acacia nervosa — Lemon-yellow — Jun-Sep
Ribbed wattle — Woodlands — Common
Shrub to 0.4x1m, spreading, stems whitish, angular, with green to brown stripes. Phyllodes 35x7mm, banana-shaped in outline, spreading, with pointed tip, prominent midrib and two small thorns in axils. Flower heads spherical 8mm across on stalks 12mm up to three in the phyllode axils. Page 82

Acacia saligna — Orange-yellow — Aug-Sep
Orange wattle — Damp areas — Common
(See Chapter 2, Trees and Tall to Medium Shrubs, page 14).

Acacia dentifera — Yellow — Sep-Oct
Toothed wattle — Damp areas — Common
(See Chapter 2, Trees and Tall to Medium Shrubs, page 14).

Medium to Small Shrubs   73

Acacia divergens	Yellow	Sep-Oct
Sailboat wattle	Broad drainage lines	Uncommon

(See Chapter 2, Trees and Tall to Medium Shrubs, page 14).

4B Flowers not yellow, or if yellow, not pom-pom or sausage-shaped
MYRTACEAE: Beaufortia Calothamnus Darwinia [Grp 5]
Melaleuca Verticordia [Grp 2b]
Groupings for identification are:
- 4B-1 Stamens grouped on more than five stalks page 73
- 4B-2 Stamens grouped on five or fewer stalks, some broad strap-shaped page 73
- 4B-3 Stamens separate page 74

■ **4B-1 Stamens grouped on more than five stalks**

Beaufortia macrostemon	Scarlet	Sep-Dec
	Woodlands; slope shrublands	Uncommon

Shrub to 35cm branched and spreading. Leaves 10x2mm narrowly oval to oblong, hairy, crowded on stem. Flowers with stamen bundles 18mm, yellow green at base, clustered in rounded heads at the ends of stems and branchlets, petals 3mm.

Beaufortia purpurea	Purple	Nov-Jan
Purple beaufortia	Slope shrublands	Rare

(See Chapter 2, Trees and Tall to Medium Shrubs, page 15).

■ **4B-2 Stamens grouped on five or fewer stalks, some broad, strap-shaped**

CALOTHAMNUS - One Sided Bottlebrushes

Calothamnus sanguineus	Bright red	Mar-Jul
Pindak	Gravelly woodlands	Uncommon

(See Chapter 2, Trees and Tall to Medium Shrubs, page 15).

Calothamnus torulosus	Red	Aug-Oct
	Slope shrublands	Rare

Shrub 0.5x2.5m, twiggy. Leaves 35x1mm, pointed tips, crowded round stem, pine-like. Flowers 2.5cm, made up of four bundles of anthers, the upper two wider and longer than the lower two, clustered along 6cm of one side of the stem, hidden.

Calothamnus hirsutus	Red	Sep-Nov
One-sided bottlebrush	Slope shrublands	Rare

(See Chapter 2, Trees and Tall to Medium Shrubs, page 15).

Calothamnus quadrifidus	Red	Sep-Nov
One-sided bottlebrush	Woodlands; slope shrublands	Common

(See Chapter 2, Trees and Tall to Medium Shrubs, page 15).

Melaleuca radula	Pinky-mauve	Sep-Nov
Graceful honeymyrtle	Slope shrublands	Common

Shrub to 1.5m, straggly. Leaves 35x3mm, grey-green, opposite. Flowers in pairs, opposite, 2cm across with fringed, spreading petals. Woody capsules persistent lower on stems.

■ 4B-3 Stamens separate

Melaleuca parviceps	Shocking pink	Sep-Dec
Rough honeymyrtle	Gravelly woodlands; slope shrublands	Very common

Erect shrub to 75cm. Leaves 15x1mm, cylindrical, minutely knobbly (scabra = rough), scattered to crowded on stems. Flowers with stamens to 1cm, crowded in rounded heads at the ends of stems. Page 82

Melaleuca incana	Cream	Oct-Dec
Grey honeymyrtle	Swampy streamsides	Rare

Shrub to 1m. Leaves 10x2mm tapering to blunt point, grey-hairy. Flowers with stamens to 8mm in cylindrical clusters at or near the ends of stems.

Melaleuca species (A)	Light pink	Nov-Dec
	Slope shrublands	Rare

Shrub to 40cm, spreading. Leaves 20x1mm cylindrical, hairy, silvery. Flowers with stamens to 1.5cm, few in rounded heads at or near the ends of stems.

GROUP 5
Flowers individually inconspicuous

CASUARINACEAE:	*Allocasuarina*
EUPHORBIACEAE:	*Monotaxis Stachystemon*
HALORAGACEAE:	*Gonocarpus*
MYRTACEAE:	*Darwinia*
PROTEACEAE:	*Stirlingia [Grp 2d]*
RHAMNACEAE:	*Trymalium*
SANTALACEAE:	*Leptomeria*
SAPINDACEAE:	*Dodonaea*

Groupings for identification are:
- ■ 5-1 Flowers scattered along stems, at ends or midway along, page 74
- ■ 5-2 Flowers grouped in heads at ends of stems, page 75
- ■ 5-3 Flower heads surrounded by coloured bracts, nodding, page 75
- ■ 5-4 Flowers in loose clusters on branched stalks from leaf axils, page 76
- ■ 5-5 Flowers dangling singly on stalks, page 76

■ 5-1 Flowers scattered along stems, at ends or midway along
CASUARINACEAE - Sheoaks (For fuller description see Chapter 9, Page 222)

Allocasuarina humilus	Red/Brown	Aug-Sept
Scrub sheoak	Open woodland, slope shrublands	Common

(See Chapter 2, Trees and Tall to Medium Shrubs, page 29).

Allocasuarina microstachya	Red/Brown	Sep-Oct
Dwarf Sheoak	Slope shrublands	Very Rare

Shrub to 50cm, intricately-branched, dense. Branchlets in short sections 5mm or less with four tiny teeth (scale leaves) at each join.

SANTALACEAE - *Sandalwoods*
(see also Chapter 2, Trees and Tall to Medium Shrubs, p.28)

A family of root-parasitising plants closely related to mistletoes.

Leptomeria cunninghamii — Yellow-brown — Aug-Oct
Fingerbush — Woodland — Uncommon
  Shrub to 50cm with much-branched, knitted, arching stems. Leaves 9x1mm, lying along stems with tips curved inwards, scattered or absent. Flowers 1.5mm across scattered towards ends of stems in axils of leaf-like bracts. Page 91

HALORAGACEAE - *Gonocarpus*

Gonocarpus cordiger — Greeny-brown — Nov-Jan
  — Woodlands — Common
  Shrub to 30cm, erect, branched. Leaves 22x1mm, cylindrical, rough. Flowers 3mm across borne singly in axils of shield-like bracts along unbranched flower stalks.

EUPHORBIACEAE - *Spurge Family* (For fuller description see Chapter 9, page 223)

Stachystemon vermicularis — Maroon — Nov-May
Wormflower — Open woodlands — Rare
  Shrub to 40cm, erect, sparsely branched. Leaves 15x2mm cylindrical, keeled. Flowers 3mm across along unbranched ends of stems giving worm-like (vermicularis) appearance.

■ 5-2 Flowers grouped in heads at ends of stems

Monotaxis grandiflora — White — Sep-Nov
Diamond of the desert — Woodlands — Uncommon
  Shrub to 15cm, erect, much branched stems. Leaves 15x1mm cylindrical, tips pointed. Male and female flowers 4mm across on stalks, male 3mm, female near stalkless, clustered in the axils of the crowded upper leaves.

■ 5-3 Flower heads surrounded by coloured bracts, nodding

MYRTACEAE - *Darwinia*

Darwinia citriodora — Red — Jun-Nov
Lemon-scented darwinia — Rock outcrops — Common
  (See Chapter 2, Trees and Tall to Medium Shrubs, page 29)
  This can also be a small, rock-hugging shrub.

Darwinia apiculata — Green — Aug-Sep
Scarp darwinia — Open woodland — Very rare
  Shrub to 30cm, much-branched, spreading, cushion-form. Leaves 8x0.5mm, cylindrical, pointed, yellowy-green, crowded on stem. Flowers 3mm long, up to six in the head surrounded by narrow, pointed bracts, 12x2mm. Extremely restricted distribution. Page 92

Darwinia thymoides — White or red — Sep-Nov
  — Damp areas — Uncommon
  Mat-forming shrub to 10cm resembling the herb, thyme (thymoides). Leaves 8x3mm oval, spreading, blue-green. Flowers 4mm long, up to six in the head surrounded by broad bracts, 6x4mm. Page 83

■ 5-4 Flowers in loose clusters on branched stalks from leaf axils
RHAMNACEAE - *Trymalium*

The tiny creamy flower parts of Trymalium are the sepals; the petals are minute hoods over the stamens.

Trymalium ledifolium	Cream	May-Sep
	Gravelly woodland; slope shrublands	Very common

Shrub to 1m, erect, branched. Leaves 20x4mm, oblong, shiny dark green above, edges curled under and white underneath. Flowers 3mm across, scattered on branched sprays to 10cm long at ends of stems and branchlets. Very floriferous. Produces abundant fine seed and is a good coloniser of disturbed areas. Page 96

Trymalium floribundum	Cream	Aug-Sep
Karri hazel	Rock outcrops; streamsides	Uncommon

(See Chapter 2, Trees and Tall to Medium Shrubs, page 28).

■ 5-5 Flowers dangling singly on stalks

SAPINDACEAE - *Dodonaeas*
The most striking feature of Dodonaeas is their seed capsule rather than the inconspicuous flowers.

Dodonaea ericoides	Brown	Feb-Apr
	Slope shrublands	Rare

Shrub to 50cm, erect with hairy branchlets. Leaves 10x2mm narrowly oblong, edges curled under, hairy, toothed beyond middle. Flowers 5mm across on short, hairy curved stalks borne singly at the ends of stems and branchlets. Fruit four-angled seed capsule 7mm across, densely hairy. A species at the southern edge of its distribution.

Dodonaea ceratocarpa	Brown	Jul-Oct
	Rock outcrops	Rare

Shrub to 1.5m, spreading, rounded. Leaves 30x8mm glossy, rounded, edges curled under, with point at tip. Flowers 6mm across on short stalks up to four on branched stalk at the ends of stems. Fruit three to four capsules, horned, 8cm across, brown.F

GROUP 6
Flowers clustered in tight HEADS [Most are referred to previous Groups]

|6A| Flower heads nodding

RUTACEAE:	*Diplolaena*
MYRTACEAE:	*Darwinia [Grp 5]*
THYMELAEACEAE:	*Pimelea [Grp 3a]*

Diplolaena drummondii	Red-green	Jul-Sep
	Lower slope shrublands	Very rare

Shrub to 1m. Leaves 40x10mm, felty, densely hairy. Flowers in nodding heads 2cm across with stamens protruding. Page 89

| 6B | Flower heads not nodding

ASTERACEAE: *Olearia [Grp 3c]*
MIMOSACEAE: *Acacia [Grp 4a]*
MYRTACEAE: *Beaufortia [Grp 4b] Callistemon [Grp 1c]*
Calothamnus [Grp 4b] Melaleuca [Grp 4b]
PAPILIONACEAE: *Pultenaea [Grp 1a] Sphaerolobium [Grp 1a]*
PROTEACEAE: *Conospermum (Pale blue flowers) [Grp 1e]*
Dryandra Isopogon [Grp 3a] Petrophile [Grp 3a]

Dryandra sessilis   Pale yellow   Mar-Nov
Parrot Bush   Gravelly woodlands   Very common
   (See Chapter 2, Trees and Tall to Medium Shrubs, page 26).

Dryandra armata   Yellow   Jun-Sep
Prickly Dryandra   Gravelly woodlands;   Common
                           slope shrublands
   (See Chapter 2, Trees and Tall to Medium Shrubs, page 26).

Dryandra lindleyana   Greeny-brown   Jun-Sep
Couch Honeypot   Woodlands   Very common
   Spreading shrub to 30cm with trailing to semi-erect stems covering up to several square metres.
   Leaves 25x1cm, with pointed, toothed margins cut to near midrib, twisting, shiny green above,
   snow (nivea) white underneath. Flowers 4cm long in densely clustered, pot-like heads 6x3.5cm
   surrounded by numerous oblong bracts 2x0.5cm at the ends of stems surrounded by leaves.
   Nectar at the base of the flower heads gives the common name of Honeypot.   Page 80

Dryandra squarrosa   Pale yellow   Aug-Nov
Pingle   Woodlands   Uncommon
   (See Chapter 2, Trees and Tall to Medium Shrubs, page 26).

Dryandra bipinnatifida   Brown-yellow   Oct-Nov
Ground dryandra   Woodlands   Common
   Shrub stem underground with leaves to 30cm. Leaves twice-divided (bipinnatifida) 30x10cm,
   lobes flattened, dark green above, dull white underneath, fern-like. Flowers 3cm long densely
   clustered in head 10cm long, 6cm across, cone-shaped, half-buried in the ground, surrounded
   by broad strap-shaped, brown, stiff, papery bracts 6x1cm.

Hakea myrtoides
Myrtle hakea

Leucopogon pulchellus
Beard-heath

Verticordia huegelii
Variegated featherflower

Isopogon asper
Flat-topped coneflower

Andersonia aristata
Rice flower

Medium to Small Shrubs 79

Ricinocarpos glaucus
Wedding Bush

Boronia cymosa
Granite boronia

Hemiandra pungens — Snakebush

Andersonia lehmanniana

Leucopogon capitellatus
Clustered heath

Boronia ovata
Heart-leaved boronia

Hypocalymma angustifolium
White myrtle

Hemigenia sericea
Silky hemigenia

Dryandra lindleyana
Couch Honeypot

Medium to Small Shrubs 81

Hybanthus floribundus
Showy hybanthus

Olearia paucidentata
Autumn scrub daisy

Hybanthus floribundus
Showy hybanthus

Baeckea camphorosmae
Camphor myrtle

Boronia tenuis
Blue boronia

Hibbertia hypericoides
Yellow buttercup

Grevillea wilsonii
Native fuchsia

Chorizema dicksonii
Yellow-eyed flame pea

Acacia nervosa
Ribbed wattle

Melaleuca parviceps
Rough honeymyrtle

Medium to Small Shrubs 83

Hibbertia commutata

Grevillea bipinnatifida
Fuchsia grevillea

Darwinia thymoides

Astroloma foliosum
Candle cranberry

Persoonia angustiflora
Shrub persoonia

Acacia teretifolia

Scaevola platyphylla
Broad-leaved fan flower

Stirlingia simplex

Hibbertia spicata

Calytrix glutinosa
Sticky calytrix

Medium to Small Shrubs 85

Calytrix variabilis

Hibbertia pachyrrhiza

Astroloma ciliatum
Moss-leaved heath

Hovea chorizemifolia
Holly-leaved hovea

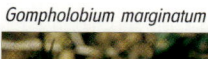

Gompholobium marginatum

Bossiaea ornata
Broad-leafed brown pea

Synaphea gracillima
Synaphea

Hakea myrtoides
(with a Wanderer butterfly)
Myrtle hakea

Grevillea quercifolia
Oak-leaved grevillea

Synaphea pinnata
Helena synaphea

Medium to Small Shrubs 87

Rulingia cygnorum

Gompholobium knightianum

Synaphea gracillima
Synaphea

Styphelia tenuiflora
Common pin-heath

Tetratheca hirsuta
Black-eyed Susan

Daviesia preissii

Asterolasia pallida

Daviesia rhombifolia

Daviesia decurrens
Prickly bitter-pea

Daviesia horrida

Medium to Small Shrubs 89

Pimelea ciliata
White banjine

Diplolaena drummondii

Pultenaea ericifolia
Woolly-heads

Thomasia foliosa

Hakea auriculata
Hairbrush hakea

Astroloma pallidum
Kick bush

Conospermum huegelii
Slender Smokebush

Grevillea synapheae
Catkin grevillea

Adenanthos barbiger
Hairy jugflower

Medium to Small Shrubs 91

Templetonia biloba
Horn-leaved bossiaea

Leptomeria cunninghamii
Fingerbush

Scaevola platyphylla
Broad-leaved fan flower

Petrophile striata

Petrophile seminuda

Acacia anomala
Grass-wattle

Dillwynia species

Phyllanthus calycinus
False boronia

Hibbertia pachyrrhiza

Darwinia apiculata
Scarp darwinia

Medium to Small Shrubs 93

Goodenia fasciculata
Bristly scaevola

Hibbertia amplexicaulis

Labichea punctata
Lanced leaf labichea

Pimelea suaveolens
Scented banjine

Mirbelia dilatata

Verticordia plumosa
Granite featherflower

Thomasia glutinosa
Sticky thomasia

Hypocalymma robustum
Swan River myrtle

Verticordia pennigera

Medium to Small Shrubs 95

Cryptandra arbutiflora
Waxy cryptandra

Thomasia grandiflora
Potato flowered thomasia

Philotheca spicata
Pepper and salt

Grevillea pilulifera
Woolly flowered grevillea

Lechenaultia biloba
Blue lechenaultia

Jacksonia restioides
Rush Jacksonia

Trymalium ledifolium

Sphaerolobium medium

Lechenaultia biloba
Blue lechenaultia

CHAPTER 4

Scramblers, Climbers and Perchers

This chapter includes all genuine climbers along with plants which can more appropriately be described as scramblers.

There are also species which, in the absence of support to climb or scramble up, form perfectly satisfactory shrubs or clumps. These too are included here.

Finally, there is a very small group, all semi-parasitic plants, which are rooted in woody species, sometimes high above the ground.

GROUP 1
SCRAMBLERS AND CLIMBERS
Flower Parts in threes page 100

Sub-Group	Families	Genera
1A Showy, petals purple, fringed page 100	Anthericaceae	Thysanotus
1B Inconspicuous, yellow to pale yellow flower parts: page 100.	Dioscoreaceae Lauraceae	Dioscorea Cassytha

GROUP 2
Flower Parts four page 101

Sub-Group	Families	Genera
2A REGULAR arrangement of parts, WHITE page 101	Ranunculaceae	Clematis
2B IRREGULAR, petals in two pairs, PINK, rarely white page 101	Stylidiaceae	Stylidium

GROUP 3
Petals five, IRREGULAR flowers - petals not all with shield-like similar page 101

Sub-Group	Families	Genera
3A PEA flowers (i.e. standard petal, forward-projecting wing and keel petals) purple, red, pink, yellow, orange. page 101	Papilionaceae	Hardenbergia Gompholobium Kennedia
3B Flowers with two prominent wing petals but no shield-like standard petal: BLUE page 102	Polygalaceae	Comesperma

GROUP 4
Petals five, REGULAR flowers - all petals similar   page 102

Sub-Group	Families	Genera
4A Flowers white, leaves with sticky-glandular hairs page 102	Droseraceae	Drosera
4B Flowers white, purple, blue or greeny-yellow, leaves flattened, green, without sticky glands page 103	Pittosporaceae	Billardiera Cheiranthera Pronaya Sollya
	Polygonaceae	Muehlenbeckia
	Rosaceae	Rubus

GROUP 5
PERCHERS: Flowers Funnel-Shaped page 104

Sub-Group	Families	Genera
	Convolvulaceae	Convolvulus

GROUP 6
Perchers page 104

Sub-Group	Families	Genera
6A Showy: Flowers bright orange; on wattles and gum trees in Feb-Jul page 104	Loranthaceae	Amyema
6B Inconspicuous: Flowers small, breaking through stem surface, dark red. Plant not visible. page 105	Rafflesiaceae	Pilostyles

GROUP 1
Flower Parts in Threes

1A Showy, petals purple, fringed

ANTHERICACEAE:	*Thysanotus*	
Thysanotus patersonii	Purple, fringed	Aug-Dec
Climbing fringed lily	Woodlands; slope shrublands	Common

Leafless, branching slender green stems, less than 1mm diameter, climbing over 1m amongst shrubs. Parts in threes, the larger, the petals, purple and fringed. Flowers 1.5x1.5cm clustered on branchlets. Thysanotus manglesianus, previously a variety but now a recognised species, is similar but with larger flowers. The other fringed lilies are described in Chapter 5, Plants with Grasslike Leaves page 128
Page 107

1B Inconspicuous, yellow to pale yellow flower parts

DIOSOREACEAE: *Dioscorea*
LAURACEAE: *Cassytha*

    Groupings for identification are:
    ■ 1B-1 Leaves arrowhead-shaped page 100
    ■ 1B-2 No obvious leaves page 100

■ **1B-1 Leaves arrowhead-shaped**

DIOSCOREACEAE:	*Dioscorea*	
Dioscorea hastifolia	Yellow	May
Native Yam, Warrine	Slope shrublands	Common

Occurs in large patches giving a yellow tinge to the slopes when flowering. Flowers 1.5mm across, many on flower stalks, 8cm long, borne on long, trailing stems with several leaves shaped like arrowheads (hastifolia). The three-seeded fruits with extended wings are characteristic, ending on stalks. The tuber of this species which belongs to the tropical yam family is thin and short.
Page 106

■**1B-2 No obvious leaves**

LAURACEAE:	Cassytha	
Cassytha spp.	White and yellow	
Dodder Laurels	Woodlands; slope shrublands	Common
Cassytha racemosa	White to pale yellow	Oct-Jan
Cassytha glabella	White to pale yellow	Nov-Jan
Cassytha flava	Lemon yellow	Dec-Jan

Matted pale yellow to brown-yellow leafless stems straggling over shrubs and grasses, often almost covering them, attached by suckers (haustoria) semi-parasitic. Flowers often grouped, 1mm, single, stalkless on hairless stems (C. glabella) or two to three, shortly-stalked, on slightly hairy stems (C. racemosa), or in stalked tight heads of about 10 very yellow flowers (C. flava). Developed fruits, 3x1mm, pear-shaped, green-yellow.

GROUP 2
Flower Parts Four

2A REGULAR arrangement of parts, WHITE
RANUNCULACEAE: *Clematis*

Clematis pubescens	White	Sept-Oct
Old man's beard	Forests	Uncommon

Robust scrambler and climber, stems 2mm diameter, with three-part leaves, 50x20mm, each leaflet with smooth or toothed margin. Conspicuous tresses of white flowers, 4x4cm with stamens. Flower stalks hairy. In fruit, several seeds with long hairy ends on each flower head (old man's beard). Page 108

2B IRREGULAR, petals in two pairs, PINK, rarely white
STYLIDIACEAE: *Stylidium*

Stylidium repens   Pink, sometimes white   Sporadic
Matted triggerplant   Woodlands; slope shrublands;   all year
    rock outcrops   Common

Spreading thread-like stems, 0.5mm, a few centimetres above the ground forming extensive mats, several metres across which can trip the unwary. Leaves 0.5x5mm, narrow, cylindrical, in tufts, 1x1cm, at intervals with descending aerial roots. Flowers 1cm scattered across the mat, with two pairs of petals and sensitive column underneath or when triggered, across the petals.

GROUP 3
Petals Five, IRREGULAR flowers- petals not all similar

3A PEA flowers (i.e. with shield-like standard petal, forward-projecting wing and keel petals) purple, red, pink, yellow, orange.

PAPILIONACEAE: *Hardenbergia Gompholobium Kennedia*

PAPILIONACEAE - Peas (For fuller description see Chapter 9, page 224)

Hardenbergia comptoniana   Purple   Jul-Aug
Native wisteria   Forests   Uncommon

Robust scrambler and climber, stems 2mm diameter. Leaves compound with three leaflets 3x1cm not toothed. Pea flowers, 1x1cm, with white spot at base of standard petal, in conspicuous tresses. Long, narrow, pointed pea pods, 7x100mm. Uncommon in the Hills, common on the Coastal Plain.

Kennedia coccinea   Orange and pink   Aug-Sep
Coral pea   Woodlands   Very common

Scrambler and climber, stems, 1.5mm diameter. Leaves compound with three leaflets 4x2cm, usually rounded, short white hairs underneath but occasionally can be long and narrow. Flowers 13mm across, several in heads at the ends of flower stalks. Improbable colour combination of an orange standard petal setting off the pink wings. Fruiting pod short, hairy, 4x30mm.

| Kennedia prostrata | Pillar box red | Aug-Sep |
| Running postman | Slope; disturbed areas shrublands | Uncommon |

Prostrate scrambler, 1m or more across on bare ground. Leaves compound with three leaflets 4x2cm, rounded, dark blue-green, with wavy edges. Flowers, 2x2cm, borne singly. Pods, 4x40mm. Page 108

| Kennedia stirlingii | Rust red | Aug-Sep |
| Rusty Kennedia | Wandoo woodlands; slope shrublands | Uncommon |

Scrambler to over 1m across, sometimes upright and semi-shrubby. Leaves compound with three leaflets 4x2.5cm pale green with obvious leafy triangles (stipules) at the join of leaf stalk and stem. Flower, 1.5x1.5cm, partly hidden amongst leaves, borne singly. Pods 40x4mm.

| Gompholobium polymorphum | Yellow, orange or rust red | Sep-Dec |
| Variable Gompholobium | Woodlands; slope shrublands | Common |

Climber to over 1m with orange-red flowers on slopes; bushy plants, 40cm, with lemon-yellow flowers, in the woodlands. Leaves five finger-like leaflets, 15x2mm, often dark blue-green. Flowers 1x1cm stalked, striking, borne singly but several on each plant with standard petal held very erect. Pods spherical, 1x1cm with over 10 seeds. Page 106

3B Flowers with two prominent wing petals but no shield-like standard petal: BLUE

POLYGALACEAE: *Comesperma*

| Comesperma ciliatum | Deep blue | Sep-Dec |
| Love creeper | Slope shrublands; streamsides | Uncommon |

Stems often twisting together to make an almost upright self-climber to 1m. Leaves 7x2mm. Flowers with spreading, boat-shaped wings, 7x5mm, crowded at the top of the stem in a spike. See Chapter 7, Herblike Plants and Annuals page 165 for other comespermas.

GROUP 4
Petals Five, REGULAR flowers - all petals similar

4A Flowers white or red, leaves with sticky-glandular hairs

DROSERACEAE: *Drosera*

DROSERACEAE - Sundews   (For fuller description see Chapter 9)

| Drosera macrantha | White | Jun-Sep |
| Bridal sundew | Slope shrublands | Common |

Climbs in shrubs, stems to 1.5m, glistening green. Leaves, round discs, 6mm across, covered with sticky glandular hairs, and attached in threes to the stem by reddish stalks, one stalk longer 45mm, than the other two 12mm. Flowers, 1.5x1.5cm, crowded at the top with sepals and flower stalk glandular-hairy.

| Drosera pallida | White | Aug-Sep |
| Pale sundew | Woodlands | Common |

Similar to D. macrantha but without glandular hairs on sepals and flower stalk. D. microphylla has red flowers. Page 107 & 106

4B Flowers white, purple, blue or greeny-yellow, leaves flattened, green, without sticky glands

PITTOSPORACEAE: *Billardiera Chieranthera Pronaya*
POLYGONACEAE: *Muehlenbeckia*
ROSACEAE: *Rubus*

PITTOSPORACEAE

Billardiera bicolor	Cream, streaked brown	Feb-Mar
Painted billardiera	Wandoo woodlands; slope shrublands	Uncommon

Shrub with climbing tendency 1.5x2m or more with twisting dark red stems, 3mm diameter. Leaves, 20x3mm, oblong. Flowers, 2x2cm, petals spreading with lengthwise brown streaks, densely clustered. Cultivated. Page 107

Marianthus coeruleo-punctatus	Pale sky-blue with dark spots	Apr-May
Spotted billardiera	Woodland	Uncommon

Scrambling at ground level, 1m across and up shrubs to 1m in the slender 1mm wiry, twisting stems. Leaves, 20x2mm, oblong, pointed. Flowers, 1x1cm, with dark blue spots (coeruleo-punctata), borne singly to three in leaf axils, well-separated. Anthers blue, shortly, oblong.

Billardiera drummondiana	Purply blue	Aug-Sep
Drummond's billardiera	Woodlands; slope shrublands	Uncommon

Similar to B. coeruleo-punctata but with leaf edges notched or toothed and petals 15x6mm, a uniform purply blue, not spotted. Anthers yellow, oval.

Billardiera variifolia	Purply blue	Sep-Oct
Variable billardiera	Woodlands, damp areas	Uncommon

Can climb on itself to form a 2m shrub. Similar to B. drummondiana but with larger leaves, 3x1cm, more wedge-shaped, often notched and very variable to small upper leaves. Usually with more flowers, up to five, at the tips of the stems.

Marianthus candidus	White	Oct-Nov
White spray	Streamsides	Common

Robust climber to 4m on tall shrubs and trees, stems 5mm diameter. Leaves 5x2cm, oval, tapered. Flowers 2cm across in conspicuous tresses. Tip of style narrows to a point.

Billardiera floribunda	White	Oct-Nov
Showy billardiera	Slope shrublands	Uncommon

Scattered plants to 1m climbing over shrubs. Leaves 9x4cm, oval, tapered. Flowers, 3cm across, clustered at the ends of branches. Tip of style fat and rounded.

Cheiranthera preissiana	Blue-purple	Sep-Oct
Preiss's cheiranthera	Slope shrublands	Uncommon

Scrambling amongst shrubs, 1x0.5m, thin stems, 2mm. Leaves, 30x2mm. Flowers, 1x1cm, single or a few on individual stalks, with spreading, oval, pointed petals. Each flower has five long narrow anthers together, hand-like (Cheiranthera), to the side of the stigma.

Pronaya fraseri	Pale purple	Dec-Mar
Elegant pronaya	Woodlands; slope shrublands	Common

Scrambling at ground level in small patches, 0.5m across occasionally ascending to 0.5m with stout, twisting stems 2mm diameter. Leaves, 20x3mm, oblong, pointed. Flowers, 1x1cm clustered at tips of stems, petals spreading with distinct points on otherwise blunt tips. Anthers long and narrow, rolled up and spread around the flower centre - not all on one side.   Page 107

Sollya heterophylla	Sky blue	Oct-Feb
Australian bluebell	Forest and woodlands	Common

(See Chapter 2, Trees and Tall to Medium Shrubs, page 24)

POLYGONACEAE (For fuller description see Chapter 9, page 225)

Muehlenbeckia adpressa	Greeny yellow	Sep-Dec
Climbing lignum	Slope shrublands	Uncommon

Weedy-looking scrambler, almost self-supporting with stout, twisting stems, 3mm diameter. Leaves, 4x3cm, rounded at tip but squared-off, shield-like, at leaf stalk. Small, dull-coloured flowers, 6x4mm, crowded on a single stalk at each leaf axil over the upper 50cm of stem. Separate male and female flowers.   Page 108

Rubus aff. selmeri*	White	Nov-Dec
Blackberry	Steamsides and roadsides	Uncommon

(See Chapter 2, Trees and Tall to Medium Shrubs, page 24)

GROUP 5
Flowers Funnel-Shaped

CONVOLVULACEAE: *Convolvulus*

Convolvulus erubescens	Pink	Oct-Feb
Pink bindweed	Slope shrublands	Uncommon

Slender scrambler-climber, stems 1.5mm diameter, often unsighted because scrambling through shrubs. Leaves 10x0.5mm stalked, arrowhead-shaped. Funnel-shaped flowers, 12x5mm, borne singly.

Convolvulus arvensis*	Cream	Dec-Mar
Field bindweed	Waste places	Uncommon

Stout scrambler-climber, stems 3mm diameter, up to 3m. Leaves 3x1cm stalked, arrowhead-shaped. Funnel-shaped flowers, 2x1cm, borne singly. Native to Europe.

GROUP 6
Perchers

6A Showy: Flowers bright orange; on wattles and gum trees in February-July

LORANTHACEAE: *Amyema*

Amyema preissii	Flame orange	Feb-Mar
Narrow-leaved mistletoe	Woodlands	Uncommon

Spreading shrub, 1x1m, with dark green cylindrical stems attached to branches of wattles; semi parasitic. Leaves, 40x3mm, round in cross section. Flowers, 4x4cm, hanging in groups of three, with parts spreading. Fruits, a pale pink berry spread by mistletoe birds. Most familiar on Eastern States wattles including Acacia podalyriifolia (Mt Morgan Wattle) and A. decurrens (Green Wattle) which eventually succumb. Page 106 & 108

Amyema miquelii	Orange-red	Mar-Jul
Broad-leaved mistletoe	Woodlands	Uncommon

Similar to Amyema preissii except with flattened leaves, 6x1cm. On Eucalyptus species, especially E. calophylla and E. wandoo. Page 106

6B Inconspicuous: Flowers small, breaking through stem surface, dark red. Plant not visible.

RAFFLESIACEAE: *Pilostyles*

Pilostyles hamiltonii	Dark red	Nov-Apr
Stem flower	Woodlands	Very rare

Appearing as flowers and accompanying bracts, 2mm across, many, crowded, poking through 10-20cm of stem surface of Daviesia decurrens and rarely D. rhombifolia (see Chapter 3, Medium to Small Shrubs, p. 46). Look at older wood of these Daviesias, especially if they appear unhealthy, for the flowers or small knobbly fruit.

Helena Valley

Welshpool Road Scarp

Dioscorea hastifolia
Native Yam, Warrine

Drosera pallida
Pale sundew

Amyema preissii — Narrow-leaved mistletoe

Gompholobium polymorphum
Variable Gompholobium

Amyema miquelii
Broad-leaved mistletoe

Scramblers, Climbers and Perchers 107

Drosera erythrorhiza
Red Ink sundew

Drosera pallida
Pale sundew

Billardiera bicolor Painted billardiera

Pronaya fraseri
Elegant pronaya

Thysanotus patersonii
Climbing fringed lily

Amyema preissii
Narrow-leaved mistletoe

Muehlenbeckia adpressa
Climbing lignum

Kennedia prostrata
Running postman

Clematis pubescens
Old man's beard

CHAPTER 5

Plants with Grasslike Leaves

The key features of the plants with grasslike leaves is that they are herbaceous, not woody, which separates them from trees and shrubs and their leaves are long and narrow usually with parallel veins. Most often the leaves are flattened, but occasionally, they may be round in section and so appear needle-like.

Many of the grasslike plants have inconspicuous flowers, although the flowerheads are obvious enough thanks to the clustering of bracts around the flowers. But there are several plants with grasslike leaves which have conspicuous flowers, usually found with parts in threes (mostly six).

Many species in this section are Monocotyledons - see Chapter 9 for fuller explanation.

GROUP 1

Flowers inconspicuous: in HEADS largely hidden by bracts, usually greenish or straw-coloured, sometimes with pink, feathery stigma noticeable. LEAVES with TWO PARTS - stem-sheathing base and blade with distinct junction between the two marked by papery extension of sheath part or fringe of hairs. GRASSES page 114

Sub Groups	Families	Genera
1A Grass head compact. page 114	Poaceae	Amphipogon Arundo* Cortaderia* Cymbopogon Cynosurus* Danthonia Ehrharta* Holcus* Imperata Lagurus* Neurachne Pennisetum* Phalaris* Stipa
1B Grass head spreading. page 115		Agrostis Aira* Aristida Arrhenatherum* Avena* Briza* Bromus* Eragrostis Festuca Poa* Rhynchelytrum* Stipa Themeda
1C Grass head with spikelets stemless on single flower stalks. page 117		Eragrostis Hordeum* Lolium* Stenotaphrum* Tetrarrhena Vulpia*
1D Grass head with spikelets stemless on two or more flower stalks. page 118		Cynodon* Hyparrhenia* Paspalum

Plants with Grasslike Leaves 111

GROUP 2

Flowers inconspicuous: in HEADS largely hidden by bracts, brown to dark brown; sometimes greenish or straw-coloured. LEAVES tiny papery scales at stem joints or green, clasping and continuous with stem NO papery extension or fringe of hairs marking junction of leaf blade and stem sheath. page 118.

Sub Groups	Families	Genera
2A Leaves: papery scales at stem joints page 118	Restionaceae	Anarthria Lepidobolus Leptocarpus Loxocarya
2B Leaves: green, flattened cylindrical. Some plants tiny, in seasonally damp places. page 119	Centrolepidaceae Cyperaceae Haemodoraceae Juncaceae Plantaginaceae	Apheliaor Centrolepis Baumea Carex Chorizandra Cyathochaeta Cyperus Gahnia Isolepis Lepidosperma Mesomelaena Schoenus Tetraria Haemodorum Juncus Luzula Plantago

GROUP 3

Flowers inconspicuous: not hidden by bracts, plants either STEMLESS with leaves emerging at ground-level and flowers hidden in their bases or erect, leafless, or stemmed with fleshy flattened leaves on stems continuing into tall, branched flower-stalk. page 122

Sub Groups	Families	Genera
	Dasypogonaceae	Lomandra
	Haemodoraceae	Haemodorum
	Juncaginaceae	Triglochin

GROUP 4

Flowers showy: parts SEPARATE in three's, usually three sepals and three petals, often similar appearance. page 124

Sub Groups		Families	Genera
4A	SIX parts similar in appearance Page 124	Anthericaceae	Agrostocrinum
			Borya
			Caesia
			Chamaescilla
			Laxmannia
			Sowerbaea
			Tricoryne
		Colchicaceae	Burchardia
			Wurmbea
		Dasypogonaceae	Chamaexeros
			Lomandra
		Haemodoraceae	Tribonanthes
		Iridaceae	Babiana*
			Hesperantha*
			Homeria*
			Orthrosanthus
			Romulea*
		Phormiaceae	Dianella
			Stypandra
		Xanthorrhoeaceae	Xanthorrhoea
4B	THREE parts similar in appearance. page 128	Anthericaceae	Arthropodium
			Thysanotus
		Iridaceae	Patersonia

Plants with Grasslike Leaves 113

GROUP 5
Petals and sepals joined to form TUBULAR flower. page 131

Sub Groups	Families	Genera
5A Flowers REGULAR page 131	Haemodoraceae	Conostylis
5B Flowers IRREGULAR page 132	Haemodoraceae	Anigozanthos
	Iridaceae	Freesia*
		Gladiolus*
		Romulea*
		Watsonia*

GROUP 6
Flowers showy, or if inconspicuous, not hidden by bracts. Parts in twos. page 133

Sub Groups	Families	Genera
	Hypoxidaceae	Hypoxis
	Philydraceae	Philydrella
	Stylidiaceae	Stylidium

GROUP 1

Flowers inconspicuous: in HEADS largely hidden by bracts, usually greenish or straw-coloured, sometimes with pink, feathery stigma noticeable. LEAVES with TWO PARTS - stem-sheathing base and blade with distinct junction between the two marked by papery extension of sheath part or fringe of hairs.

GRASSES

POACEAE: Austrodanthonia Austrostipa Aira Amphipogon Arrhenatherum Arundo Avena Briza Bromus Chloris Cortaderia Cymbopogon Cynodon Digitaria Ehrharta Eragrostis Holcus Hordeum Hyparrhenia Lagurus Lolium Microlaena Neurachne Pennisetum Phalaris Poa Melinis Stenotaphrum Tetrarrhena Themeda Vulpia

POACEAE - Grasses (For fuller description see Chapter 9, page 225)

Grasses are a somewhat specialist group, but are quite prominent in the bush. Some are very colourful (e.g. Red Natal Grass, Rhynchelytrum repens). They are often sought for floral arrangements. Descriptions are given for the more prominent of the 43 grass species recorded for the Hills.

1A Grass head compact

POACEAE: *Amphipogon Arundo Cortaderia Cymbopogon Cynosurus Danthonia Ehrharta Holcus Imperata Lagurus Neurachne Pennisetum Phalaris Stipa*

Cortaderia selloana* Pale fawn Feb-Mar
Pampas grass Streamsides; roadsides Uncommon
   Tussocks to 3m. Leaf blades 1mx1cm with rough-sharp margins. Flower heads 30x10cm on stalks to 3m, feathery. Native of South America.

Arundo donax* Pale fawn Apr-Jun
Giant reed Streamsides; damp areas Uncommon
   Tussocks to 3m often mistakenly referred to as bamboo, perennial. Leaf blades 40x6cm, in two rows along flowering stem. Head 15x5cm. Native to the Mediterranean region.

Amphipogon laguroides Brown-red Oct-Nov
   Woodlands Uncommon
   Tight tussocks to 30cm, perennial. Head 1x1cm but brown-red tinge to the bracts. Three species, of which this is the most common.

Cymbopogon obtectus Dense white hairs Oct-Nov
Silky heads Slope shrublands Uncommon
   Loose tussocks to 1.5m, perennial. Leaf blades 150x7mm with 4mm ligule. Head 3x2cm, cluster of spikelets dominated by white hairs and short 1mm awns.

Cynosurus echinatus* Green-tinged Oct-Nov
Rough dogstail Waste places Uncommon
   Loose tussocks to 30cm, perennial. Leaf blades 200x8mm. Head 7x1.5cm of closely packed spikelets. Native to southern Europe and western Asia favoured by frequent fires, spreading into bushland on lighter soils.

Plants with Grasslike Leaves 115

Austrodanthonia caespitosa   Rapidly straw-coloured   Oct-Nov
Common Wallaby grass   Woodlands   Very common
    Loose tussocks of wiry leaves to 20cm, perennial. Leaf blades 120x2mm. Head 5x1.5cm.

Ehrharta calycina*   Pale rose tinged   Oct-Nov
Veldt grass   Spreading from waste places   Common
    Loose tussocks to 1.5m, perennial. Leaf blades 70x5mm. Head 15x5cm. Native to South Africa favoured by frequent fires, spreading into bushland on lighter soils.

Holcus lanatus*   Tinged green,   Oct-Nov
Yorkshire fog grass   soon straw-coloured   Uncommon
                                    Waste places
    Loose tussocks to 25cm, perennial. Leaf blades 80x7mm, noticeably soft, grey-green with dense soft short hairs. Head 6x1cm, awns (1mm). Introduced.

Lagurus ovatus*   Straw coloured to white   Oct-Nov
Hare's tall grass   Waste places   Uncommon
    Loose tussocks to 30cm, annual. Leaf blades. Distinctive soft oval Heads 4x2cm with soft spreading awns, 2mm. Generally on lighter sandy soil. Native to the Mediterranean region.

Neurachne alopecuroidea   Steely grey   Oct-Nov
Foxtail mulga grass   Woodlands; slope   Very common
                                    shrublands
    Tight tussocks to 40cm, perennial. Leaf blade 45x5mm roughly hairy. Heads 1x2cm.

Page 140

Pennisetum villosum*   Light rose tinged   Oct-Nov
Feathertop   Waste places   Uncommon
    Loose tussocks to 1.5m, perennial. Large blades 20x5cm. Heads 10x1cm. Slender bottle brushes, tending to nod slightly. Native to South Africa.

Austrostipa compressa   Tinged green and brown   Oct-Nov
Compact needlegrass   Slope shrublands   Common
    Loose tussocks to 50cm, perennial. Leaf blades 20x15mm. Heads up to 300mm long. As typical of Stipas, awns ('needles') long (2cm), the head of this species remaining moderately compact. (See also Stipa elegantissima.)

| 1B | Grass head spreading

POACEAE: *Agrostis Aira Aristida Arrhenathrum Avena Briza Branus Eragrostis (some) Festuca Poa Rhynchelytrum Stipa Themeda*

Melinis repens*   Rose-pink   Apr-Jun
Red Natal grass   Waste places   Common
    Loose tussocks to 30cm, perennial. Leaf blades 25x1cm. Heads 20x10cm, feathery pink, one of the most distinctive introduced grasses. Native to South Africa.

Aira caryophyllea*   Tinged brown-red   Oct-Nov
Silver grass   Slope shrublands,   Very common
                                    rock outcrops

Delicate, 15cm, single or loosely branching annual. Leaf blades 10cmx1m. Head 4x2cm. Individual spikelets 0.5mm. Native to the Mediterranean region.

Aristida sp	Tinged brown-red	Oct-Nov
Three awn grass	Slope shrublands	Uncommon

    Loose tussocks to 50cm, perennial. Leaf blade 100x1mm. Head 5x11cm. Spikelets 3 awned. Tenacious in clothing.

Arrhenatherum bulbosum*	Tinged brown and green	Oct-Nov
False oat grass	soon straw-coloured	Common
	Waste places	

    Very loose tussocks to 1.5m annual. Good grass to observe leaf blade of hanging spikelets, leaf sheath, ligule (3mm), and clasping auricle characteristics of grasses. Head broad, awns 3mm. Native to the Mediterranean region.

Avena fatua*	Tinged green soon straw	Oct-Nov
Wild oats	coloured	Common
Avena barbata*	Waste places	
Bearded oats		

    Single stemmed to very loose tussocks to 1.5m annual. Leaf blades 250x5mm. Head 20cm long hanging spikelets 25mm, awns 3mm. Spreads into bushland especially where soil fertility has been increased by rubbish dumping. Native to the Mediterranean region.

Briza maxima*	Tinged green soon straw	Oct-Nov
Blowfly grass	coloured	Very common
Briza minor*	Waste places, slope	
Shivery grass	shrublands, rock outcrops	

    Single-stemmed delicate 25cm annuals. Two species, Briza maxima (25cm) the more common, and B. minor (15cm), both native to South Africa.   Page 136

Bromus spp	Green-tinged	Oct-Nov
Brome	Waste places	Uncommon
(incl. soft brome, rip-gut brome)		

    Loose tussocks to 45cm, annuals. Leaf blades 150x7mm with sparse hairs spreading from edges. Flower heads 6x3cm with awns projecting from bracts. Awns rough - rip-gut brome; awns smooth - smooth brome. Native to Europe.

Eragrostis curvula*	Tinged green and brown	Oct-Nov; Mar-Apr
African love grass	Roadsides	Common

    Robust tussock grass to 1.5m, perennial. Leaf blades 250x3mm. Heads 25x20cm with spikelets 1mm. Native to South Africa.

Poa (three species)*	Tinged green	Oct-Nov
	Woodlands, waste places,	Uncommon
	shrublands	

    Weakly tussocked grasses up to 30cm. Leaf blades with tips boat-shaped. Range from Poa annua (winter grass) 10cm, an introduced annual of waste places, shrublands and lawns, to the tall Poa pratense, a native perennial, straggling weakly through shrubby undergrowth in woodlands.

Plants with Grasslike Leaves 117

Austrostipa elegantissima	White-fringed	Oct-Nov
Feather-spear	slope shrublands	Common

Weak stems growing through shrubs to 1m, perennial. Leaf blades 120x2mm. Heads 15x20cm widely spread spikelets one of the most distinctive and beautiful of the native perennial grasses. With awns 3.5cm fringed with feathery white hairs. Page 135

Themeda triandra	Tinged green and rose-pink	Oct-Nov
Kangaroo grass	Slope shrublands	Common

Loose tussocks to 1m, perennial, often in extensive patches several square metres. Head of nodding spikelets, awns 5mm. Widespread across Australia. Susceptible to frequent burning and overgrazing. Page 139

1C Grass head with spikelets stemless on single flower stalk

POACEAE: Eragrostis (some) Hordeum Lolium Stenotaphyrum Tetrarrhena Vulpia

Hordeum spp.*	Tinged green soon	
Barley Grass	straw-coloured	Oct-Nov
	Waste places, damp areas	Uncommon

Single-stemmed, often crowded into swards, 20cm, annual. Leaf blades 10cmx8mm. Heads 10cm barley-like, spikelets arranged opposite in two rows, awns 5mm. Two species, Hordeum leporinum and H. marinum, the latter indicating saltier conditions. Native to the Mediterranean region.

Lolium spp.*	Tinged green	Oct-Nov
Rye Grass	Waste places	Uncommon

Pasture grass, weakly-tussocked to 75cm. Leaf blades 150x7mm. Heads 20x1cm, spikelets alternating. Lolium rigidum, Wimmera , an annual and L. perenne, Perennial . Native to the Mediterranean region and north-west Europe.

Tetrarrhena laevis	Tinged green becoming	Oct-Nov
Forest ricegrass	straw-coloured	Very common
	Woodlands	

Straggling through shrubby undergrowth to 50cm, perennial. Leaf blades 4cmx5mm at about 90o to stem. Head 50x5mm, spikelets widely-spaced. Page 137

Vulpia myuros*	Tinged green soon	Oct-Nov
Rat's tail fescue	straw-coloured	Common
	Waste places, slope	
	shrublands; rock outcrops	

Slender, single-stalked 15cm annual. Leaf blades 120x3mm. Head 4cmx5mm, spikelets acutely-angled soon becoming brittle and breaking off. Native to the Mediterranean region.

| 1D | Grass head with spikelets stemless on two or more flower stalks

POACEAE: *Cynodon Hyparrhena Paspalum*

Paspalum dilatatum*   Green tinged   Year-round
Paspalum   Streamsides; damp places   Very common
   Loose tussocks to 2.5m, perennial. Leaf blades 300x9mm. Head with five flower stalks coming from different levels down the main stalk. Has taken over much of the streamside habitat. Native of South Africa.

Hyparrhenia hirta   Grey-green tinged   Jul-Sep
Tambookie Grass   Waste places, roadsides   Common
   Robust tussocks to 1.5m, perennial. Leaf blades 250x3mm. Head with two flower stalks. Native of South Africa.

Cynodon dactylon   Green and brown tinge   Oct-Nov
Couch grass   Waste places   Uncommon
   Spreading, prostrate, 15cm, perennial. Leaf blades 6cmx3mm. Head with up to five radiating flower stalks. Native of Europe.

GROUP 2

Flowers inconspicuous: in HEADS largely hidden by bracts, brown to dark brown sometimes greenish or straw-coloured. LEAVES tiny papery scales at stem joints or green, clasping and continuous with stem. NO papery extension or fringe of hairs marking junction of leaf blade and stem sheath

---

| 2A | Leaves: papery scales at stem joints
RESTIONACEAE: *Anarthria Lepidobolus Leptocarpus Loxocarya*
RESTIONACEAE -

   All have tough, cylindrical or slightly flattened, wiry stems, straight or curled. The stems are green to grey green and often with obvious joints (nodes) each with a small, brown or straw-coloured leaf appearing as a scale. All have separate male and female plants.

Anarthria prolifera   Pink-brown   Sep-Oct
Ribbon Twine Rush   Damp places   Uncommon
   Tufted rush to 30cm. Stems branched at nodes. Leaves 50x4mm. Flowers in loose heads.

Loxocarya/Desmocladus spp.   Straw-coloured   Oct-Nov
Twine Rushes   Woodlands   Common
   Three species all conspicuous and attractive in their growth form. Desmocladus flexuosus (green) and L. cinerea (grey-green, shortly hairy) occur in large patches extending over some square metres from underground stems. Both species have wiry, erect, twisting stems 2.5cm, with the flower heads at the ends. Desmocladus fasciculatus (bright green) is less common, 15cm in smaller patches.   Page 139

Plants with Grasslike Leaves 119

Leptocarpus/Chaetanthus spp. Reddish-brown Oct-Nov
Twine rush Seasonal swamps Uncommon
    Chaetanthus aristatus, a plant of winter-wet swamps is uncommon because its habitat is infrequent. It often grows in extensive swards to 30cm with attractive drooping flower heads from the last few nodes (male), or at the ends of upwards stems (female). L. tenax is similar but taller (50cm) and with spikes of flowers in the female plant from the top few nodes. The flower heads of the male plants wave on longer stalks.

Lepidobolus spp. Dark red-brown Oct-Nov
Bristle headed Slope shrublands Uncommon
chaff rush rushes
    Stout, wiry, twisting stems to 20cm in untidy patches. The scale leaves of both species are straw-coloured (chaff-like), with a prominent point, pressed to the stem. L. preissianus occurs on lighter sandy soil. It is more common on the Coastal Sand Plain. Its single flower head (male plant) contrasts with L. chaetocephalus which has two or more flower heads on the flower stalk.

2B Leaves: green, flattened or cylindrical. Some plants tiny, in seasonally damp places

CENTROLEPIDACEAE:	Aphelia Centrolepis
CYPERACEAE:	Baumea Carex Chorizandra Cyathochaeta Cyperus Gahnia Isolepis Lepidosperma Mesomelaena Schoenus Tetraria
HAEMODORACEAE:	Haemodorum [Grp 3]
JUNCACEAE:	Juncus Luzula
PLANTAGINACEAE:	Plantago
CENTROLEPIDACEAE -	Dwarf sedges

A family of tiny, annual, sedge-like plants. All are associated with damp conditions from wheel ruts in clay on the Scarp face to the extensive winter-wet areas of broad drainage lines.

Aphelia spp. Green-tinged and brown Oct-Nov
  Damp places Common
    Tussocks to 5cm sometimes growing closely to form a sward, annuals. Flower heads consisting of opposing spikelets on an erect (Aphelia brizula) or zig-zagged (A. cyperoides) flower-head stalk, or set at about 45° to the flower stalk (A. drummondii).

Centrolepis spp. Green and brown-tinged Oct-Nov
  Damp places Common
    Tussocks to 6cm. Centrolepis aristata, the most common of dwarf sedges occurs on damp clay in otherwise dry habitats such as the slope shrublands and near rock outcrops. The small tussocks often form small patches with the enclosing bract extending crab-claw like beyond the flower head. Related C. drummondiana is slighter, more restricted to extensive damp areas, and lacks the prominent point on the flower-head bract.

CYPERACEAE - Sedges

These plants have brown, occasionally straw-coloured, flower heads at the ends of flower stalks. The flower stalks of the sedges are often leaf-like, or only occasionally with leaves along their length. Usually, both flower stalks and leaves come from the base of the tussock or from a crown or horizontal stem near ground level. Sedge leaves are flattened and folded, or circular in cross-section (hence, needle-like), and may or may not have a midrib or central vein running lengthwise.

Gahnia decomposita	Brown	Sep-Oct
Saw sedge	Damp places	Uncommon

Tussock sedge 3x1.5m. Leaves 200x1cm, drooping, finely saw-toothed edges, easily cutting skin and making passage difficult. Page 138

Lepidosperma tetraquetrum	Brown	All year
Square sedge	Streamsides	Common

Swards with graceful flower stalks to 2.5m. Leaves and flower stalks four-angled, H-girder in section. Also, along streamsides with flattened leaves to 1m is Lepidosperma longitudinale (uncommon). Other large streamside species are Baumeas. There are several smaller species of Lepidosperma on the slopes and in the woodlands.

Cyathochaeta avenacea	Straw-coloured	All year
Grass sedge	Woodlands	Common

Sparse tussocks of cylindrical leaves and persistent, grasslike flower stalks to 1.5m. Grass-like with leaves both on the flower stalk and from the base.

Cyperus alterniflorus	Pink and green tinged	All year
Leaf sedge	Streamsides	Uncommon

Tussocks to 1m. Leaves grasslike, flattened, keeled. Flower stalks triangular with a tuft of spreading flower spikes with two or three leaf-like bracts extending from their point of attachment.

Mesomelaena tetragona	Dark brown	All year
Semaphore sedge	Woodlands	Very common

Robust tussocks to 75cm. Leaves 500x5mm, flat but often inrolled. Flower heads with two bracts extending beyond in semaphore-signalling fashion.

Lepidosperma spp.	Light to dark brown	All year
Sword sedges	Woodlands; slope shrublands, rock outcrops	Very common

Several species occur. When in fruit they produce small nuts with shiny brown heads. L. squamatum occurs as tussocks to 30cm, leaves flattened, common in the woodlands along with L. tenue, which has leaves needle-like, 50cm. L. tuberculatum is uncommon, occurs in the slope shrublands as loose tussocks, leaves 700x5mm with tiny brown nobs along the edges. Also uncommon is L. drummondii occurring as tussocks to 1m at base of granite boulders. Similar to the previous species but without the nobs, with broader leaves, and taller, to 1m. Page 138

Schoenus spp	Light to dark brown	Aug-Nov
	Woodlands; slope shrublands, winter wet depressions	Very common

A few species occur. When in fruit the nuts are three-angles usually three ribber or with three distinct lines. S. unispiculatus is up to 65cm high and has only one terminal spikelet,

S. globifer has atenural head of many spikelets and is up to 45cm tall. S. benthamii has flattened stems and an inflorescence of 1-10 spikelets.

Tetraria octandra	Dark brown	Oct-Nov
Eight-anthered sedge	Slope shrublands	Common

Tussocks to 25cm. Leaves spreading, recurved, bright green, V-shaped in cross-section. Flower heads 1.5cm long, several, borne along slightly curved flower stalks.   Page 135

Isolepis spp.	Green to straw-coloured	Oct-Nov
Club rush	Seasonal swamps	Common

Small grasslike tussocks. Isolepis marginata occurs as spreading tussocks to 20cm, larger than the associated dwarf sedges. Flower spikes, three to five at the end of each flower stalk.

JUNCACEAE - Rushes

Rushes occur as tussocks, their leaves are usually needle-shaped or grooved hollow and coming from the base of the tussock. Flower heads often appear from below the tip of the stalk although, when expanded, can look as if occurring at the end of the stalk.

Juncus holoschoenus	Light brown	All year
Jointed-leaf rush	Streamsides	Common

Tussocks of pliable, hollow but jointed leaves to 1m. Flower heads 20cm long, several on branching stalks emerging from below the end of the flower stalk. Attractive for floral decoration.

Juncus pallidus	Straw-coloured	Oct-Nov
Pale rush	Streamsides	Uncommon

Tussocks of cylindrical leaves to 1.5m. Flower heads 15cm long from 2-3cm back from the tip of the flower stalk.

Juncus effusus	Brown	Oct-Nov
	Woodlands; waste places	Uncommon

Tussocks of overgrazed pastures with stiff cylindrical leaves to 1m. Flower heads from below the end of the flower stalk.

Luzula meridionalis	Light brown	Oct-Nov
Field woodrush	Woodlands	Uncommon

Loose tussocks, 20cm. Leaves 200x5mm flat, soft, with hairs extending from margins. Several flower heads 5mm at the ends of stalks of varying length from the end of the flower stalk.

PLANTAGINACEAE - Plantain

Plantago lanceolata*	Black	Mar-May
Ribwort plantain	Waste places	Uncommon

Leaves 20x1.5cm with strong parallel veins as a rosette ascending from ground level. Flower head, 30x6mm, of tiny densely clustered flowers, at end of stalk to 75cm. Native of north-west Europe.

GROUP 3

Flowers inconspicuous: not hidden by bracts, plants either STEMLESS with leaves emerging at ground-level and flowers often hidden in their bases or stemmed with fleshy flattened leaves on stems continuing into tall, branched flower-stalk

DASYPOGONACEAE: *Lomandra*
HAEMODORACEAE: *Haemodorum*
JUNCAGINACEAE: *Triglochin*

DASYPOGONACEAE - Mat rushes (most)

All mat rushes have male and female plants. The female plants generally have the simpler flower head with the individual flowers stalkless on an unbranched stem. The male plants usually have a spreading, branched flower head with the flowers open with individual stalks.

| Lomandra hermaphrodita | Pale brown | Apr-May |
| Curly-leaved mat rush | Woodland | Common |

Slight tussocks to 15cm. Leaves 150x2mm, strap-shaped, blue-green often straw-coloured at the tips. Frequently cork-screwed, especially when dead when they may also have a rosy tinge. Flowers on stalks to 3cm within tussock base.

| Lomandra drummondii | Purply-brown | May-Jun |
| Drummond's mat rush | Forests | Uncommon |

Tussocks to 40cm. Leaves 40x1cm, strap-shaped with rounded end. Flowers of both male and female plants on upper 15cm of branching flower stalk to 50cm.

| Lomandra preissii | Greeny-yellow or purple | May-Jun |
| Preiss's mat rush | Forests; woodlands | Common |

Tussocks to 15. Leaves 250x4mm. Flowers 2mm stalkless along top 4cm of stalks 25cm. The two colour forms, greeny-yellow or purple grow together.   Page 138 & 139

| Lomandra caespitosa | Grey-white | Jun-Jul |
| Tufted mat rush | Woodlands | Common |

Tussocks to 20cm. Leaves 200x2mm, grooved, slightly twisted, of bright green. Flowers, 2mm across on stalks to 4cm within tussock base.   Page 139

| Lomandra nigricans | White, purple-tipped | Jun-Jul |
| | Forests; woodlands | Common |

Tussock to 20cm. Leaves 300x5mm. At very base, some black, shredding into fibres, peppery, sheathing leaves. Flower heads 8cm across, branched, spreading, extended above leaves to 30cm. Scented.

| Lomandra spartea | Greeny-white | Jun-Jul |
| Needle-leaved mat rush | Woodlands | Uncommon |

Rush (Juncus)-like tussocks to 40cm. Leaves 400x2mm, cylindrical, needle-like, grey-green. Flowers 2.5mm on stalks 4cm anthers tussock base.

| Lomandra sericea | Purple | Jul-Aug |
| Silky mat rush | Woodlands | Common |

Robust tussocks to 30cm. Leaves 300x5mm, strap-shaped, blue-green. Sparse silky hairs (sericea) at the leaf bases. Flowers 3mm in loose heads 2cm across on stalks to 6cm within tussock base.

| Lomandra micrantha | Pale brown | Aug-Sep |
| Small flower mat rush | Woodland | Common |

Robust tussocks to 30cm. Leaves 300x2mm, strap-shaped, grey-green. Male flower heads spreading to 6cm across, much branched. Female flower heads, 1cm across, simple. Both occur at the base of the tussock.

The following two species are closely related:

| Lomandra odora | Greeny-yellow, purple-tipped | Aug-Sep |
| Tiered mat rush | Open woodlands and swamp margins | Uncommon |

Tussock to 15cm. Leaves 220x1mm, basal sheaths, leaves straw-coloured. Scented.

Page 135 & 140

| Lomandra integra | White, purple-tipped | Aug-Sep |
| | Forests | Uncommon |

Similar to Lomandra nigricans but the leaf bases remain entire, they do not shred into fibres. Scented.

| Lomandra brittanii | Green-white | Sep-Oct |
| Grass mat rush | Woodlands | Uncommon |

Tussocks to 8cm, the smallest of the mat rushes. Leaves 150x1mm, pliant, grasslike, bright green. Flowers sparsely along stalks, 8cm.

| Lomandra purpurea | Purple | Sep-Oct |
| Purple mat rush | Woodlands | Common |

Described under sub-group 4A.

Page 142

| Lomandra sonderi | Greeny-white | Oct-Nov |
| Wood mat rush | Woodlands | Common |

Tussocks, to 50cm. Leaves 500x5mm, flat. Flowers on flattened stalks almost as tall as the leaves.

Other species are L. pauciflora and L. suaveolens, uncommon, in the woodlands east of the Scarp. L. pauciflora is the only non-tussock species, forming straggly, grass-like tufts. L. suaveolens is fragrant. L. drummondii is similar to L. sonderi but flowers July to August.

HAEMODORACEAE - *Haemodorums*

The leaves are green, leek and iris-like, strap-shaped or broad and sword-like. They emerge from underground bulbs in late winter. Although with inconspicuous flowers, the plants are noticeable because of the height of their upright stems, most exceed 40cm.

| Haemodorum paniculatum | Brown | Sep-Oct |
| Strap-leaved haemodorum | Woodlands | Common |

Solitary strap-shaped fleshy green leaves, 400x7mm emerging from laterite soils in late winter followed by brown flower stalk to 1m with several flower clusters on much-branched top. Flowers 3mm across, rarely fully opening.

Page 138

Haemodorum simplex	Brown	Sep-Oct
Scented haemodorum	Near rock outcrops	Common

Sparse tussock of flattened somewhat rounded leaves, 150x7mm with dark brown flower stalk to 40cm. Flowers 8mm across, scented on branching flower stalk.

Haemodorum brevisepalum	Dark brown	Oct-Nov
	Slope woodlands	Uncommon

Sparse tussocks to 30cm. Robust flower stalks 8.5mm long.

Haemodorum laxum	Brown	Oct-Nov
Broad-leaved haemodorum	Slope shrublands	Uncommon

Sparse tussock of broad basal leaves, 20x2cm, flattened in a single direction (not spiral) with thick flower stalks to 40cm. Small, broad, leaf-like bracts with narrow papery margins on sparsely-branching flower stalks. Flowers 5mm with distinguishable petals and sepals. Another closely-related undescribed species, has not been separated here.

Haemodorum simulans	Greeny-black	Nov-Dec
	Rock outcrops	Uncommon

Sparse tussock of flat basal leaves, 20x1.4cm, in two opposite ranks. Stem leaves several. Flowers 12-14mm long, tipped orange inside.

Haemodorum spicatum	Brown	Nov-Dec
	Slope shrublands	Uncommon

Unbranched, stout brown flower stalk to 1m from sparse tussock of flattened leaves 250x7mm. Flowers 2mm across, sepals and petals pointed sparsely scattered along stalk. It is the flower stalk which is unbranched, not the leaves.

JUNCAGINACEAE - Water rushes

Triglochin lineare	Green	Oct-Nov
Water ribbons	Shallow water	Uncommon

Submerged loose tussocks to 25cm. Leaves 250x3mm weak, flattened. Flowers 2mm across sparsely scattered along flower stalk emerging above the water.

GROUP 4

Flowers showy: parts SEPARATE in threes, usually three sepals and three petals, often similar This Group, of plants with showy flowers, and parts in threes includes all the Lilies and Irises.

4A ■ SIX parts similar in appearance

ANTHERICACEAE:	*Agrostocrinum Borya Caesia Chamaescilla Laxmannia Sowerbaea Tricoryne*
COLCHICACEAE:	*Burchardia Wurmbea*
DASYPOGONACEAE:	*Chamaexeros Lomandra*
HAEMODORACEAE:	*Tribonanthes*

IRIDACEAE: *Babiana Hesperantha Homeria Orthrosanthus Romulea*
PHORMIACEAE: *Dianella Stypandra*
XANTHORRHOEACEAE: *Xanthorrhoea*

Laxmannia sessiliflora	White	May-Jul
Nodding lily	Woodlands	Common

Semi-upright plant with stems forming open cushions to 10cm. Leaves 70x0.5mm, soft, cylindrical, pointed, in tufts. Flowers 3mm across clustered in heads 8mm without stalks (sessile, hence sessiliflora), one in each tuft of leaves.

Laxmannia ramosa	White	Jun
Branching lily	Slopes	Uncommon

Branched, straggling plant with wiry, prostrate stems, occurring in patches. Leaves 25x1mm, soft, recurved, needle-like leaves, in tufts at intervals along the stems. Flowers 3mm across, Borya-like, clustered on stalks, 3cm, from the leaf tufts.

Laxmannia squarrosa	White	Jun-Aug
False borya	Woodlands and slopes	Common

Upright, branching stout stems forming open cushions to 8cm. Leaves 25x1mm, recurved, flexible, cylindrical, pointed, not rigid and sharp. Flowers 3mm across clustered in tight heads 1cm across widely varying from stalkless amongst the tuft of leaves to being on an unbranched stalk to 10cm.   Page 140

Tribonanthes brachypetala	Dull yellow	Jul
Yellow tribonanthes	Damp places on slopes	Common

Upright, unbranched plants to 20cm. Leaves, 250x2mm, and flower stalks, 30cm, renewed annually. Flowers 3mm across, about seven, at end of stem in loose head, 2.5cm across, stalks and flowers hairy.   Page 134

Burchardia multiflora	Creamy white	Jul-Aug
Dwarf burchardia	Damp areas	Common

Upright cluster to 25cm of basal leaves, 8cmx7mm, stout, fleshy. Flowers 25mm across compactly clustered at the ends of flower stalk, 25cm, stout, pale brown, fleshy. Anthers dark purple.   Page 136

Tribonanthes spp.	Hairy white	Jul-Aug
White tribonanthes	Damp places on slopes	Common

Upright, unbranched plants to about 20cm. Three species, with T. longipetala the most common. Leaves broad, tapering, 70x5mm, with bases clasping the flower stalk, white-hairy to 25cm, with two to three flowers borne separately on loose 3cm-long branches topping the stalk. Flowers 3cm across with spreading white-hairy petal-like parts. Less common is T. australis with similar leaves, flower stalk to 35cm, flowers in loose head, each flower 2cm across. Least common, T. violacea, smaller, to 8cm, with more slender leaves, 120x3mm, flower stalk and leaf bases tinged with violet, ending in a single flower, 1.5cm across, with spreading, rounded, white-hairy, petal-like parts.   Page 134 & 137

Wurmbea tenella	White	Jul-Aug
Early Nancy	Damp places	Common

Delicate plants 10cm. Leaves 25x5mm, fleshy, broad, stalk-clasping at base, tapering to long point. Flower stalk 10cm bearing one or two flowers 1cm across with a transverse marking (glands) half-way down the petals and sepals, one or two on the unbranched flower stalk. Page 141

Chamaescilla corymbosa	Deep sky blue	Aug
Blue Squill	Woodlands	Common

Pair of broad fleshy green leaves, 3.5x1.5cm, pressed to the ground with slender, dark flower stalk to 15cm bearing two to six flowers, 1.2cm across. The leaves, which have purple-red undersides, are often mistaken for orchid leaves. Page 141

Borya sphaerocephala	White	Aug-Sep
Pin cushions	Granite outcrops, ironstone gravels	Very common

Tussocks 15x30cm of branching stems ending in tufts of recurved leaves, 25x1mm, with sharp points, green in winter, straw-coloured to orange in summer. Flowers 8mm across clustered in spherical heads, 15mm across at ends of unbranched flower stalks to 10cm. A resurrection plant: capable of reconstituting its chlorophyll and so turning apparently dead straw-coloured to orange leaves green again following rewetting by rain. Page 135 & 139

Burchardia umbellata	Creamy white	Aug-Sep
Milkmaids	Woodlands	Common

Upright cluster to 75cm of basal leaves 100x7mm fleshy. Flowers 25mm across in a loose cluster (umbrella-like - umbellata) at the ends of slender brown flower stalks with bright yellow anthers. Drying off after flowering.

Homeria spp.*	Pink or yellow to orange	Aug-Sep
Cape tulips	Disturbed damp places	Uncommon

Two species, with leaves 50cmx12mm from a corm underground. The two-leaved, Homeria miniata, with pink flowers and a yellow centre, has bulbils at the join of leaf and stem. The one-leaved, H. flaccida, with solitary leaf of similar size, has yellow-orange flowers. Native to South Africa.

Caesia micrantha	Light grey-white,	Oct-Nov
Pale grass lily	purple-tinged Woodlands	Common

Erect curving flower stalk, 50cm, with spreading branches from a cluster of basal leaves, 80x7mm, fleshy, shallow V in cross-section coming to a point. Flowers somewhat inconspicuous, 5mm, opened and partly opened, suspended on stalks, 2mm, scattered along upper part of flowering stalk.

Orthrosanthus laxus	Pale sky blue	Aug-Sep
Morning iris	Woodlands	Common

Loose tussocks with basal leaves, 12cmx7mm, green, pliant, as well as flower stalk leaves. Flowers 2.5cm across up to six occurring at intervals along the flower stalk, 75cm. Fully out in morning. Page 134

Sowerbaea laxiflora	Pale purple	Aug-Sep
Purple tassels	Lower slopes and damp areas	Common

Dense tussocks of leek-like leaves, 120x4mm, with simple flower stalks radiating to 20cm ending in a loose tassel of flowers, 7mm across, on individual stalks, 1cm.   Page 137

Stypandra glauca	Sky blue or creamy white	Aug-Sep
Blind grass	Rock outcrops	Common

Loose tussock 75cm. Leaves 10x1cm, sword-shaped, soft, green, often bent over, continuing, overlapping, up the flower stalk. Flowers 1cm across, numerous on individual stalks 1cm on uppermost 5cm of flower stalk.   Page 136 &137

Romulea rosea*	Pink	Aug-Oct
Guildford grass	Waste places, damp lower slopes	Common

Slight tuft of needle-shaped leaves 300x1mm appearing annually from a corm below ground. Flowers 1.5cm across borne singly at the ends of stalks, 10cm. Native to South Africa.

Tricoryne humilis	Yellow	Sep
Dwarf yellow autumn lily	Damp places	Rare

Tuft 10cm. Leaves 50x5mm, opposite, fleshy. Flowers 1cm across on stalks, 1cm, in loose heads on simple 5cm flower stalks.

Agrostocrinum scabrum	Royal blue	Sep-Oct
False blind grass	Woodlands	Common

Loose tussock to 1m. Basal leaves 15x1cm, pliant, sword-shaped. Flowers 15mm across with black hairs on outer surface of sepals, two to six flowers on dark red, stalk, 1m, roughened (scabrous) on uppermost few centimetres and with two to three leaves.   Page 142

Babiana angustifolia*	Purple	Sep-Oct
Baboon flower	Waste places	Uncommon

Tuft of pleated leaves and single flower stalk to 20cm appearing annually from a corm below ground. Leaves 15x2cm, tapered at each end. Flowers 2.5cm across, shortly tubular, 1cm, by comparison with the lobes, 2x1cm, several in sequence to one side of sparsely branched flower stalk. Native to South Africa.

Chamaexeros serra	Yellow	Sep-Oct
Saw false mat rush	Slope shrubland	Rare

Tussock of basal leaves to 30cm, mat-rush like (all Group 3). Leaves 300x2mm, margins with small white teeth (serra = saw). Flowers 3mm across on individual stalks 1cm, clustered in heads at ends of flower stalks, 5cm, hidden in the tussock base.

Hesperantha falcata*	Creamy white, sepals with reddish backs	Sep-Oct
Evening iris	Disturbed places incl. lowerslopes	Uncommon

Slight tussocks to 30cm. Leaves 100x5mm, mostly basal, bend over towards tips (falcate) appear annually from corms. Flowers 15mm across, opening in late afternoon or evening; up to six at intervals along straw-coloured flower stalks to 30cm. Native to South Africa.

Lomandra purpurea	Purple	Sep-Oct
Purple mat rush	Woodlands	Common

Robust tussocks to 50cm, leaves 50x1cm, strap-shaped, blue-green. Flower stalk up to 1.5m. Numerous flowers 1mm across, the purple petals and sepals providing a striking background to the six bright yellow anthers.

Tricoryne elatior	Yellow	Sep-Dec
Yellow autumn lily	Woodland	Common

Tangled slender green stems forming domed cushions 50x50cm. Leaves reduced to inconspicuous brown scales. Flowers 1cm across, starry, in small groups with individual stalks, 5mm, sparsely scattered amongst plant. Page 137 & 138

Xanthorrhoea gracilis	White	Oct-Nov
Slender balga	Woodlands	Common

Trunkless tuft of leaves, to 40cm, remaining at ground level. Flowers, 2mm across massed in a head, 20x4cm, on the flower stalk 1.5m. Page 142

Dianella revoluta	Pale blue	Nov-Dec
Flax lily	Woodlands	Common

Loose tussock to 30cm, leaves 30x3cm, broad, stiff, sword-shaped, light blue-green, often inrolled from the edges. Flowers 1cm across hanging downwards on individual delicate stalks, rarely more than two to four flowers open at any one time. Flower stalks to 1m. Page 141

4B ■ THREE parts similar in appearance

ANTHERICACEAE: *Arthropodium Thysanotus*
IRIDACEAE: *Patersonia*

Dichopogon capillipes	Pale mauve	Nov-Mar
Nodding lily	Woodlands	Common

Loose tussocks 75cm. Leaves 10x1cm, fleshy, drying off after flowering. Flowers 1.5cm, two to three out at a time. Flower stem 75cm, curved. The petals spreading, the sepals arched back, hanging on stalks 1cm in threes, scattered along flower stem, common A. preissii is similar but flowers single on flower stem, not in threes. Page 141

THYSANOTUS - Fringed lilies

These have the petals broader than the sepals, various intensities of purple and with a fringe of spreading hairs along the petal margins. All but the climbing species, Thysanotus patersonii and Thysanotus manglesianus (see Chapter 4 Scramblers, Climbers and Perchers, page 97) are described below.

Thysanotus thyrsoideus	Purple	Aug-Sep
Fringed lily	Woodlands	Uncommon

Erect cylindrical, fleshy, ribbed, grey-green leaf, 150x2mm, alongside flower stalk to 25cm topped by flowers, 15mm across, on indivdual stalks, 8mm, crowded in loose spray on upper third of the flower stem.

Plants with Grasslike Leaves

Thysanotus dichotomus	Purple	Sep-Oct
Branching fringed lily	Streamsides	Uncommon

Tangled, apparently leafless, stiff, cylindrical green stems forming loose cushions to 2x1m, the stems dividing equally into two at each branching (dichotomus branching). Leaves 10cmx2mm, few, withered before flowering. Flowers 2cm across on stalks to 7mm up to three at the ends of stems.

Thysanotus multiflorus	Purple	Sep-Oct
Fringed lily	Woodlands; disturbed places	Common

Dense tussocks to 20cm of leek-like leaves, 4mm across, grooved. Flowers 2cm across on individual stalks 1.5cm, many radiating from the ends of the flower stems, 25cm. Flowers with three stamens. Page 142 & 140

Thysanotus gracilis	Purple	Sep-Oct
Slender fringed lily	Rock outcrops	Rare

Tufts of leaves to 6cm, with flowering stems to 25cm. Leaves 60x1mm, slender, cylindrical. Flowers 1.2cm across on stalks 6mm, up to two at the ends of the flowering stems.

Thysanotus tenellus	Purple	Sep-Oct
Dwarf fringed lily	Woodlands	Uncommon

Tussock a tuft of short, 5cm, flattened, 2mm, basal leaves with branching flower stalk to 10cm. Leaves with papery wings at base and small knobs along margins. Flowers 1cm across on stalks, 8mm, up to four at the ends of the flower stems.

Thysanotus arbuscula	Purple	Sep-Nov
	Forests	Rare

Erect stem to 35cm, shortly hairy, cylindrical, upper part branched, leafless. Flowers 1.5cm across on stalks 3mm, up to four clustered at the ends of the stem and branchlets.

Thysanotus triandrus	Pale purple	Oct-Nov
Dwarf leek fringed lily	Woodlands	Uncommon

Similar to T. dichotomus but smaller, leaves 15cm variable, flattened to channelled, hairy, and flower stalks to 20cm.

Thysanotus asper	Purple	Oct-Nov
Hairy fringed lily	Slope shrublands	Rare

Tuft of leaves to 120x1mm, and sparingly-branched flowering stems to 30cm. Leaves with papery wings at the base, hairy, with blunt tips. Flowers 2cm across, on stalks, 8mm, up to four in clusters at the ends of branchlets of the flowering stems.

Thysanotus scaber	Purple	Oct-Nov
Rough fringed lily	Woodlands	Uncommon

Tuft of few leaves, 20cm, and flowering stem to 35cm, much-branched in upper part. Leaves 2mm across, cylindrical with channel, round-tipped, rough with short hairs and sheathing at base. Flowers 1.2cm across on stalks 1cm, up to five clustered at the ends of branchlets in loose tress-like heads.

Thysanotus fastigiatus	Purple	Nov-Dec
	Woodlands	Uncommon

Tangled, apparently leafless, curving, weak green stems forming untidy cushions, 20x20cm. Flowers 1cm across on short stalks, 2mm, borne singly at the ends of stems. Occurring only in the Hills.

Thysanotus sparteus	Purple to whitish-purple	Nov-Jan
Broom fringed lily	Woodlands	Common

Loose spreading tussocks to 1m of cylindrical, leafless stems. Flowers 2cm, on stalks, 4mm, four or more in clusters along the stems.

Thysanotus anceps	Purple	Dec
Two-sided fringed lily	Forests	Uncommon

Erect stem to 40cm, flattened above, sparsely branching. Leaves absent at flowering, 30x2mm, channeled, hairy. Flowers 2cm across on individual stalks, 6mm, scattered along and at the ends of the stems.

PATERSONIA - Native Iris (For fuller description see Chapter 9, page 223)

Patersonia occidentalis	Purple	Aug-Sep
Purple flag	Woodland	Common

A very variable species. Tussocks of leaves, 400x8mm, broad, smooth, scimitar-shaped. Flower stalks smooth, 35cm ending in a flower 'purse' from which a sequence of single flowers, 4cm across, emerge.   Page 140

Patersonia umbrosa	Purple or yellow	Sep-Oct
Yellow flags	Woodlands; streamsides	Common

Loose tussocks to 60cm. Leaves 600x5mm, graceful, tapering to a point. Flower stalk to 75cm, slender, ending in flower 'purse' from which one delicate flower, 4.5cm across, appears at a time. Shrivelled remains of earlier flowers may be apparent.   Page 141

Two varieties, var. xanthina with bright yellow flowers in the woodlands and var. umbrosa with purple flowers occurring in the Hills along streamsides.

Patersonia rudis	Purple	Sep-Oct
Hairy flag	Woodland	Very Common

Open tussocks of broad, stiff leaves, 500x7mm, often curled and twisting with minutely hairy margins and pale, red-brown, clasping leaf bases. Flower stalk dark red-brown, covered with white velvety matting, slightly shorter than longest leaf. Topped by flower 'purse' with flowers, 3cm across, emerging singly, in succession.

Patersonia pygmaea	Purple	Sep-Oct
Dwarf patersonia	Woodland	Common

Tussock of overlapping, sword-like leaves, 150x2mm, smooth. Flower stalk 8cm with pale brown flower 'purse' from which a sequence of single flowers, 3cm across, emerge.

Patersonia babianoides	Purple	Sep-Oct
Rib-leaved patersonia	Woodland	Uncommon

Single leaf, 8cmx4mm, pleated, very hairy, narrowed at tip and base, 80x4mm. Flower stalk very hairy,

2cm, with flower 'purse' 2.5cm from which a sequence of single flowers, 3cm across, emerge.

Patersonia juncea	Purple	Oct
Rush leaf patersonia	Woodland	Uncommon

Loose tussocks of leaves, 200x1mm. Flower stalk 15cm with red-brown flower 'purse' from which a sequence of single flowers, 2cm across, emerge.

GROUP 5
Petals and sepals joined to form TUBULAR flower

5A Flowers REGULAR
HAEMODORACEAE: *Conostylis*
CONOSTYLIS - Cottonheads

Conostylis androstemma	Creamy white	Jun-Jul
Trumpets	Woodland and slopes	Common

Dense tussocks 15x20cm of stiff, needle-shaped, wiry leaves, 150x1mm. Flowers 35x10mm, trumpet-shaped, shortly-stalked, 2mm, several borne singly amongst the leaves. Flower lobes spreading to 3cm, anthers and style protruding from the trumpet. Page 135

Conostylis aculeata	Creamy-yellow	Aug
Prickly conostylis	Woodlands	Uncommon

Tufts of leaves to 12cm. Leaves 120x4mm grey green and ribbed. Flowers 1cm long in loose heads at end of the flower stem, 15cm.

Conostylis caricina	Pale creamy-yellow	Aug-Oct
Sedge conostylis	Woodlands; slope shrublands	Uncommon

Tussocks to 10cm on flower stalks to 5cm. Leaves 100x3mm, sword-like, slightly curved, with fringe of short hairs pressed along the margin. Flowers 15mm long, about six clustered in heads, 2.5cm across, downy-hairy.

Conostylis setigera	Pale creamy yellow	Aug-Oct
Bristly cottonhead	Woodlands; slope shrublands	Very common

Tussocks 8x10cm. Leaves 30x2mm with long spreading hairs. Flowers 1cm long in cluster of four to five flowers in head 1.5cm across at the end of stem, 8cm, both matted with short white hairs. Page 134

Conostylis setosa	White sometimes pink-tinged	Sep-Oct
White cottonhead	Woodlands	Common

Basal leaves flat, tapering, 3004mm, with prominent white spreading marginal hairs. Flowers, 18mm long, very white - hairy, several in head 5cm across on flower stalks 25cm, dark coloured but white hairy. Page 136

Conostylis serrulata	Creamy yellow	Sep-Oct
	Woodlands	Uncommon

Tussocks 25x10cm. Leaves 250x5mm with prominent veins, grey-green with hairs pressed lengthwise along margins. Flowers 8mm long loosely clustered at end of stalk 10cm.

Conostylis aurea	Rich yellow	Oct-Nov
Golden conostylis	Woodlands	Uncommon

Tufts of leaves to 18cm. Leaves 180x1.5mm, blue-green. Flowers 18mm long densely packed in spherical heads, 3cm across, at the ends of stems to 22cm, woolly-hairy.

5B Flowers IRREGULAR

HAEMODORACEAE: *Anigozanthos*
IRIDACEAE: *Freesia Gladiolus Romulea Watsonia*

Groupings for identification are:
- 5B-1 Parts in six as obvious petals and sepals but fused to form a broad tube in the lower half of the flower page 132
- 5B-2 Parts in six as teeth at the ends of broad tubes which form the main part of the flower page 132

■ **5B-1 Parts in six as obvious petals sepals but fused to form a broad tube in the lower half of the flower**

Watsonia meriana var. bulbillifera*	Brick red to salmon pink	Oct-Dec
Bugle lily	Streamsides; ditches	Common

Robust erect tussocks with flower stalk to 1.5m. Often in dense swards choking out native vegetation: a serious invader of streamside communities. Basal leaves 70x3cm robust, sword-shaped. Flowers 5cm long narrowly trumpet-shaped to 8mm across at open end, crowded on uppermost parts of flower stalk in the axils of bracts, 2x1cm, with bulbils lower down. Can be controlled by slashing and the weed-killer, Round-Up. Native of South Africa.

Other Watsonias*	Pink, pale magenta,	Oct-Nov
Watsonias	brick-red	Common
	Ditches; disturbed places	

All similarly robust to the previous species but none bearing bulbils. Garden escapes and not seriously invasive of native bushland. W. meriana has distinctive brick-red flowers, 7x3cm, with obtuse bracts to 2cm. W. versfeldii has pink to pale magenta flowers, 8x1cm, and spear-shaped bracts to 2cm.

Gladiolus caryophyllaceus*	Pink	Sep-Oct
Wild gladiolus	Slope shrublands; woodlands	Common

Erect narrow tussocks to 75cm. Leaves 60x1cm spirally twisted. Flowers 8x6cm, tube funnel-shaped, about six on stout flower stalk to 75cm. A successful invader from South Africa where it is comparatively rare.

Freesia hybrid*	Creamy white, some yellow	Aug-Oct
Freesia	Waste places	Uncommon

Erect slender tussocks to 20cm. Leaves 100x5mm few, basal, pliant, sword-shaped. Flowers, 3x2cm, four to seven on wiry flower stalk to 20cm, strongly fragrant, often shaded purple on outside of the tube. Naturalised garden plant originating from South Africa.

■ **5B-2 Parts in six as teeth at the ends of broad tubes which form the main part of the flower** This sub-group includes all the showy members of the Haemodoraceae, amongst them, Kangaroo Paw.

Plants with Grasslike Leaves 133

Anigozanthos manglesii Green and red Aug-Sep
Kangaroo paw Woodlands Uncommon
    Erect narrow tussocks to 1m. Basal leaves 250x6mm, overlapping, as well as progressively shorter stem leaves. Flowers 7cm long with red swollen base (ovary) and dark green tube, all prominently hairy, 10 or more developing flowers coming from one side of the curved top of the flower stalk. Less common in the Hills than on the Coastal Plain, usually indicating patches of lighter, sandy soil. The Western Australian floral emblem.

Anigozanthos bicolor Yellow-green and red Jul-Oct
Little Kangaroo paw Seasonally damp places Common
    Erect narrow tussocks to 25cm. Basal leaves 70x3mm. Flowers 3.5cm long with flower tube having a slightly narrower section before flairing out, three to five spreading from the top of the flower stalk. Sometimes occurring in extended patches over several square metres.Page 142

Anigozanthos humilis Red and yellow Sep-Oct
Cat's paw Damp sandy patches Uncommon
    Erect narrow tussocks to 25cm. Leaves tapering, 150x5mm. Flowers 4cm with points prominent and widely spreading, hairy, three to six spreading at the ends of the flower stalks.

GROUP 6
Flowers showy parts in twos (two or four)

HYPOXIDACEAE:	*Hypoxis*	
PHILYDRACEAE:	*Philydrella*	
STYLIDIACEAE:	*Stylidium*	

Philydrella pygmaea Yellow Nov
Butterfly plant Damp places Uncommon
    Flower stalk 15cm, up to eight flowers, 17x10mm, on upper 6cm, one to two out at once, petals two, fan-shaped up and down. Each flower with bract. Basal leaf 2x60mm, tapering, stalk leaf midway up. Page 134

Hypoxis occidentalis Yellow Jul-Oct
Yellow star Damp places Common
    Flower stalk 16cm, flower, 15x15mm, four spreading petal-like parts, occasionally six. Basal leaves, three to four, 1x190mm, tapering, single flower stalk bract 1.5x30mm midway up. Hypoxis glabella, similar, usually with six petal-like parts, flower stalk 10cm, basal leaves, 1x120mm, and two opposite flower stalk bracts midway up, one, 1.5cm, slightly longer than the other.

Stylidium affine Pink Sep-Oct
Queen trigger plant Woodland Common
    Tussocks of leaves 250x3mm, basal, grasslike leaves, hairy flower stalks, 30cm with side branches with up to five flowers, 15x25mm, not all in flower at once, with four, rounded-squarish petals, the upper pair larger than the lower pair. Lower branches longer (e.g. 4.5cm) than the more crowded, upper branches (e.g. 0.5cm). Page 136

Stylidium schoenoides Creamy-yellow Sep-Oct
Cowkicks Woodland Uncommon
    (See Chapter 7, Herblike Plants and Annuals) page 170

Tribonanthes variabilis
White tribonanthes

Tribonanthes brachypetala
Yellow tribonanthes

Conostylis setigera
Bristly cottonhead

Philydrella pygmaea
Butterfly plant

Orthrosanthus laxus
Morning iris

Plants with Grasslike Leaves 135

Borya sphaerocephala
Pin cushions

Lomandra odora
Tiered mat rush

Conostylis androstemma
Trumpets

Austrostipa species
Feather-spear

Tetraria octandra
Eight-anthered sedge

Conostylis setosa
White cottonhead

Stypandra glauca
Blind grass
(White flowered form)

Burchardia multiflora
Dwarf burchardia

Stylidium affine
Queen trigger plant

Briza maxima
Blowfly grass

Plants with Grasslike Leaves 137

Tricoryne elatior
Yellow autumn lily

Stypandra glauca
Blind grass

Sowerbaea laxiflora
Purple tassels

Tribonanthes longipetala
White tribonanthes

Tetrarrhena laevis
Forest ricegrass

Lomandra preissii

Gahnia decomposita
Saw sedge

Haemodorum paniculatum Strap-leaved haemodorum

Tricoryne elatior
Yellow autumn lily

Lepidosperma angustatum
Sword sedge

Plants with Grasslike Leaves 139

Lomandra preissii
Preiss's mat rush

Themeda triandra
Kangaroo grass

Borya sphaerocephala　　　　Pin cushions

Lomandra caespitosa
Tufted mat rush

Desmocladus flexuosus
Twine rush

Neurachne alopecuroidea
Foxtail mulga grass

Patersonia occidentalis
Purple flag

Laxmannia squarrosa
False borya

Thysanotus multiflorus
Fringed lily

Lomandra odora
Tiered mat rush

Plants with Grasslike Leaves 141

Dichopogon capillipes
Nodding lily

Wurmbea tenella
Early Nancy

Chamaescilla corymbosa
Blue squill

Patersonia umbrosa
Yellow flags

Dianella revoluta
Flax lily

Xanthorrhoea gracilis
Slender balga

Lomandra purpurea
Purple mat rush

Agrostocrinum scabrum
False blind grass

Anigozanthos bicolor
Little Kangaroo paw

Thysanotus multiflorus
Fringed lily

CHAPTER 6

Orchids

The orchids, as a group, are the most confusing of all. As monocotyledons, they all basically have parts in threes. However, one of these may be modified to produce a lip (labellum) leaving five obvious parts. Still others have parts fused and hooded, when they simply appear 'odd'; and some have their parts taking different shapes with some reduced in prominence, in which case only one or two parts may appear prominent.

Their leaves also can be non grasslike, with some being broad and heart-shaped, occurring singly, and pressed to the ground.

Some of the modifications can be difficult to interpret. The following scheme illustrates the modifications and is designed to help interpretation and provide a foundation for the sequence in which the various orchids are described.

ORCHIDS   *Burnettia Caladenia Cyanicula Cyrtostylis Diuris Drakaea*
ORCHIDACEAE: *Elythranthera Eriochilus Leporella Lyperanthus Microtis Monadenia*
                   Paracalaena Prasophyllum Spiculea
(For fuller description see Chapter 9)

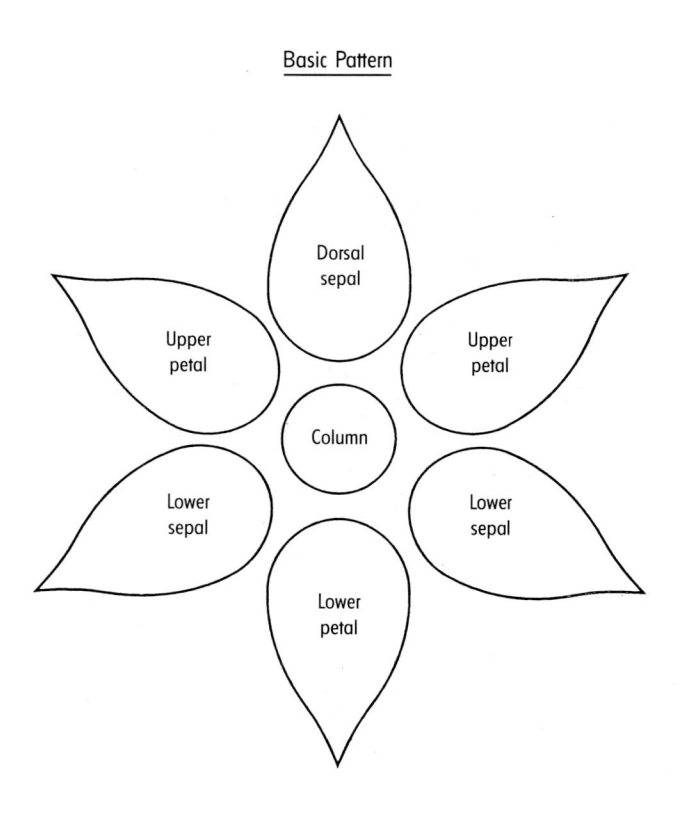

Basic Pattern

(Diagram showing a flower with: Dorsal sepal at top, two Upper petals, two Lower sepals, Lower petal at bottom, and Column in the centre.)

1A		Six parts but dissimilar
1B		Six parts similar
2A		Lower petal becomes labellum
2B		Flowers hooded
	2B-1	Dorsal sepal becomes a hood, also sometimes fused with upper petals
	2B-2	Dorsal sepal becomes a hood, several small flowers crowded on a stalk
2C		Flower is borne upside down with lower sepals on top, often fused
2D		Upper petals prominent, ear-like
2E		Lower sepals prominent
2F		Labellum the most prominent part, often cantilevered, other parts reduced

These variations on the regular, three plus three theme are used in separating the different orchids for identification.

Types of Orchid Flowers

Type	Flowers	Size	Parts	Genera	Page
1A	6 parts dissimilar	Several	Small plants		Cyrtostylis	146
1B	6 parts similar		Several	Showy	Thelymitra	146
2A	Parts in fives	Few per stalk	Showy	Long tapering points	Caladenia (Spider orchids)	147
				Short points or rounded	Caladenia Cyanicula (Fairy orchids etc)	
				Rounded, shiny	Elythranthera	
2B-1	Hooded by hood	Dominated		Hood obscuring labellum and column	Pterostylis	149
				Tufted labellum visible	Burnettia Lyperanthus	
2B-2	Hooded flowers	10s	Tiny		Microtis Monadenia	150
2C	Parts in fours rarely	10s to 100s	Small flowersfives	Upside down	Prasophyllum	151
2D	Pair of prominent	Few to many		Upward projecting	Caladenia (1) Diurisparts Leporella	152
2E	Pair of prominent parts	Few	Downward projecting		Eriochilus	153
2F	Cantilevered parts	Few plants	Small prominent	Labellum	Drakaea Spiculaea Paracaleana	153

Groupings for identification are summarised on page 144
1   Parts in six
1A   Parts in six, dissimilar
1B   Parts in six, similar
2   Parts five, with sixth, the lower petal modified as a labellum
2A   Showy, five parts
2B   Flowers hooded
    2B-1   Dorsal sepal a prominent hood, few to many large flowers
    2B-2   Flowers hooded, tiny, several crowded on flower stalk
2C   Flowers upside down, parts appearing as four (lower sepals, now uppermost, partly fused; when not, parts appear as five) small, several crowded on stem
2D   Pair of upward-pointing prominent parts, few flowers
2E   Pair of downward-pointing prominent parts, few flowers
2F   Labellum prominent, parts cantilevered

1A Parts in six, dissimilar

One small species, the Mosquito orchid, inconspicuous because of its size.

Cyrtostylis huegelii	Brown and green	Jul-Sep-Oct
Mosquito orchid	Woodland	Uncommon

Single leaf pressed to the ground 3x2.5cm, heart-shaped, translucent. Usually growing in colonies, sometimes over 100 plants per square metre. Single, slender flower stalk to 10cm with three to seven flowers well separated, 1.5cm across.   Page 155

1B Parts in six, similar

ORCHIDACEAE: *Thelymitra*
THELYMITRA - Sun Orchids

Because they are fully-opened when in bright sunshine, the warmth causing them to open.

Thelymitra antennifera   Pale yellow   Jul-Sep
Vanilla orchid   Rock outcrops; swamps   Common

Basal flower stalk to 20cm, slender, typically arching away from the leaf 70x2mm tapering. Two to three flowers 2.5cm across. Two dark brown, dish-like antennae (hence, antennifera) extending above each side of the anther arch are quite distinctive.   Page 155

Thelymitra flexuosa   Lemon yellow   Aug-Sep
Twisted sun orchid   Swampy places   Uncommon

Similar to the previous species with bending flower stalk at leaf axil. Two flowers, 8mm across with rounded, yellow lobes of column drooping downwards on either side of the anther arch.

Thelymitra ?pauciflora   Blue or white   Sep-Oct
Slender sun orchid   Winter wet swamps   Uncommon

Plants grow in small clumps. Basal leaf 250x3mm, long and channelled. Flower stalk 35cm with up to six self pollinating flowers which only open for short periods on hot days. Page 161

Thelymitra crinita   Sky blue   Sep-Nov
Blue lady orchid   Woodland   Common

Leaf single, broad, erect, close to flowering stalk, blade dark green 8x4cm tapering into 5cm sheath at base. Otherwise similar to Thelymitra macrophylla, flower stalk 35cm, but flowers with less prominent anther over a tuft of purple hairs.   Page 162

Thelymitra macrophylla   Blue to violet blue and pink   Sep-Nov
Scented sun orchid   Woodlands; rock outcrops   Common

Leaf single, variable in length but tending to be grass-like, pleated, 150x5mm up to 40mm, dying off. Solitary flower stalk 35cm with up to 25 spreading flowers, 3cm across, out at any one time. Column an arch of glistening orange yellow and black over a tuft of white hairs.
Page 162

Thelymitra benthamiana   Yellow with palebrown dots   Oct-Nov
Leopard orchid   Slope shrublands; winter   Uncommon
   wet areas

Similar to T. crinita. Leaf blade light green, 8x3cm, sheath 5cm. Flower stalk 35cm, more robust and noticeably more fleshy than for the previous two species. A variety, var. stellata, the Bronze orchid, is similar but with pale brown spots coalescing to cover most of the sepals and petals leaving just streaks of yellow. Page 160

| Thelymitra dedmaniarum | Golden yellow | Oct-Nov |
| Cinnamon sun orchid | Woodland; granite slopes | Rare |

Basal leaf 150x3mm. Flower stalk 45cm, with 2-15 or more cinnamon scented flowers.

| Thelymitra mucida | Dull blue | Oct-Nov |
| Plum orchid | Streamsides, swamps | Uncommon |

Flower stalk 300x2mm, slender, delicate, with two to three flowers, 1cm across. Single basal leaf long and narrow, 120x2mm, often shrivelled by flowering time. Yellow anther arch over a forked tuft of creamy-white hairs.

| Thelymitra stellata | Golden brown | Oct-Nov |
| Star orchid | Jarrah forest | Rare |

Base leaf 150x3mm. Flower stalk 25cm with two to twelve or more flowers. Found in the lateritic loams of the jarrah forest.

2A Showy, five parts

This includes the Caladenias and the Enamel orchids, Elythranthera. Some Caladenias, popularly called Spider orchids, have long points to their parts, others have shortly pointed or rounded parts.

Cyanicula deformis	Purply blue	Jul-Aug
Blue Beard	Labellum: blue	Common
	Slope shrublands; rock outcrops	

Single basal leaf, 2x60mm, strap-shaped. Flower stalk 11cm, single flower 3x3cm, strap-shaped spreading parts, 3x15mm. Labellum semi-tubular, 2x5mm, tuft purple hairs at tip. Page 160

Caladenia denticulata	Creamy-white, or pale	Jul-Aug
Yellow spider orchid	Labellum: Red streaks	Uncommon
	Yellow, some red	
	Slope shrublands	

Single basal leaf tapering, 4x60mm, sometimes twice this length. Flower stalk 25cm, often less (15cm), one or two flowers, 8x8cm due to long, thread-like extensions to sepals and petals. Labellum 5x5mm, very short marginal teeth.

Caladenia reptans	Pink	Jul-Aug
Dwarf pink fairy	Labellum: striped	Uncommon
	Near granite outcrops	

Single basal leaf 8x45mm, strap-shaped. Flower stalks 12cm, one to two flowers, 2x2.5cm, parts 5x1.5mm early broad, tapering. Labellum 2x5mm, pink tip, rest white with short marginal teeth. Can be very small, half the flower stalk and leaf sizes given. Page 161

Caladenia hirta	Cream to pink	Aug-Sep
Sugar candy orchid	Labellum: pink/red	Very rare
	Woodlands; sandy soil	

Single basal leaf, 1.2x6cm, tapering. Flower stalk 20cm, hairy, one to two flowers, 2.5x3cm, strap-shaped parts tapering to rusty-brown tips, 2mm. Labellum semi-tubular, 2x5mm, short fringe and surface projections, darker.

Caladenia longiclavata	Greeny-white, red tinges	Aug-Sep
Clubbed spider orchid	Labellum: Deep red tip	Uncommon
	Slope shrublands	

Single basal leaf tapering, 7x120mm, hairy. Flower stalk 45cm, one or two flowers 7x10cm, tips narrowed then broadening into clubbed ends, 1x15mm, dark-coloured. Labellum 15x20mm, 5mm of tip solidly coloured, marginal projections 4mm, four rows of surface projections. Page 159

Caladenia macrostylis	Greeny cream	Aug-Sep
Leaping spider orchid	Labellum: Centre dark red	Uncommon
	Woodlands; slope shrublands	

Single basal leaf tapering, 6x130mm, hairy. Flower stalk 15cm, single, occasionally two flowers, 4x5cm, tips dark red, 1mm, ending in long points. Labellum 6x7mm, central part with crowded projections, grape-like. Page 159

Cyanicula sericea	Purply blue	Aug-Sep
Silky blue orchid	Labellum: white/blue	Common after fire
	Woodlands; slope shrublands	

Single basal leaf, 1.8x5.5cm, oval. Hairy flower stalk 20cm, one to two flowers, 3.5x3.5cm, parts oval, tips rounded. Labellum semi-tubular, 3x10mm, sparsely dotted at mouth. Flowers best after summer fires. Page 157

Caladenia discoidea	Green and red	Sep
Dancing orchid	Labellum: Red and green	Rare
	Woodlands, sandy soil	

Single basal leaf, 6x140mm, tapering, hairy. Flower stalk 16cm, one to three flowers, 3x2.5cm, parts pointed but not extended. Labellum 8x10mm, flared marginal threads, 3mm, and closely set rows of short, projections.

Caladenia falcata	Red and green	Sep-Oct
Fringed mantis orchid	Labellum: red tip, greeny yellow	Very rare
	Woodlands	

Single basal leaf, 6x120mm, tapering, hairy. Flower stalk 15cm, one to two flowers, 3x4cm, laid back with extended points curving upwards. Labellum 8x10mm, marginal projections pointing forward, shorter projections spotting throat.

Caladenia flava	Bright yellow, some red	Sep-Oct
Cowslip orchid	Labellum: yellow, red	Common
	Woodland	

Single basal leaf, 1.2x10cm, strap-shaped. Hairy flower stalk 10cm, usually two flowers, 3x4cm, parts early broad then tapering 8x20mm, lower sepals larger, upper petals and sepal varyingly streaked with red. Labellum 5x5mm, with coarse marginal teeth, paler. Page 158

Orchids 149

Cyanicula gemmata	Deep blue	Sep-Oct
Blue china orchid	Labellum: white, streaked blue	Common after fire
	Woodlands; slope shrublands	

Single basal leaf 1x2cm, oval, stiffly hairy. Hairy flower stalk 9.5cm, one to two flowers, 3.5x3.5cm, oval rounded parts, 7x15mm. Also occurs cream coloured. Labellum, rounded, 3x4mm. Flowers abundantly after summer fires. Page 156

Caladenia longicauda	Creamy-white	Sep-Oct
White spider orchid	Labellum: white fringed red	Common
	Woodlands; slope shrublands	

Single basal leaf, tapering, 150x8mm, with long 3mm hairs, single, occasionally two or three flowers 15x10cm due to long, thread-like extensions to the sepals and petals on stalk 50cm. Labellum 2x1cm, with thread-like, red projections 7mm at edges, shorter ones on surface. Page 157

Elythranthera brunonis	Lacquered light purple	Sep-Oct
Purple enamel orchid	Labellum: white, purple	Common
	Woodlands; slope shrublands	

Single basal leaf broadly strap-shaped, 1.1x8cm, hairy. Flower stalks 40cm, two to three flowers, 3x3.5cm, widely spaced on upper 12cm with pointed tips darker, curled backwards; backs of parts with purple spots on white. Page 157

Caladenia marginata	White	Oct
White fairy orchid	Labellum: fringed	Rare
	Seasonally wet places	

Single basal leaf, 1.5x7.5cm, tapering. Hairy flower stalk 12cm, two flowers, 2.3x2cm, strap-shaped parts tapered at base and tip, tips darker with short dusky hairs. Labellum 2x3mm, coarsely toothed margin. Page 162

Elythranthera emarginata	Lacquered pink	Oct-Nov
Pink enamel orchid	Labellum: white, purplish-pink	Common
	Woodlands; slope shrublands	

Single basal leaf, broad, rounded, 1x4.5cm. Flower stalk 20cm, one to two flowers, 4.5x3.5cm, widely spaced on upper 7cm, spreading gently arching backwards. Pink colour made up of closely spaced dots. Backs of parts with widely spaced pink dots on white. Page 161

■ 2B-1 Dorsal sepal a prominent hood, few to many large flowers

Oligochaetochilus sanguineus	Red-brown	Jun-Aug
Dark banded greenhood	Granite rocks	Common

Similar to Pterostylis vittata but differs in broad, flat sepals. Page 159

Oligochaetochilus vittatus	Green and white	Jun-Aug
Banded greenhood	Woodland	Common

Leafy stalks 25cm translucent green, sometimes red-brown, four to ten flowers, 1.5x2cm, nodding forward, lower sepals downward-pointing. Stem leaves 3.5x10mm, broadest above stem-clasping base, tapering to point. Non-flowering plants, a rosette, 3cm across, of heart-shaped, translucent green leaves pressed against the ground. Page 160

Plumatichilos barbatus	Green and white	Aug-Sep
Bird orchid	Labellum: Bearded, orange-yellow	Common
	Woodland	

Flower stalk 18cm, single flower, bird-shaped from side, lower sepals pointing down and outwards. Labellum tip projecting 2cm, clubbed, 2mm, dark, wiry, with bright orange, 2mm, hairs. Leaves 8x30mm crowded towards stem base, triangular, stem-clasping, netted green and white. Page 157

Pterostylis pyramidalis	Green and white	Aug-Sep
Dwarf greenhood	Woodland	Uncommon

Shortly-hairy flower stalks 8cm, single flower, 7x15mm, with two upward pointing, antennae-like lower sepals, adding 1.5cm. Hood beaked, nodding forward and slightly downward. Basal leaves 1x1cm, three or four, flat on ground, translucent, heart-shaped, two to three flower stalk leaves. Page 158

Pterostylis aspera, has larger darker leaves

Pterostylis recurva	Green and white	Aug-Sep
Jug orchid	Woodland	Common

Leafy stalks 50cm, translucent-green, up to five upright flowers 2x3cm with eight recurved sepals. Several leaves 4x35mm, pointed, on the flower stalk, clasping it at their base. Page 161

Pyrorchis nigricans	Red and white	Sep
Red Beaks	Woodlands	Common, rare in flower

Single leaves, 6x10cm, heart-shaped plain green pressed to the ground scattered in colonies over some square metres. Flowers infrequently without fire, sometimes well following fire. Single flower stalk 18cm, three to four flowers, 3x3cm, with prominent sheathing bracts. Plant turns black (nigricans) when dried off. Flowers after summer fires. Page 156

Lyperanthus serratus	Red-brown	Sep-Oct
Rattle Beaks	Woodlands	Uncommon

Flower stalks 50cm through shrubby groundcover, four to six flowers, 4x3cm, in a gentle spiral to the stalk tip. Each flower with sheathing bract. Sinister appearance because of hood and four other parts 'waving' beneath from the centre dominated by the white-tufted labellum. Single basal leaf 1.5x45cm, tapered. Page 156

■ **2B-2 Flowers hooded, tiny, several crowded on flower stalk**

Microtis media	Yellowy-green	Sep-Nov
Common mignonette	Damp places	Common

Flower stalk 35cm overtopped by single leaf 45cm, tubular, enclosing emerged flower stalk, its upper 10cm crowded with flowers, 5x5mm, each with a forward-pointing hood. Remaining flower parts less prominent than the larger, swollen seed-case, 2x5mm, between these and the stalk.

Microtis alba	White	Oct-Nov
White mignonette	Slope shrublands; damp places	Uncommon

Flower stalk 50cm, as for M. media except that hoods white and the forked, fringed labellum is prominent below each hood. Seed case less prominent. Strongly perfumed. Flowers abundantly after summer fire. Page 158

Microtis atrata	Green-yellow	Oct-Nov
Swamp mignonette	Swamps	Uncommon

Flower stalk 8cm, all but 2cm enclosed by tubular leaf, 8cm. Flowers, 2x3mm, crowded on top 2cm of flower stalk, tiny green hoods 1mm on prominent seed cases, 1.5x1mm. Turns black when dry.

Disa bracteata*	Creamy green	Oct-Nov
Brown finger orchid	Woodlands; slope shrublands	Common

Leafy flower stalk 35cm, stout, 6mm diameter, uppermost 10cm crowded with flowers, 5x5mm, each with a green, triangular, leafy bract, to 2.5cm long. Lower leaves to 15cm long, sword-shaped, with prominent mid-vein persists. Brown-coloured when dried off. Native of South Africa. Page 156

⎯⎯⎯

2C Flowers upside down, parts appearing as four (lower sepals, now uppermost, partly fused; when not, parts appear as five) small, several crowded on stem.

PRASOPHYLLUM - Leek Orchids

There are nine species all with tubular, leek-like leaves part of enclosing the flower stalks. The five taller species are rather similar requiring careful observation of the labellum (now the upper, central structure with the column below) petals and sepals for identification.

Prasophyllum parvifolium	Green sometimes brown-tinged	Jun-Aug
Autumn leek orchid	Slopes	Common

Flower stalk 25cm, leaf 20cm enclosing stalk for 17.5cm; small part, 2.5cm, of leaf free (parvifolium). Flowers, 10x8mm, crowded on uppermost 5cm (>15), five parts, spreading. Labellum white, arched back. Page 160

Prasophyllum fimbria	Olive green	Jul-Sep
Fringed leek orchid	Woodlands	Common

Flower stalk 1m, dark green, otherwise similar to the previous species. Sepals and petals olive green, spreading. Labellum with white frilly edge, raised central plate, pink tinged. Flowers abundantly after fire.

Prasophyllum gracile	Green with some red	Aug-Oct
Laughing leek orchid	Rock outcrops	Common

Flower stalk 18cm, leaf 20cm, enclosing stalk for 10cm. Flowers, 4x6cm, on uppermost 6cm of stalk, 12 or more. Sepals partly fused, the uppermost as two arching points 1.5mm. Petals small and narrow, lowermost sepal broad. Labellum and petals sometimes red-tinged, otherwise, not prominent.

Prasophyllum giganteum	Greeny-bronze and white	Sep-Oct
Bronze leek orchid	Slope shrublands	Common

Flower stalk 1m bronzed-brown enclosed by tubular leaf to 75cm with its upper, 5x250mm, part free from the flower stalk. Flowers, 1x1.5cm, on uppermost 25cm, stalked 12mm on slender seed cases. Fused sepals prominent, 3x8mm, surrounding labellum with broad wavy margin, petals slight, narrow, clasping. Very strong sweet scent. Flowers after summer bushfires.

Prasophyllum hians	Green or reddish brown and white	Sep-Oct
Yawning leek orchid	Damp places	Uncommon

Flower stalk 25cm, green or reddish-brown, leaf 20cm enclosing stalk for 10cm. Flowers 1x1cm, crowded on uppermost 6cm, dominated by white clasping petals and upward pointing white labellum; sepals smaller, green or brown. Flowers usually after bushfires.

Prasophyllum plumiforme	Greeny-white	Sep-Oct
Little leek orchid	Damp places; slope shrublands	Uncommon

Flower stalk 35cm, single leaf 25cm enclosing stalk for 12cm. Over 20 flowers, 5x5mm, spreading, on uppermost 12cm of flower stalk. Parts five, not four, because upper sepals not fused. Labellum with broad wavy edge.

Prasophyllum elatum	Greeny-white	Sep-Nov
Tall leek orchid	Woodlands; slope shrublands	Common

Flower stalk 1m, green or black, top 25cm with flowers. Leaf similar to P. giganteum; flowers similar except fused sepals more blunt, lower sepal similar size and labellum both with wavy margin and inner raised plate. Flowers abundantly after fire. Page 156

Prasophyllum brownii	Greeny-white, brown streaked	Nov
Brown's leek orchid	Swamps; granite outcrops	Uncommon

Flower stalk 1m, browny-green, otherwise similar to P. giganteum and P. elatum. Sepals and petals with central brown streak, fringed green; curved inwards, cupping. Labellum greeny-white with wavy margin and less prominent raised central plate. Flowers in absence of fire.
Page 155

2D Pair of upward-pointing prominent parts, few flowers

Leporella fimbriata	Light brown and green	Apr-Jun
Hare orchid	Woodlands; damp places	Common

Flower stalk 25cm, slender, two to three flowers, 10x23mm on upper 8cm. Petals, 1cm, light brown erect, ear-like, above hooded sepal; lower sepals similar but descending close together. Labellum 1cm, dark-brown, fringed with green centre. Basal leaf, rarely two, 8x20mm, small heart-shaped, flat on ground. In colonies. Page 160

Diuris brumalis	Yellow and green-brown	Jul-Aug
Common donkey orchid	Woodlands; slope shrublands	Common

Flower stalk 45cm, robust, up to 12 flowers, 3x4cm, on the uppermost 18cm. Stalked, oval, pointed petals extend above the broad, rounded sepal. Lower sepals 10x0.5mm crossed-over, leg-like. Labellum yellow tinged red-brown with small lip and two prominent wings. Leaves, 1x25cm, basal, tapering, pointed. Page 162

Diuris laxiflora	Yellow, brown and green	Sep-Oct
Bee orchid	Rock outcrops	Uncommon

Flower stalk 22cm, slender, two flowers, 1.5x2cm, on stalks 2cm. Two petals, rounded, yellow, erect on brown stalks. Lower sepals narrow, downward-pointing, green, not crossing. Labellum with fan-like centre, larger than wings. Basal leaf, 2x80mm, about 4cm free. Page 155

Diuris longifolia	Mauve	Sep-Oct
Purple pansy orchid	Edge of scarp	Rare

Flower stalk 35cm, robust up to seven flowers, 4x2cm, on the uppermost 20cm. Stalked, oval, petals extend above the broad, rounded sepal. Lower sepals 10x5mm. Labellum mauve, tinged yellow with small lip and two prominent wings. Leaves, 20cm, basal, tapering, pointed.

Diuris magnifica	Rich yellow and green-brown	Sep-Oct
Pansy orchid	Woodlands; slope shrublands	Uncommon

Was included in D. corymbosa but with many differences: later flowering; petals more rounded; labellum yellow-tinged pink-purple, lip enlarged to similar size as wings; colouring different. Flower stalk 25cm, rarely more than five flowers, 2x3cm, on upper 10cm of flower stalk, leaves 15cmx7mm.

Diuris setacea	Yellow, brown and green	Oct
Bristly donkey orchid	Woodlands	Rare

Flower stalk 30cm, up to four flowers, 2x2.5cm, on upper 6cm. Like D. laxiflora but petals more elongated. Labellum pointed with markings lighter brown on yellow, wings almost inconspicuous. Upper sepal yellow, forward-pointing, matching labellum in length. Basal leaves 1x12cm, tapering and twisting, sheathing stalk for 4cm.

Leptoceras menziesii	White and plum red	Sep-Oct
Rabbit orchid	Damp areas, sandy	Rare

Flower stalk 18cm, one to two flowers, 3x2cm, two plum red petals, erect, ear-like, two white, lower sepals horizontal, forward-pointing. Top sepal, hooded, plum red. Labellum 3x3mm, not prominent. Basal leaf 2x6.5cm, tapering. In colonies. Flowers best after summer fire.

2E Pair of downward-pointing prominent parts, few flowers

Although several orchids have downward pointing parts, only those of the Bunny orchids (Eriochilus) are prominent and dominating.

Eriochilus dilatatus	White, green and brown	Mar-Jun
White bunny orchid	Woodlands; rock outcrops	Uncommon

Flower stalks 40cm, slender, two to eight flowers, 15x15mm, on upper 8cm. Lower sepals 1.2cm, white, spreading. Other parts not prominent. Basal leaf on stalk 13cm, blade 9x35mm oval, pointed at tip, contracted at stalk end.   Page 159

Eriochilus scaber	Pink	Jul-Sep
Pink bunny orchid	Damp places	Rare

Flower stalk 8cm, one to two flowers, 1.5x1.5cm. As for E. dilatatus but all parts pink. Leaf blade 10x7mm, on stalk 1cm. Flowers after fire.   Page 159

2F Labellum prominent, parts cantilevered

Included here are the Flying Duck orchid (Paracalaena), the Elbow orchid (Spiculaea) and the Hammer orchids (Drakaea).

Drakaea gracilis	Browny-green	Aug-Sep
Unnamed hammer orchid	Woodland	Rare

Species (Hoffman and Brown (1984) p.218-219) similar to D. livida but with labellum all purple and with more prominent hairs at the tip.

Paracalaena nigrita   Green, pink-tinged   Aug-Sep
Flying duck orchid   Woodlands   Very rare

    Flower stalk 12cm, flower 1x1cm, upside-down. Sepals and petals 1x5mm, finger-like projections, around inflated, translucent, green column. Labellum 1x5mm, dark purple, glistening, grape-textured, labellum (duck's head), up stout, curved, stalk (duck's neck). Basal leaf, 7mmx1cm, heart-shaped, flat on ground, green tinged with pink.   Page 162

Drakaea livida   Pinky-green   Sep-Oct
Warty hammer orchid   Woodland   Rare

    Flower stalk 20cm, slender, flower, 2.5x2cm. Sepals and petals 12x0.5mm. Labellum purple and white, 5x10mm, suspended 10mm from flower centre, resembling wingless female native wasp with tilted tail and spotted thorax. On contact with male wasp, swings on hinge to collide with column. Basal leaf 1.5x2cm, heart-shaped, flat on ground surface, with reddish veins against green.   Page 158

Spiculaea ciliata   Browny-green   Nov-Feb
Elbow orchid   Labellum: Browny-green and purple   Uncommon
            Rock outcrops

Flower stalk 15cm, succulent, up to seven flowers, 1x1.5cm, on upper 9cm. Flowers slender, parts projecting in all directions. Sepals and petals, 0.5x7-10mm, upper sepal arched over clawed column, other parts arched backwards. Hinged labellum, 1x2mm, hangs downwards with purple tuft at one end and pale brown at the other. Basal leaf, 3x10mm, absent at flowering. Sufficient sustenance in stem to support flowering and seed development.   Page 155

Lesmurdie Scarp

Orchids 155

Prasophyllum brownii
Brown's leek orchid

Diuris laxiflora
Bee orchid

Spiculaea ciliata — Elbow orchid

Thelymitra antennifera
Vanilla orchid

Cyrtostylis huegelii
Mosquito orchid

Lyperanthus serratus
Rattle Beaks

Cyanicula gemmata
Blue china orchid

Prasophyllum elatum   Tall leek orchid

Pyrorchis nigricans
Red Beaks

Monadenia bracteata
Brown finger orchid

Orchids 157

Cyanicula sericea
Silky blue orchid

Caladenia longicauda
White spider orchid

Plumatichilos barbatus
Bird orchid

Elythranthera brunonis
Purple enamel orchid

Microtis alba
White mignonette

Caladenia flava
Cowslip orchid

Drakaea livida
Warty hammer orchid

Pterostylis pyramidalis
Dwarf greenhood

Pterostylis aspera

Orchids 159

Eriochilus scaber
Pink bunny orchid

Eriochilus dilatatus
White bunny orchid

Oligochaetochilus songuineus Dark banded greenhood

Caladenia macrostylis
Leaping spider orchid

Caladenia longiclavata
Clubbed spider orchid

Cyanicula deformis
Blue Beard

Oligochaetochilus vittatus
Banded greenhood

Prasophyllum parvifolium   Autumn leek orchid

Thelymitra benthamiana
Leopard orchid

Leporella fimbriata
Hare orchid

Orchids 161

Elythranthera emarginata
Pink enamel orchid

Thelymitra pauciflora
Slender sun orchid

Pterostylis recurva
Jug orchid

Caladenia reptans
Dwarf pink fairy

Thelymitra crinita
Blue lady orchid

Paracalaena nigrita
Flying duck orchid

Caladenia marginata
White fairy orchid

Diuris brumalis
Common donkey orchid

Thelymitra macrophylla
Scented sun orchid

CHAPTER 7

Herblike Plants and Annuals

Plants in this Chapter all have non-woody, pliable parts. Most of the smallest plants in the Hills are found here.

Many are annuals (growing from seed each year). Others, while perennial (lasting more than one year) renew heir aboveground parts annually. Ferns are included here.

GROUP 1

Flowers showy: IRREGULAR, four petals as two pairs, rarely near-regular (Triggerplants) page 168

Sub-Groups	Families	Genera
1A to 1E	Stylidiaceae	Levenhookia Stylidium

GROUP 2

Flowers showy: regular or irregular, IN HEADS. page 172

Sub-Groups	Families	Genera
2A Tight compact heads of flowers page 172	Asteraceae	Arctotheca* Asteridea Brachyscome Chthonocephalus Cotula Craspedia Dittrichia* Gnaphalium Hedypnois* Helichrysum Hyalospermum Hypochaeris* Lagenifera Lawrencella Leptorhynchos Millotia Pithocarpa Podolepis Podotheca Ptesochaeta Rhodanthe Senecio Siloxerus Sonchus* Taraxacum* Tolpis Trichocline Ursinia* Vellereophyton Waitzia
2B Domed, spherical or cylindrical heads of individually distinguishable flowers, often at ends of stalks. NOT daisies. page 176	Amaranthaceae Apiaceae Lamiaceae	Ptilotus Actinotus Eryngium Foeniculum Pentapeltis Platysace Schoenolaena Trachymene Xanthosia Mentha

GROUP 3

Flowers showy: IRREGULAR appearing to have two, five or other number of petals but NOT four (includes PEA flowers). Parts may be separate or joined to form a tube. page 178

Sub-Group	Families	Genera
3A Petals five, separate PEA flowers. page 178	Papilionaceae	Gompholobium Isotropis Jacksonia Kennedia Lathyrus* Lotus Lupinus* Medicago* Melilotus* Trifolium*
3B Petals five, separate or joined at base, but NOT forming a prominent tube. Petals sometimes UNEQUAL as three larger (lower) and two much smaller (upper) petals OR two larger 'wing' petals OR just one prominent large lower petal. page 180.	Geraniaceae Goodeniaceae Lobeliaceae Polygalaceae Lentibulariaceae Fumariaceae	Erodium Geranium Pelorgonium Dampiera Goodenia Scaevola Velleia Grammatotheca Isotoma Lobelia Monopsis Comesperma Utricularia Fumaria*
3C Parts joined to form TUBE with petals as unequal lobes, sometimes not readily distinguishable in number. page 184	Scrophulariaceae Lamiaceae Orobanchaceae	Bartsia* Dichisma* Gratiola* Misopates* Parentucellia* Stachys* Orobanche

Herblike Plants & Annuals

GROUP 4
Flowers showy: REGULAR, parts in four, five or more; separate or joined. page 186

	Sub-Group	Families	Genera
4A	Appearing regular. Actually a composite head of many flowers, the outer, often white and strap-shaped, irregular, the inner, yellow, tubular and regular. page 186	Asteraceae	Daisies [Grp 2] page 172
4B	Petals five, (one species eight) separate sometimes inconspicuous but grouped in umbrella-shaped clusters. page 186	Apiaceae	[Grp 5] page 193 or in heads [Grp 2] page 176
		Caryophyllaceae	Cerastium* Petrorhagia* Silene* Spergularia* Stellaria
		Droseraceae	Drosera
		Euphorbiaceae	Monotaxis
		Linaceae	Linum
		Loganiaceae	Logania
		Menyanthaceae	Villarsia
		Oxalidaceae	Oxalis*
		Primulaceae	Anagallis* Samolus
		Ranunculaceae	Ranunculus
		Scrophulariaceae	Verbascum
4C	Petals five, joined to form a tubular, bell- or cup-shaped base page 191	Boraginaceae	Echium*
		Campanulaceae	Wahlenbergia
		Gentianaceae	Centaurium*
		Solanaceae	Solanum
		Stackhousiaceae	Stackhousia Tripterococcus
4D	Petals four, regular, separate page 192	Brassicaceae	Brassica* Raphanus
		Haloragaceae	Glischrocaryon
		Rutaceae	Boronia

GROUP 5

Flowers inconspicuous, clustered in greenish, blackish, straw-coloured or yellow heads or borne.

Sub-Group		Families	Genera
5A	Flowers in composite heads. DAISIES. page 193	Asteraceae	Angianthus Chthonocephalus Dittrichia* Gnaphalium Millotia Podotheca Siloxerus Vellereophyton Waitzia
5B	Flowers clustered in domed, spherical cylindrical or umbrella-shaped heads NOT DAISIES. page 193	Amaranthaceae Apiaceae Euphorbiaceae Plantaginaceae Rosaceae Rubiaceae Stylidiaceae	Alternanthera Xanthosia Poranthera Plantago* Acaena Galium Opercularia Levenhookia
5C	Flowers borne singly or if clustered, in loose heads page 194	Apiaceae Caryophyllaceae Crassulaceae Euphorbiaceae Gentianaceae Haloragaceae Lamiaceae Lobeliaceae Loganiaceae Polygonaceae Portulacaceae Scrophulariaceae Urticaceae	Daucus Homalosciadium Hydrocotyle Trachymene Stellaria* Crassula* Monotaxis Cicendia Haloragis Gonocarpus Myriophyllum Stachys* Grammatotheca Monopsis Mitrasacme Polygonum Rumex Calandrinia Dischisma* Gratiola Parietaria
5D	Flowers NONE. FERNS page 198	Ferns	Adiantum Cheilanthes Lindsaea Ophioglossum Pteridium Selaginella Sphaeropteris

GROUP 1

Flowers showy: IRREGULAR, four petals as two pairs, rarely near-regular

STYLIDIACEAE: *Levenhookia, Stylidium*

STYLIDIACEAE - Triggerplants (For fuller description see Chapter 9, Page 226)

Triggerplants get their name from their pollination mechanism.

Groupings for identification are:

- [1A] Small (5cm) annuals, single-stemmed, with few noticeable leaves. (Leaves 1-2mm close to the ground in a rosette, often absent at flowering. Flowers singly at tips of branching upper part of stem. Often scattered in colonies.). page 168
- [1B] Plants with several distinct, even if sometimes short stems. Leaves in tufts at tips of several stems. Some form dome-shaped cushions with a tuft of leaves at the tips. page 169
- [1C] Leaves in rosette at ground level, plants without stems but a single rosette of many leaves at ground level (rarely on stems then supported by aerial roots), each leaf ending in a long, fine white hair. page 170
- [1D] As for 1C but leaves without long hair-tip. page 170
- [1E] Leaves in rosette at ground level. page 171

[1A] Small annuals

Stylidium calcaratum	White or pink	Sep-Oct
Book triggerplant	Woodlands; slope shrublands	Common

Erect slender plants 10cm, scattered in colonies. Leaves 2mm flat on ground, not prominent. Flowers in bright sunlight with vertically-paired petals, upper pair three-pointed, lower pair resembling feet. Column from below. The flowers close book-like at night and in dull weather.
Page 200

Stylidium emarginatum	White	Sep-Oct
	Woodlands; slope shrublands	Uncommon

Similar to S. calcaratum but all four petals are foot-like from above.

Stylidium petiolare	Cream	Sep-Oct
Horn triggerplant	Slope; shrublands; rock outcrops	Common

Similar to S. calcaratum, smaller (8cm) with the upper pair of petals horn-like, curved, pointed. Column from above.   Page 204

Stylidium inundatum	White or pink	Oct-Nov
	Swampy	Uncommon

Similar to S. perpusillum. Flowers of almost equal, vertically paired, elongated, rounded petals.

Levenhookia pusilla	Pink	Oct-Nov
Midget stylewort	Open woodland on gravel	Common

Similar to S. stipitata. Flowers clustered, stalkless, in heads made dark red with the bracts and calyces, 1mm.   Page 208

Stylidium perpusillum	White	Nov-Dec
Tiny triggerplant	Rock outcrops	Uncommon

Similar to S. calcaratum, but 3cm tall, petals hardly visible, 2mm.

Levenhookia stipitata	Pink	Nov-Dec
Common stylewort	Open woodland on gravel	Common

Erect plants 6cm, pink petals, 3mm, almost forming a square on stalked flowers with a bract at the base.

1B Stemmed with leaf tufts

Stylidium bulbiferum	Salmon pink to cream	Oct-Nov
Circus triggerplant	Open woodlands; slope shrublands	Common

Domed cushions, 20cm, of meshing reddish stems. Leaves, 10mm, cylindrical, tufts. Flowers 1cm, massed with unequally-paired, spreading petals, red-spotted towards their bases, the larger pair, 6mm, with the column set behind the smaller pair. Page 201

Stylidium breviscapum	Red and white	Nov-Dec
Boomerang triggerplant	Slope shrublands and granite outcrops	Uncommon

Similar to S. bulbiferum, more straggly, 20cm. Flowers with unequally-paired, spreading petals, larger pair 6mm curved strongly upwards, boomerang-like, with the column set between them, the smaller pair 2mm, near circular. Page 203

Stylidium dichotomum	Yellow-Orange	Nov-Dec
Pins-and-needles	Slope shrublands and granite outcrops	Uncommon

Plants in patches to 1m^2, shortly stalked with loose tufts of leaves to 3cm, flowers stalkless, loosely clustered on flower-stem to 15cm, petals spreading, 5mm, red-dotted near centre often with red central streak on reverse.

Stylidium leptophyllum	Pink	Nov-Dec
Needle leaved triggerplant	Open woodlands	Uncommon

Similar to S. dichotomum but growing on gravel.

Stylidium rhyncocarpum	White to pinkish white	Nov-Dec
Black beaked triggerplant	Woodlands	Uncommon

Robust, dark, somewhat upright, leafy-stemmed, to 30cm with flowers, stalkless, clustered at ends of stems, petals equally paired, 5mm, red-dotted at base, with calyx distinctively curved and narrowing towards the flower-base (beaked).

Stylidium repens	Pink, sometimes white	Sporadic
Matted triggerplant	Woodlands; slope shrublands; rock outcrops	all year Common

(See Chapter 4, Scramblers, Climbers and Perchers, page 101).

1C Stemless, Rosette Leaves ending in White Hairs

Stylidium hispidum	White	Sep-Oct
White butterfly triggerplant	Open woodland	Common

Lower flower stem hairless; 10-40cm leaf margins comb-like with short hairs; petals unequal, somewhat oblong, the upper pair the larger; large flowers, 2cm.

Stylidium piliferum	Off-white	Sep-Oct
Common butterfly triggerplant	Open woodland	Common

Lower flower stem hairless; 15-50cm leaf margin with transparent fringe but without prominent comb-like hairs; petals rounded, pairs similar.

Stylidium pubigerum	Yellow	Sep-Oct
Yellow butterfly triggerplant	Slope shrublands	Uncommon

Flower stem hairless, 8-25cm reddish below the flowers; leaf margin with transparent fringe but no prominent comb-like hairs; petals unequal, the upper pair oblong and the larger, the lower, oval.

Stylidium ciliatum	Cream	Oct-Nov
Golden triggerplant	Open woodland	Common

Flower stem densely covered with yellow (golden) glandular hairs, 40cm. Leaf margins comb-like with a row of short hairs. Petals rounded, pairs similar.

1D Stemless, Rosette Leaves with Hairless Tips

Stylidium affine	Pink	Sep-Oct
Queen triggerplant	Woodland	Common

(See Chapter 5, Plants with Grasslike Leaves. page 133)

Stylidium schoenoides	Cream	Sep-Oct
Cowkicks	Woodlands	Uncommon

Flowers upright, 3cm, two or three on stem to 15cm, petals in unequal, oblong pairs, the upper arching round slightly, the lower, close and parallel. Column strong, 1mm broad, arched back between upper pair of petals, releasing with vigour. Smooth, grasslike leaves, many longer than flower stem, to 20cmx2mm. Page 200

Stylidium canaliculatum	Fawn (washed-out yellow)	Oct-Nov
Delicate triggerplant	Damp places	Uncommon
	(slope seepages and valley floors)	

Flower stems to 10cm, flowers 1cm with narrow petals, nearly equal pairs, vertically spreading, the small column set between the lower pair, the throat with six appendages. Leaves 60x2mm, noticeably soft and green in basal tufts. Page 207

Stylidium carnosum	White	Oct-Nov
Fleshy-leaved triggerplant	Slope shrublands and woodlands	Uncommon

With tendency to flower after fires, the rosette of smooth, dark blue-green, spoon-shaped leaves, 5x3cm may be more familiar. Striking in flower with stem to 1m, flowers many, stalkless along the dark stem, petals somewhat crinkled, pairs almost equal, column set to the side of the flower.

Stylidium crassifolium	Pink-white	Oct-Nov
Thick-leaved	Damp valley floors	Rare
triggerplant		

    Similar to S. pycnostachyum but without hairs and plant larger: leaves 12x1.5cm; flower stem to 60cm.

Stylidium junceum	White	Oct-Nov
Reed triggerplant	Woodlands	Very common

    Distinctive because flowers clustered in conical head, petals with bright rose mark at base, pairs equal, rounded; column set to side. Flower stem to 50cm with sparsely scattered bracts. Rosette of leaves each to 40x2mm, pointed, stiff and pressed to ground.   Page 200

Stylidium lineatum	Yellow	Oct-Nov
Sunny triggerplant	Open woodlands	Uncommon

    Rosettes of grey-green, spoon-shaped leaves, glandular-hairy, broader towards tips, to 2x1cm. Flower stem to 30cm, sparsely hairy, flowers shortly stalked to stem, petals unequally paired, oval-rounded, the larger 5mm; column set to side between the smaller.

Stylidium pycnostachyum	White	Oct-Nov
Downy triggerplant	Slope shrublands	Uncommon

    Flower stem to 25cm, downy-hairy, flowers crowded in groups of up to three on short stalks with bract at stem; petals with purple spot at base, pairs nearly equal, column set to side. Stout basal rosette of soft, hairy leaves, 8x1cm.

1E Stemless, Rosette-leaved with Leaf Whorls on Flower Stem

Stylidium brunonianum	Pink	Sep-Nov
Pink fountain	Woodlands	Very Common
triggerplant		

    Slender, grey-green, smooth, flower stem with shortly-stalked, upright flowers, 6mm; upper pair of petals slightly longer than lower pair; column set between upper pair. Rosette of grey-green, limp leaves, 30x2mm.

Stylidium amoenum	Lilac to whitish	Oct-Nov
Lovely triggerplant	Woodlands	Very Common

    Flower stem to 50cm with single whorl of leaves, lower part hairless, angled to near-upright flowers, 8mm; pair of petals nearly equal; column set to side. Rosette of smooth, slightly fleshy, dark green, pointed leaves, 40x5mm, broadest nearer tip.   Page 202

Donkey triggerplant	Open woodlands	Common

    Delicate plant with flower stem to 15cm, with single whorl of grasslike leaves low, others scattered higher; flowers 6mm, singly-stalked, petal pairs nearly equal, oval, column set to side between smaller pair. Leaves fresh-green, grasslike, to 30x1mm.

Stylidium diversifolium	White	Oct-Nov
Touch-me-not	Forest	Uncommon

Similar to S. amoenum. Flowering glistening white, usually three whorls of leaves on the lower stem to 80cm.

Stylidium rigidifolium	Yellow	Oct-Nov
	Open woodlands	Uncommon

Similar to S. amoenum, to 30cm, flowers 15x8mm, petals with violet spot at base. Leaves spoon-shaped, 30x6mm, whitish-green with a waxy bloom. A rare species occurring only in the Kalamunda Hills.

GROUP 2
Flowers showy: regular or irregular, IN HEADS

2A Tight compact heads of flowers

ASTERACEAE: Arctotheca Asteridea Brachyscome Chthonocephalus Cotula Craspedia Dittrichia Gnaphalium Hedypnois Helichrysum Hyalosperma Hypochaeris Lagenifera Lawrencella Leptorhyncos Millotia Pithocarpa Podolepis Podotheca Pterochaeta Rhodanthe Senecio Siloxerus Sonchus Taraxacum Tolpis Trichocline Ursinia Vellereophyton Waitzia

ASTERACEAE - Daisies (For fuller description see Chapter 9, Page 222)

Groupings for identification are:
- 2A-1   Leafy up a stem, 'petals' papery bracts. Everlastings page 172
- 2A-2   Leafy up a stem, 'petals' soft, strap-shaped, fused petals page 173
- 2A-3   Leaves in a basal rosette, petals as in 2A-2. Mainly weeds page 174
- 2A-4   No obvious petals. Ray florets absent. Plants often dwarf, less than 4cm page 175

■ 2A-1 Leafy up a stem, 'petals' papery bracts. Everlastings

Lawrencella rosea	Pink	Sep-Oct
	Slope shrublands; rock outcrops	Common

Upright, sparingly-branched stems to 20cm ending in flower heads 15mm across with yellow centres and with thread like, cylindrical leaves, 10x1mm.

Rhodanthe manglesii	Pink	Sep-Nov
	Slope shrublands	Uncommon

Upright simple or branched stems to 50cm ending in flower heads 25mm across and with broad, stem-clasping leaves, 3x1.5cm.

Waitzia nitida	Golden yellow	Sep-Nov
Rhodanthe citrina	Lemon yellow	Sep-Nov
	Woodlands; slope shrublands	Uncommon

Similar, usually single-stemmed annuals to 20cm with cottony-hairy leaves, 20-30x1mm, and flower heads 2-5mm across, not fully opening.

Hyalosperma cotula	White	Oct-Nov
	Woodlands; slope shrublands	Very Common

Usually unbranched, upright stems to 15cm with threadlike, cylindrical leaves, 8x1mm, and topped by 15mm diameter heads with yellow centres.

Rhodanthe corymbosa   White   Nov-Dec
                                       Woodlands; slope shrublands   Uncommon
    Branching, upright stems to 30cm with flattened leaves, 10x2mm, and many heads, 5mm across, sparsely bracted.   Page 200

Waitzia suaveolens   White   Nov-Dec
                                       Slopes   Uncommon
    Upright, unbranched stems to 30cm, similar to Hyalosperma cotula but with white centres to the flower heads, 20mm across, remaining top-shaped, not flat, and with leaves stem-clasping at their bases.

Helichrysum macranthum   Pinky-white   Nov-Dec
                                       Woodlands   Common
    Largest of the local Everlastings. Leaves, lance-shaped, 5x1cm. Upright, sparingly branched, slightly hairy plant to 60cm. Yellow-centred flower heads to 3cm.   Page 202

Pithocarpa corymbulosa   White   Dec-Apr
                                       Woodlands; slope shrublands   Common
    Straggling, knitted, branched, white-haired stems tending to be woody at the base and with short cylindrical leaves, 1x5mm scattered along the stems. Flower heads, 5mm across, at the stem tips with the outside of the outer bracts sometimes dark-red tinged.   Page 200

■ **2A-2 Stems with Leaves and Obvious Soft 'Petals'**

Sonchus oleraceus*   Yellow   Aug-Nov
Common Sowthistle   Disturbed places   Common
    Weedy. Upright, stout, hollow, largely smooth, stems to 80cm with stem-clasping, irregularly-toothed leaves, 6x2cm. Flower heads many on shortly-branched, tops of stem, each 2cm across. Milky sap from broken leaf-end. Native of Europe, Asia and North Africa.

Asteridea pulverulenta   White   Sep-Oct
                                       Slope shrublands   Common
    Upright, sparingly-branching, hairy stems to 30cm ending in flower heads 25mm across with strap-shaped petals squared-off at tips and three-lobed. Leaves hairy, flat, 20x2mm. Flower heads enclosed by narrow bracts ending in hair-like tips.   Page 203

Brachyscome iberidifolia   Magenta   Sep-Oct
Swan River Daisy   Slope shrublands   Uncommon
    Upright, branching stems to 20cm with deeply-divided leaves to 5cm with long, narrow segments. Flower heads 15mm across with yellow centre, several.

Podolepis gracilis   White (to pink-tinged)   Sep-Oct
                                       Slope shrublands   Uncommon
    Upright, sparingly-branched, smooth, shortly-hairy, wiry stems to 30cm ending in flower heads 25mm across, strap-shaped petals rounded, two or three-lobed. Leaves shortly-hairy, broadly flat, 30x5mm. Bracts enclosing flower heads broad, 1.5mm across, transparent-papery.

Ursinia anthemoides* Fawn (off-yellow) Sep-Dec
 Woodlands; slope shrublands Very common
Upright, much-branched stems to 30cm with deeply-divided leaves to 3cm each lobe finger-like, 1mm across, and strongly aromatic when crushed. Flower heads ending leafless upper parts of stems, 1.5cm across; strap-shaped petals with rounded ends. Seeds attached to round, five-lobed, papery, petal-like scales. Native of South Africa. Page 204

Senecio lautus Yellow Nov-Dec
A groundsel Slope shrublands Common
Semi-upright, twisting, smooth, slightly fleshy stem to 50cm with tapering, notched, flat, leaves, 5x2cm. Flowers heads on short stalks towards end of stem, 12mm across with strap-shaped petals round-ended.

■ **2A-3 Leaves in Basal Rossette; Heads with Large Soft 'Petals'**

Arctotheca calendula* Yellow Jul-Sep
Capeweed Disturbed places Uncommon
Flower stalk roughly hairy extending from semi-upright, weak, juicy, partly-leafy stem, 10cm, with flower head 4cm across, strap-shaped petals tapering to blunt point from midway, and with dark centres. Rosette leaves stalked, lobed, at broadest beyond midway, 10cmx3cm, densely white-hairy underneath. Native of South Africa.

Dandelions* Bright yellow Jul-Dec
 Disturbed places Common
Four species of dandelion-like weed species, all with lobed, basal-rossette leaves with milky sap when broken. Very common is Hypochaeris glabra, or Flatweed with two or three heads on smooth stems to 50cm, the rossette leaves, roughly-hairy. Occurring in every habitat in disturbed places. Native of the Mediterranean region. More restricted to disturbed places on the slopes, and in order of more to less common are: Tolpis barbata, Yellow Hawkweed, with woolly-hairy, branched stem to 30cm, several flower heads with square-tipped, strap-shaped petals and bracts of flower head becoming hard and upwardly pointed with age. Hedypnois rhagadioloides, Cretan Weed, with roughly-hairy, upright stem to 40cm with heads on long, smooth flower stalks usually hollow and swollen near top. Both species are native of the Mediterranean region. Taraxacum officinale, Dandelion, flower stem and leaves smooth or very sparsely hairy; spreading flower heads to 2.5cm. Origin unknown.

Lagenophora huegelii White, pink-tinged Sep-Nov
 Woodlands Common
Hairy flower stalk 20cm from flat rosette of stalked, softly-hairy, lobed leaves, 7x1.5cm. Flower head 5mm, strip shaped petals short, 1mm long.

Trichocline spathulata Creamy-white Nov-Jan
Native Gerbera Woodlands Common
Flower stalk to 70cm with single head, 6cm across, with narrow, strap-shaped petals, 2cmx2mm, minutely three-lobed at tips, and with yellow centre. Rosette of up to five, stalked, semi-upright, spoon-shaped leaves, 6x1.5cm, with slightly toothed, wavy edges and densely covered with white, cottony hairs especially on underside.

■ 2A-4 No Obvious 'Petals'

Here, the 'flower' is a head of tubular flowers (disc florets) without extending ray florets or brightly coloured bracts.

Cotula coronopifolia	Yellow	Year-round
Waterbuttons	Damp places, often salt affected	Uncommon

　　Straggling fleshy stems to 10cm. Leaves 20x5mm, fleshy, hairless, two-three toothed. Flower wads, flat disk 8cm across. On salt affected ground.

Dittrichia graveolens*	Yellow	Mar-Dec
Stinkwort	Roadsides and disturbed places	Very common

　　Bright green stems to 50cm with many side-branches, pyramid-like in outline. Leaves decreasing in size up stem, but about 30x5mm, sticky, glandular-hairy, sickly-sweet smelling when crushed. Flower heads 5mm across in each leaf axil. Can cause dermatitis. Native of Europe and Africa.

Senecio spp.	Yellow	Mar-Dec
Fireweeds	Open woodlands and slopes	Common

　　Three species: Senecio hispidulus, S. quadridentatus and S. ramosissimus, all with milky sap, stems usually exceeding 50cm, sparingly-branched, heads about 5mm across, the species differing in details of leaves, flowers and bract numbers.

Craspedia variabilis	Pale lemon	Jul-Aug
	Woodlands	Common

　　Flower heads domed, 2cm across, single on upright stems to 70cm. Basal leaves spoon-shaped, stalked, 17x1.5cm; stem leaves stalkless, 9x1.5mm.　　　　　　　　　　Page 201

Podolepis lessonii	Bright yellow	Sep-Nov
	Slopes and granite outcrops	Common

　　Flower heads 1cm enclosed by broad, 1mm, translucent, overlapping bracts, on characteristic red-brown, wiry, branched, somewhat-twisting stems to 20cm. Leaves scattered along stem, 20x7mm, stem-clasping.　　　　　　　　　　　　　　　　　　　　　　　　　Page 204

Millotia spp	Pale fawn	Oct-Nov
	Open woodland gravels	Common

　　Millotia myosotidifolia, upright, white-hairy stems to 12cm, leaves, 30x3mm tapering to 3mm, grey green, flower heads 5mm on stout stalks. Millotia tenuifolia, similar, but to 6cm, leaves, 15x1mm and flower heads 10x2mm.

Podotheca angustifolia	Yellow	Oct-Nov
	Open woodland and slopes	Very common

　　Ground-hugging plant with narrow, 3cmx2mm leaves with head nearly stemless, tall-pointed to 3cm with green-bracted sides and flowers emerging at narrow, 3mm diameter, tip. After seeding, opened-out bracts form shiny, straw-coloured stars, 4cm across.

Dwarf daisies	Translucent-papery, pale fawn, brown	Oct-Nov
	Various open places	Very common

　　Very small plants less than 4cm. Chthonocephalus pseudevax in colonies of white domed buttons 2cm, rock outcrops appearing as brain-coral under the hand lens. Hyalosperma demissum appears like Chthonocephalus but shortly stemmed, to 2cm, and lacking the brain-coral appearance under the hand lens. Pterochaeta paniculata, upright, whitish, woolly stems to 4cm with flower heads tucked in the leaf axils, pale fawn.

Euchiton sphaericus	Inconspicuous	Oct-Dec
Cudweeds	Open woodland	Uncommon

Grey hairy annual to 70cm high. Leaves without stalks. Flower heads clustered, up to 1.5cm in diameter.

Vellereophyton dealbatum*	Inconspicuous	Oct-Dec
	Damp places	Uncommon

Both white, densely-woolly stems to 30cm, branched from the base, with leaves similarly densely woolly, 4x1cm (Gnaphalium) or 15x3mm (Vellereophyton) with several, woolly-white flower heads, shortly stalked, 3mm across, clustered at tops of stems. Vellereophyton weedy. Native of South Africa.

2B Domed, spherical or cylindrical heads of individually distinguishable flowers, often at ends of stalks. NOT daisies.

AMARANTHACEAE:	Ptilotus
APIACEAE:	Actinotus Eryngium Foeniculum Pentapeltis Platysace Schoenolaena Trachymene Xanthosia
LAMIACEAE:	Mentha

AMARANTHACEAE - Mulla mullas

Ptilotus drummondii	White and hidden pink	Oct-Nov
Narrowleaf mulla mulla	Damp places	Uncommon

Stems upright, clumped, to 50cm with soft, smooth, 15x2mm leaves ending in fluffy head, 1x1cm, of flowers.

Ptilotus esquamatus	White and hidden pink	Oct-Nov
	Slopes	Uncommon

Erect, hairless stems to 50cm, sparingly-leaved, leaves 15x1mm and ending in fluffy head, 3x2.5cm, of flowers.   Page 208

Ptilotus spathulatus	White	Oct-Nov
	Woodlands	Uncommon

Stems arching, to 10cm, with flower head stalkless, 3x2.5cm, between a pair of leaves each 2x1cm.

Ptilotus manglesii	Rose-pink and white	Oct-Jan
Rose-tipped mulla mulla	Woodlands	Common

Irregular rosettes of stalked leaves with spoon-shaped blades 10x5cm, shiny, dark-green, with red veins: like beetroot. Flower stalk fleshy, semi-trailing, with scattered, smaller leaves, ending in erect, fluffy heads, 5x2cm, of pink-tipped sepals amongst white, hairy bracts.   Page 208

Ptilotus declinatus	White	Nov-Dec
Curved mulla mulla	Rock outcrops	Uncommon

Prostrate to weakly ascending, unbranched stems, to 20cm with many flat leaves, 10x5mm, ending in erect, fluffy, upright, flower heads, 3x2cm, flowers in-curved, often lasting after the leaves have withered.

APIACEAE - Carrot Family *(For fuller description see Chapter 9, Page 222)*

Platysace compressa	White	Jan-Apr
Tapeworm plant	Woodlands	Common

Erect to leaning, flattened stems 50cm, green 5mm wide with many side branches at about right-angles. Leafless except for much-divided basal leaves which wither early. Flowers clustered in heads, 2cm, parsley like at tips of branches.

Pentapeltis peltigera	White, tinged pink	Jan-Apr
	Woodlands	Common

Leaves, 3x1.5cm, semi-circular, fan-shaped, on stalks 5cm. Weakly stemmed, straggling plant 20cm. Flowers clustered in heads 3cm, with broad bracts. Page 204

Actinotus glomeratus	White	Jun-Aug
	Woodlands	Common

Straggling stems 20cm, leaves 2.5cm, stalked, dark-green, slightly-hairy, end 1cm divided into segments 8x1mm. Flower heads, 7mm, stalkless, flannel-flower like.

Foeniculum vulgare*	Yellow	Jul-Jan
Fennel	Streamsides	Uncommon

Stems stout, solid to 2m with loose clusters of flowers, each cluster to 15cm, leaves to 30cm, much-divided with segments fine green strands. The culinary plant. Native of Europe.

Eryngium pinnatifidum	Green and purple	Sep-Nov
	Slopes and wandoo woodlands	Common

Thistle-like, blue-green leaves and stems, erect, stout stem to 50cm with stiff, divided, sharply-tipped leaves, the basal leaves to 15cm, the stem leaves to 10cm. Flowers clustered in near-spherical heads, 3cm across. Page 208

Trachymene coerulea	Light blue	Oct-Nov
Blue lace flower	Slopes	Uncommon

Erect, hairy, branched stems to 60cm with heads of flowers to 5cm across and leaves to 5cm, divided into three, each segment again so-divided with pointed tips. The only other Trachymene is the tiny annual, T. pilosa, the Native parsnip.

Xanthosia spp.	Greeny-white	Oct-Nov
	Woodlands	Common

They are all somewhat weakly-stemmed, straggling plants, 30cm across or less. Xanthosia huegelii which can be somewhat upward-growing with leaf blades divided into three segments each about 2cmx4mm and leaf stalks enlarged at their base. Xanthosia ciliata to 15cm with leaf blades undivided, 10x2mm, on short stalks broadened at their bases and fringed with long hairs. Xanthosia candida to 10cm with leaf blades more rounded, 15x10mm on slender stalks and leaf blades crumby-white underneath. Xanthosia pusilla to 10cm with leaf blades divided into three segments, somewhat pointed, 1cmx3mm, with leaf stalk broadened at base, soft, downy-hairy.

Actinotus leucocephalus	White	Nov-Dec
Flannel flower	Slopes and granite outcrops	Common

Erect, sparingly branched stems 50cm. Flower heads, densely hairy, to 3cm across consisting of spreading bracts and centrally packed small flowers, annual. Leaves much divided, segmented in threes, and becoming smaller up the stem, segments, to 20x2mm. Occurs in numbers only after fire. Page 207

Xanthosia atkinsoniana	White	Nov-Mar
	Woodlands	Common

Slender, erect, branching stems 50cm. Stem-leaves divided. Flowers clustered into heads, 2cm, with broad, showy bracts, at the tips of the branches.

Platysace juncea	Cream	Dec-Jan
	Rock outcrops	Uncommon

Erect, cylindrical, leafless stems, 60cm, green, with many side-branches, produced annually without flower heads. Flower heads 5cm at tip of main stem.

Mentha spicata*	Lilac	Dec-Feb
Spearmint	Disturbed damp places	Uncommon

Smooth, erect stems 50cm, four-angled. Leaves, 3x1cm, stalkless, opposite, strongly smelling when crushed. Flowers 3mm, tubular in near-spherical clusters at stem joints on upper part of stems. Native of Europe.

Schoenolaena juncea	White	Dec-Apr
	Damp places with sedges	Rare

Stems slender, erect, sparsely-branched, to 60cm, with basal leaves to 30cm, stem leaves much shorter, to 5mm, cylindrical. Flower heads at tips of stems and at leaf axils, 1cm across. Small flowers clustered on bracts greenish-tinged beneath, darkening when dried.

GROUP 3

Flowers showy: IRREGULAR appearing to have two, five or other number of petals but NOT four (includes PEA flowers). Parts may be separate or joined to form a tube

---

3A Petals five, separate. PEA flowers

PAPILIONACEAE: *Gompholobium Isotropis Jacksonia Kennedia Lathyrus* Lotus* Lupinus* Medicago* Melilotus* Trifolium**

Kennedia species: all three, K. coccinea, K. prostrata and K. strilingii are scrambling/climbing herbaceous plants and are described in Chapter 4, Scramblers, Climbers and Perchers, page 101

Medicago polymorpha*	Yellow	Jul-Oct
Burr medic	Disturbed places	Common

The characteristic burrs (spiny, spirally twisted, pods) often caught up in dog's coats are a good indication. Weakly upright, hairless annual with stems to 20cm. Leaves with three leaflets, 15x7mm, with rounded, toothed ends. Flowers 5mm around five along stalk about 1cm.

| Lupinus species* | Blue, white or yellow | Sep-Nov |
| | Disturbed places | Common |

All are native to the Mediterranean area and were introduced for cultivating. Lupinus angustifolius, the New Zealand blue lupin, with blue flowers, and trifoliate leaves with narrow leaflets; L. albus with white flowers, and, L. luteus with yellow flowers.

| Trifolium campestre* | Yellow | Aug-Nov |
| Hop clover | Disturbed places | Uncommon |

Weakly upright stems to 15cm with sparsely-hairy, rounded leaflets, 10x5mm. Flower heads near spherical, 10x8mm, with papery, overlapping calyces giving hop appearance.

| Trifolium subterraneum* | White | Aug-Nov |
| Subterraneum clover | Disturbed places | Common |

Creeping stems to 20cm, leaflets broadly rounded, 1x1cm. Few-flowered heads 1cm across in the leaf axils. Has the habit of burying its seed pods, hence its name.

| Trifolium repens* | White | Aug-Jan |
| White clover | Disturbed places | Uncommon |

Straggling, weak green stems to 25cm, with leaflets, rounded, slightly-toothed, 2x1cm and flowers clustered into a nearly spherical head, 2cm across. Hairless plant.

| Isotropis cuneifolia | Orange | Sep-Oct |
| Lamb poison | Woodlands; damp places | Common |

Weak straggling stems 20cm. Leaves wedge-shaped, or oblong, 3x1.5cm, some with a notch out of the squared-off leaf tip. Flowers 25mm, striking, solitary on stalks 7cm, the back of the standard petal criss-crossed with dark veins.

| Trifolium arvense* | White to pink | Sep-Nov |
| Hare's foot clover | Disturbed places | Common |

Leaning to upright stems to 20cm, with leaflets 10x2mm and long spreading hairs. Flowers clustered into a softly-hairy head (Hare's foot) somewhat longer, 2cm, than broad, 1cm.

| Trifolium angustifolium* | Pink | Sep-Dec |
| Narrowleaf clover | Disturbed places | Common |

Erect, stiff stems to 50cm with pointed leaflets 30x4mm, with short stiff hairs. Flower heads mulla mulla-like, cylindrical, 8x2cm, often persisting with a grey colour after flowering.

| Lathyrus tingitanus | Pink | Oct-Nov |
| Tangier pea | Disturbed places on slopes | Uncommon |

Sweet pea like plant, stems to 1m, winged, straggly. Leaves a pair of leaflets, rounded, 3x1.5cm with arrow-shaped leafy parts (stipules) at the leaf bases. Flowers in groups up to three, 3cm across.

Lotus angustissimus* Bright yellow Nov-Jan
Narrowleaf trefoil Damp disturbed places Uncommon
    Straggling stems to 20cm, with sparse, long-hairs. Leaves with five rounded leaflets, each to 10x5mm, with central nerve shortly extended beyond the leaflet tip. Head a cluster of up to three flowers, each about 8mm across.

3B Petals five, separate or joined at base, but NOT forming a prominent tube. Petals sometimes UNEQUAL as three larger (lower) and two much smaller (upper) petals OR two larger 'wing' petals OR just one prominent large lower petal.

GERANIACEAE:	*Erodium Geranium Pelargonium*
GOODENIACEAE:	*Dampiera Goodenia Scaevola Velleia*
LOBELIACEAE:	*Grammatotheca Isotoma Lobelia Monopsis*
POLYGALACEAE:	*Comesperma*
LENTIBULARIACEAE:	*Utricularia*
FUMARIACEAE:	*Fumaria*

GERANIACEAE - Pelargonium Family

Erodium cicutarium* Pink Aug-Sep
Common crowfoot or Disturbed areas including Common
Storksbill rock outcrops
    Rosette of much-divided, parsley-type leaves, 3x1.5cm, pressed to the ground with weak, upright, hairy, reddish stems to 15cm ending in a cluster of flowers, 1.5cm across, with the upper two petals slightly longer than the three lower petals.

Erodium botrys* Blue, purple Aug-Sep
Long Storksbill Disturbed areas including Common
    rock outcrops
    Similar to E. cicutarium* but smaller, less common and with divided leaves.

Pelargonium littorale Pink Aug-Nov
Native pelargonium Near rock outcrops Uncommon
    Stems weakly upright, sparsely hairy, to 30cm. Leaves slightly lobed, 3x6cm. Flowers clustered in heads of two to five, each 1.5cm across with petals deeply two-lobed, the upper two larger than the lower three.

Geranium retrorsum Pink Sep-Oct
    Disturbed, damper areas Uncommon
    Stems weakly upright to 20cm, felty-hairy. Leaves, 2cm across, deeply divided or lobed into about five segments. Flowers regular, 1.5cm across, on stalks to 3cm.

GOODENIACEAE - Leschenaultia Family

Groupings for identification are:
- 3B-1 Large, one-sided, handlike, blue flowers - Scaevola spp. page 181
- 3B-2 Small, blue flowers, equal size petals, less than 1.5cm across. Dampiera and most Goodenias page 181
    - 3B-2a Leaves not prominent, few, small or absent page 181
    - 3B-2b Leaves obvious page 182
- 3B-3 Lobelias page 182

- 3B-4 Yellow flowers - Velleia trinervis and the tiny-flowered Goodenia claytoniacea page 183
- 3B-5 Flowers with two large 'wing' petals - Polygalaceae page 184
- 3B-6 Flowers with one prominent large lower petal page 184

3B-1 Large, handlike, blue flowers

| Scaevola glandulifera | Blue to violet-blue | Sep-Mar |
| | Slopes | Common |

Erect, hairy stem to 50cm with flowers, 2cm across, in a spike at upper end and leaves, basally, 4cmx5mm, decreasing in size up the stem. Tacky to the touch because of slightly sticky, glandular hairs.

| Scaevola calliptera | Blue | Oct-Dec |
| Royal robe | Open areas in woodlands | Common |

Straggling, hairy, weak stems often covering some square metres of ground with flowers, 3.5cm across, borne singly on stalks in the leaf axils. Leaves 4x1.5cm, stalkless, with toothed edge towards tip half.

| Scaevola pilosa | Pink-blue | Nov-Dec |
| | Woodlands and slopes | Common |

Similar to S. calliptera but less striking and covered with long, soft hairs (pilose); flowers smaller, 1.5cm across.

3B-2 Small, blue flowers, equal size petals > 1.5cm across

3B-2a Leaves not prominent, few, small or absent

Dampiera trigona	Royal blue	Aug-Oct
Angle-stem dampiera	Slope shrublands with	Uncommon
	some winter dampness	

Three-cornered, hairless green stems to 1m, weakly upright and often growing up through shrubs. Flowers, 1.5cm across, arranged along branched stalks.

Dampiera alata	Blue	Aug-Nov
Winged-stem dampiera	Slopes, slightly	Very Common
	damper areas	

Large, suckering colonies to over 1m² across of erect, hairless, winged green stems to 30cm and 5mm wide. Flowers 1cm across, scattered along stems.   Page 201

| Dampiera lavandulacea | Pale lavender blue | Sep-Oct |
| | Slopes | Uncommon |

Large, suckering colonies to over 1m² across of erect, whitish green, rounded, ribbed stems to 50cm, sparsely-leaved to leafless with leaves 10x2mm. Flowers 7mm across, a few on stalks on upper part of stems where leaves joined. Entire plant with whitish, woolly appearance; not shiny green.

| Goodenia caerulea | Deep blue | Nov-Dec |
| | Slopes | Common |

Round, erect, shortly glandular-hairy stems to 25cm, branched sparingly with ascending branches often ending in single flowers, 1cm across, with yellow throat.   Page 202

- **3B-2b Leaves obvious**

Dampiera linearis Purply blue Jul-Sep
Common dampiera Woodlands and slopes Very common
  Large suckering colonies, stems to 20cm, hairy towards tips with stalkless, very variable, shiny-green leaves, usually longer than broad, about 2.5x1cm, sometimes toothed at tip. Flowers 1cm across along hairy, bracted stalks, the two upper petals each with a forward-projecting flange. Page 203

Dampiera coronata Blue Jul-Nov
  Woodlands Common
  Erect, stems hairless, winged with shortly stalked to stalkless, very variable leaves. Flowers 1cm across, on bracted stalks.

Dampiera hederacea Blue Sep-Nov
Karri dampiera Woodlands in damper, sheltered areas Rare
  Trailing, scattered-hairy stems with stalked, ivy-shaped leaves, the leaf blade 2cm across, densely woolly-hairy on underside. Flowers, 1cm across, scattered along stalks from leaf axils.

Dampiera incana Blue Nov-Jan
  Open woodlands Uncommon
  Tuft of whitish, felty-haired stems to 15cm with similarly-hairy, rounded leaves, 15x7mm. Flowers 1cm across along bracted stalks.

■ 3B-3 Lobelias, small, 1.5cm or less, unequal sized petals

LOBELIACEAE - Lobelias

Two scarcely noticeable upper petals, and the three lower, characteristically displayed in fleur-de-lis arrangement: a prominent, projecting central petal with the two side petals curving away from it.

Lobelia alata Blue All year
  Streamsides Very common
  Straggling, weak, hairless green stems, angular or narrowly winged (alata) with pointed, sometimes slightly toothed leaves, 30x3mm. Flowers 1cm across, on short stalks scattered towards the ends of the stems, two upper petals nearly equal in length to lower petals.

Grammatotheca bergiana* Blue with white centre Mar-Apr
  Moist stream banks Uncommon
  Usually missed because of size and flowering time. Straggling, hairless stems to 10cm, leaves 30x1mm, slightly toothed. Flowers, 3mm across, appearing stalked but actually long calyx tube to 8mm, with petals as two narrow upper lobes and three rounded lower lobes. Native of South Africa.

Lobelia rhombifolia Blue Sep-Oct
  Woodlands Common
  Hairless stems in erect tuft to 20cm, the lower leaves the larger, 1cmx4mm, toothed or even lobed. Flowers, 1cm across, two to three per stem, borne singly on stalks to 4cm at the tops of the stems, the three lower petals similar in size. Flower throat white and yellow.

Herblike Plants & Annuals

Lobelia tenuior	Blue	Sep-Oct
	Slopes and woodland	Uncommon

Erect, hairless stems only to 10cm with stalked, deeply divided leaves, 20x5mm. Flowers 1.5cm across on stalks to 4cm, borne singly with the middle lower petal rounded and larger than the two lower side petals.

Lobelia rhytidosperma	Blue	Oct-Nov
	Slopes	Uncommon

Similar to Lobelia rhombifolia but differing in habitat and having the middle lower petal larger than the lower side petals.

Isotoma hypocrateriformis	White or purple-tinged	Oct-Dec
Woodbridge poison	Woodlands and slopes	Very common

Erect, hairless, often swollen, to 4mm, succulent stems to 30cm, sparsely leafy, leaves 1cmx1mm often withered when in flower. Flowers on short stalks on upper stem, to 2cm across with petals widest beyond halfway and coming to a pointed tip; petals displayed in flat arrangement. The stem base begins shrivelling up before the plant has completed setting seed, there being sufficient reserves in the stem to serve this purpose.

Monopsis debilis*	Deep blue to purple	Oct-Dec
	Slopes on winter-wet disturbed areas	Uncommon

Small, largely hairless, erect stems to 10cm with toothed leaves 15x1mm. Tiny flowers, 3mm across, borne singly on slender stalks to 2cm, petals as five lobes, fan-shaped. Native of South Africa.

Lobelia heterophylla	Blue	Oct-Jan
	Woodlands and slopes	Uncommon

Similar to Lobelia gibbosa (below) but with the three lower petals broadly spoon-shaped, the middle one especially broad to 1cm across.

Lobelia gibbosa	Blue often white centre line	Nov-Mar
	Woodlands and slopes	Common

Erect stem to 30cm with leaves 20x1mm often withered when still in flower; flowers, 1cm across, four to 10 on short stalks to side of upper stem. Somewhat elongated, larger, middle lower petal with sometimes white stripe down centre; side, lower petals curved away from middle petal.

■ **3B-4 Yellow flowers**

Goodenia claytoniacea	Yellow	Oct-Nov
	Woodlands and slopes on winter-damp areas	Uncommon

Tiny, weakly-stemmed, hairless plant to 5cm with basal leaves 20x2mm. Flowers difficult to spot, 2mm across, single, each on a threadlike, 1cm stalk.

Velleia trinervis	Yellow to orange and brown	Oct-Dec
	Valley floors: damp areas	Rare

Rosette of hairless, shiny-green leaves, spoon-shaped, 12x2cm, each with three indistinct nerves (trinervis) when viewed from underside. Flowers 6mm across on stalks to 20cm.

■ 3B-5 Flower with two large 'wing' petals

POLYGALACEAE - Milkworts (For fuller description see Chapter 9, Page 225)

One species with blue flowers is a climber: Comesperma ciliatum (see Chapter 4, Climbers, Scramblers and Perchers).

Comesperma calymega	Blue	Oct-Dec
Blue-spike milkwort	Open woodlands	Common

Hairless, erect, non-twining stem to 25cm with leaves varying from lance-shaped to circular, 15x5mm. Flowers on short, slender stalks, 5mm across, crowded on spikes towards top of stems.

Comesperma virgatum	Pink	Dec-Apr
	Open woodlands and slopes	Very common

Hairless, erect stem to 70cm with stalkless, somewhat keeled leaves, 10x2mm, pressed to the stem. Flowers on short, slender stalks, 5mm across, crowded on spikes towards top of stem
Page 203

■ 3B-6 Flowers with one prominent large lower petal

LENTIBULARIACEAE - Bladderworts (For fuller description see Chapter 9, Page 223)

Utricularia multifida	Pink	Sep-Oct
Pink petticoats	Open winter-swampy areas	Uncommon

Usually in colonies of pink flowers 1cm across borne singly on slender flower stalks to 8cm, the prominent part being the flared, two or three lobed, lower lip (the petticoat). Each plant with a rosette of leaves 6x2mm, with 1mm-long bladders on stalks at or just below the ground surface. Page 207

FUMARIACEAE - Fumitory

Fumaria capreolata*	White	Jul-Oct
Whiteflower fumitory	Disturbed places	Uncommon

Scrambling, weedy, hairless, weak green stems covering a square metre or more of ground, with much-divided leaves to 6cm, each segment three-lobed, rounded, 1cm long. Flowers on short stalks and clustered on flower stem, each about 1cm long, 2mm across, with dark tips to the outer petals. Native of Europe.

Fumaria muralis*	Pink, purple, red	Jul-Sep
Wall fumitory	Disturbed places	Uncommon

Scrambling weedy, much divided leaves, each segment three-lobed, each 1cm long. Flowers on short stalks in racemes up to 20 flowers, each flower about 1cm long, with blackish-red tips to the outer petals. Native of western Europe.

3C Parts joined to form TUBE with petals as unequal lobes, sometimes not readily distinguishable in number

SCROPHULARIACEAE: *Bellardia Dischisma Gratiola Misopates Parentucellia*
LAMIACEAE: *Stachys*
OROBANCHACEAE: *Orobanche*

SCROPHULARIACEAE - Snapdragons

Misopates orontium*   Pink   Sep-Nov
Lesser snapdragon   Slopes, damper areas   Common
    Erect, smooth stems to 30cm with opposite, stalkless, pointed leaves, 3cmx5mm. Flowers borne singly, scattered, 5mm across and 1cm long. Native of Western Asia.

Parentucellia latifolia*   Pink   Sep-Nov
Common bartsia   Slopes   Common
    Erect, hairy stems to 15cm with opposite, stalkless, rounded, toothed leaves, 10x8mm. Flowers stalkless in the leaf axils, 5mm across and 1cm long. Native of Europe.

Bartsia trixago*   White   Oct-Nov
Bellardia   Slopes and rock outcrops   Common
    Erect, glandular-hairy stems to 30cm with opposite, stalkless, sparsely-toothed leaves, 30x8mm. Flowers on short stalks in the leaf axils, 8mm across and 2cm long. Native of the Mediterranean region.

Dischisma arenarium   White   Oct-Nov
                                       Open damp areas   Uncommon
    Straggling, weak, hairless except when young, stems to 10cm with stalkless leaves, 10x2mm. Flowers 2mm across, clustered in spherical to cylindrical head, 1.5cm long.

Parentucellia viscosa*   Yellow   Nov-Dec
Sticky bartsia   Slopes   Common
    Erect, sticky-hairy stems to 30cm with opposite, stalkless, toothed leaves, 30x7mm. Flowers stalkless in the leaf axils, 7mm across and 1.5cm long. Native of Western Europe.

Gratiola pubescens   Purple   Dec-Jan
                                       Slopes, damper areas   Uncommon
    Nearly upright stem to 10cm with sticky, glandular hairs. Leaves stalkless to stem-clasping, 10x3mm. Flowers usually stalkless, 2mm across, 1cm long.

LAMIACEAE - Mint bushes

Stachys arvensis*   Pink   Aug-Dec
Stagger weed   Slopes   Common
    Weakly upright, hairy stems to 10cm with stalkless, heart-shaped, bluntly-toothed, opposite leaves, 10x6mm. Flowers, two to six, stalkless in leaf axils on upper stem, 2mm across, 3mm long. Native of Europe.

OROBANCHACEAE - Broomrapes

Orobanche minor*   Purply-white then brown   Nov-Dec
Lesser broomrape   Woodlands   Common
    Erect, stout, shortly hairy, yellowish-brown stem to 30cm lacking green colour, swollen at the base. Scale leaves brown, 1.5cmx5mm. Tubular flowers, 8mm across and 2cm long, dominating the stem, more crowded to the top, lobed lips with crinkly edges. Parasitic on roots of plants. Native of Europe.

GROUP 4

Flowers showy: REGULAR, parts in four, five or more; separate or joined

4A Appearing regular. Actually a composite head of many flowers, the outer, often white and strap-shaped, irregular; the inner, yellow, tubular and regular
ASTERACEAE - Daisies [Group 2] page 134 (For fuller description see Chapter 9, page 222)

4B Petals five (one species, eight) separate Sometimes inconspicuous but grouped in umbrella-shaped clusters

APIACEAE:	*sometimes inconspicuous [Grp 5] or in heads [Grp 2]*
CARYOPHYLLACEAE:	*Cerastium Petrorhagia Silene Spergularia Stellaria*
DROSERACEAE:	*Drosera*
EUPHORBIACEAE:	*Monotaxis*
GENTIANACEAE:	*Centaurium*
LINACEAE:	*Linum*
LOGANIACEAE:	*Logania*
MENYANTHACEAE:	*Villarsia*
OXALIDACEAE:	*Oxalis*
PRIMULACEAE:	*Anagallis Samolus*
RANUNCULACEAE:	*Ranunculus*
SCROPHULARIACEAE	*Verbascum*

Groupings for identification are:
- 4B-1 Plants covered with hairs tipped with sticky glands page 186
  - 4B-1a Leaves, basal rosette exceeding 5cm across page 186
  - 4B-1b Leaves, basal rosette not exceeding 2cm across page 187
  - 4B-1c Leaves on upright stems, sometimes also scrambling and climbing page 187

- 4B-2 Plants not covered with sticky glandular hairs page 188
  - 4B-2a Leaves on stems : opposite page 188
  - 4B-2b Leaves on stems : alternate page 189
  - 4B-2c Leaves radical (from stalks at ground-level) page 189

- **4B-1 Plants covered with hairs tipped with sticky glands**

DROSERACEAE - Sundews (For fuller description see Chapter 9, Page 222)

- 4B-1a Leaves, basal rosette exceeding 5cm across

Drosera bulbosa	White	May-June
	Lower slopes and	Common
	rock outcrops	

Similar to D. erythrorhiza but with flowers borne singly on separate weak and bending stalks, several of which come up from the centre of the rosette, and to about 5cm. The rosette is also slightly smaller and the flowers sometimes sweetly-scented.   Page 206

Drosera erythrorhiza	White	May-June
Red ink sundew	Woodlands and slopes	Very common

Leaves broadly spoon-shaped, 5x2.5cm, overlap in a flat rosette and vary in colour from yellow-green to reddish. Several rosettes usually together in a colony. The flowers, 10mm across, are clustered at the top of a single, stout, leafless stalk to 10cm from the centre of the rosette. Below ground, an orange-red (erythro-), near spherical tuber or 'root' (-rhiza).

Page 107, 205

Drosera leucoblasta   Orange   Sep-Oct
                                   Slopes and rock outcrops   Common

With four to five flowers, 7mm across, which open successively, clustered at the end of a thread-like 2cm stalk. A hand-lens is required to view the distinguishing detail of three to five dark-coloured, unbranched styles.

Drosera platystigma   Orange   Oct-Nov
                                   Open woodlands and slopes   Very common

Similar to D. leucoblasta but, with the hand-lens, the three to five dark-coloured styles can each be seen to end in a flattened, oval stigma (platystigma).

- **4B-1b Leaves, basal rosette not exceeding 2cm across**

    Some are tiny plants, so-called Pygmy Droseras, they usually grow in colonies. The frequently raised rosettes, to 1cm, have circular leaves 2mm to 3mm across and pressed to the ground, attached to the rosette by arching stalks of about 5mm. Habitat and flower details separate the four species.

Drosera pulchella   Pink   Nov-Dec, Apr-May
                                   Swamps and streamsides   Uncommon

Similar to D. leucoblasta but with four to five styles whitish and unbranched. Often beneath shrubs.

Drosera glanduligera   Orange   Sep-Oct
                                   Damp places in woodlands,   Very common
                                   slopes and rock outcrops

With distinctly yellow-green leaves and flower-stalks, the flowers, 5mm across, are grouped along the upper part of the 4cm stalk. With the hand-lens, the three reddish styles will be seen to be divided into two pointed branches.   Page 205

- **4B-1c Leaves on upright stems, sometimes also scrambling and climbing**

Two species in this group, both with white flowers, are climbers often exceeding 1m. They are Drosera macrantha and D. pallida and are described in Chapter 4 Scramblers, Climbers and Perchers, Page 102

Drosera heterophylla   White   Jun-Aug
                                   Swampy and damp places   Uncommon

Stems weak, upright, unbranched to 20cm with scattered, kidney-shaped leaves 4mm across on stalks to 1cm. Flowers 3cm across, at end of stem and with eight or more petals.

Drosera stolonifera   White   Jul-Aug
                                   Woodlands; slope shrublands   Common

Stout, upright, mostly unbranched stems to 10cm, often in a cluster, with whorls of three or four spoon-shaped leaves, 2x1cm. Flowers 1.2cm across, several (10 to 20) clustered at the top of the stem.   Page 207

Drosera neesii   Pink   Aug-Sep
                                   Open, damp woodland   Rare

Similar to D. menziesii but stem rigid, stout to 20cm.

Drosera gigantea	White	Aug-Oct
	Swampy places	Common

Stout, upright, stems 50cm, many branches at right-angles. Leaves 5mm, stalked, 1cm, scattered on branches. Flowers 1cm towards ends of upper branches. Resembles an asparagus spear when emerging in late autumn.

Drosera menziesii	Pink	Sep-Oct
	Slopes and granite outcrops	Very common

Weak, thin, mostly upright, reddish stems to 12cm with scattered leaves grouped in threes, leaf blades 4mm, two on shorter stalks, about 5mm, one on a longer stalk to 3cm. Flowers 1.5cm across at the top of the stem.   Page 206 &208

Drosera microphylla	Dark red and golden green	Sep-Oct
	Woodland and slopes	Common

Weak, upright stems to 10cm, leaves scattered, sometimes in threes like D. menziesii. Flowers 1cm across at the top of the stem with petals slightly shorter than the shiny, golden green sepals which, when the flowers are closed, close over the petals in an electric, light-bulb shape.   Page 206

■ 4B-2 Plants not covered with sticky glandular hairs
● 4B-2a Leaves on stems : opposite

CARYOPHYLLACEAE - Carnation Family

Stellaria media*	White to greeny-white	Jul-Sep
Chickweed	Woodlands in disturbed places	Uncommon

Straggling, mostly smooth stems to 10cm with usually smooth, broad, pointed leaves, 15x8mm. Flowers 3mm across on stalks to 1.5cm borne singly in loose clusters towards stem tip. Petals very deeply notched, each v-shaped, smaller than the green sepals. Native of Europe.

Silene gallica*	White/pink	Jul-Dec
French catchfly	Slopes in disturbed places	Common

Erect, slightly sticky-hairy stems to 30cm, stem leaves 15x5mm and pointed, lower leaves more spoon-shaped. Flowers 5mm across, stalkless or shortly stalked, borne singly in leaf axils on upper stem. Petals each deeply notched with a dark red mark at their narrow bases. Native of Europe. The related, but distinctive, Bladder Campion, Silene vulgaris, is less common. Of similar size, it is hairless and beneath the petals, the calyx is marked swollen, bladder-like.

Cerastium glomeratum*	White	Aug-Nov
Mouse-ear chickweed	Woodlands in disturbed places	Uncommon

Straggling, slightly sticky-hairy stems to 15cm with broad leaves, somewhat rounded, 15x8mm. Flowers, 8mm across, clustered towards stem tip and borne singly on stalks to 5mm; petals deeply notched. Native of Europe.

Spergularia rubra*	Pink	Sep-Oct
Common spurry	Woodlands in disturbed places	Uncommon

Straggling, slightly roughly-hairy stems to 15cm with pointed leaves, 20x1mm. Flowers, 5mm across, borne singly in the leaf axils on stalks to 1cm. Native of Europe.

Petrorhagia velutina*	Pink	Sep-Nov
Velvet pink	Woodlands in disturbed places	Common

Erect stems to 15cm, leaves pointed, 30x2mm. Flowers clustered in heads, 1cmx8mm, flowers 2mm across. Native of the Mediterranean region.

LOGANIACEAE - Loganias

Logania serpyllifolia	White	Sep-Dec
	Woodlands	Uncommon

Tuft of stiff, four-ribbed stems to 15cm with opposite, oval, spreading, pointed leaves, 10x5mm. Triangular flap (a stipule) between the leaf bases on each side of the stem. Flowers shortly-stalked, star-like, clustered at the end of the stem, 8mm across.

Logania campanulata	White	Oct-Jan
	Slopes	Uncommon

Rounded, smooth stem to 30cm with opposite, erect, pointed leaves, 15x4mm, joined at their bases. Flowers bell-shaped (campanulata), 1.5cm across, clustered at the end of the stem with individual stalks, up to 1cm.

● **4B-2b Leaves on stems : alternate**

LINACEAE - Flaxes

Linum trigynum*	Yellow	Sep-Dec
French flax	Woodlands and slopes	Very common

Erect, hairless, much-branched, slender stems to 15cm with stalkless, pointed, alternate leaves to 15x2mm, the larger, lower leaves shedding. Flowers borne singly at branched ends of the stem, though individually small, 5mm across, noticeable. Native of Europe.

Linum marginale	Pale blue	Oct-Nov
Wild flax	Slopes	Uncommon

Erect, hairless, sparingly-branched stems to 30cm with stalkless, pointed, alternate leaves to 20x2mm. Flowers borne singly at branched ends of the stem, 1.5cm across.

RANUNCULACEAE - Buttercups

Ranunculus colonorum	Yellow	Jul-Sep
Buttercup	Woodlands	Rare

Partly upright, somewhat straggly, softly-hairy stems to 50cm, leaves divided, 5cm across, with segments rounded and on stalks to 8cm. Flowers 2.5cm across borne singly, on stalks to 6cm in leaf axils. Petals rounded, cupped and markedly shiny on upper surface.

● **4B-2c Leaves radical (from stalks at ground-level)**

MENYANTHACEAE - Bogbeans

Villarsia albiflora	White	Oct-Nov
	Muddy, shallow parts of Helena River	Uncommon

Round, smooth, fleshy stems with leaves near-circular, 6cm across, often floating, and attached on round, smooth, fleshy stalks to 15cm. Flower stalks erect to 50cm with many flowers, 7mm across, in loose cluster on upper part of flower stalk.

OXALIDACEAE - Oxalis

Oxalis glabra*	Reddish-purple	May-Aug
	Woodlands	Uncommon

Weakly upright, slender stems to 5cm with a single flower, 1cm across, on each flower stem to 5cm. Native of South Africa.

Oxalis pes-caprae*	Bright lemon yellow	May-Aug
Soursop	Woodlands and slopes	Common

Stemless aboveground, the hairless leaves and flower-stalks, to 20cm, come from ground level. Leaves with three, heart-shaped leaflets, notched at the tip, each 1x1cm on leaf stalks to 10cm. Flowers on individual stalks to 1cm all joining the end of the leafless flower stalk together, each flower 1.5cm across. Native of South Africa.

Oxalis purpurea*	Deep pink	May-Sep
Largeflower wood sorrel	Woodlands	Uncommon

General habit similar to O. pes-caprae but with a single, larger flower, 2.5cm across, on each flower stalk. Native of South Africa.

Oxalis corniculata*	Yellow	Aug-Sep
Creeping oxalis	Woodlands and slopes	Uncommon

Similar to O. pes-caprae except it produces hairy, creeping stems and flower stalks and is smaller, with leaf and flower stalks, for example, to about 10cm. Native of South America.

PRIMULACEAE - Primroses

Anagallis arvensis*	Orange-red or blue	Aug-Dec
Scarlet or blue pimpernel	Woodlands and damp places	Common

Hairless, scrambling, weak stems to 10cm with stalkless, opposite, almost triangular leaves, to 1.5x1cm, meeting at the stem. The flowers, an almost continuous circle of overlapping, near-circular petals, are 7mm across on stalks to 2cm from the leaf axils. Sometimes considered to be two different species, the two colour forms are presently regarded as varieties of the one species. Native of Europe.

Samolus junceus	White	Oct-Nov
	Damp places	Rare

Appearing as a basal rosette of spoon-shaped leaves like Stylidium carnosum, the hairless, reed-like flower stalk grows to 50cm with a few flowers borne singly on the upper part, 8mm across.

SCROPHULARIACEAE - Snapdragons

One member, Mullein, has near-regular flowers with apparently separated petals, the lower three being just slightly the larger.

Verbascum virgatum*	Yellow	Jun-Oct
Twiggy mullein	Wandoo woodlands	Uncommon

Flower stalk to 1.5m, from basal rosette of spoon-shaped leaves, 25x10cm, all white-hairy.

Flowers 2.5cm across, many on flower stalk from one to five at each bract. Native of Europe and western Asia.

4C Petals five, joined to form tubular, bell or cup-shaped base

BORAGINACEAE:	*Echium*
CAMPANULACEAE:	*Wahlenbergia*
GENTIANACEAE:	*Centaurea*
SOLANACEAE:	*Solanum*
STACKHOUSIACEAE:	*Stackhousia Tripterococcus*

BORAGINACEAE - Borage Family

Echium plantagineum* Purple tinged pink Oct-Nov
Paterson's Curse Slopes Uncommon
Erect, slighly-branched stems to 50cm with rough-hairy, lance-shaped leaves, 5x2cm. Flowers trumpet-like to 2.5cm long and 1cm across. Native of the Mediterranean region.

SOLANACEAE - Solanum

Solanum nigrum* White All months
Black berry nightshade Waste places in woodlands Common
  and slopes
Dark-green to purplish green, much-branched stems to 35cm with shortly-hairy, stalked leaves, 5x3cm. Flowers, 1cm across, clustered on stalks between the leaves, often somewhat downward pointing, followed by bunches of black berries, 6mm across. Native of Europe.

CAMPANULACEAE - Bellflowers

Wahlenbergia stricta Pale blue Sep-Oct
  Slopes Uncommon
Upright, many-branched, weak stems to 35cm, smooth on upper parts. Leaves stalkless, rounded, slightly toothed, to 40x5mm. Flowers 5mm across and tube nearly 1cm long, borne singly on flower stalk to 5cm.

Wahlenbergia capensis* Lacquered pale blue Sep-Nov
Cape bluebell Woodland, disturbed places Uncommon
Erect, roughly-hairy stems to 35cm, leaves 40x5mm, stalkless, rough-hairy with wavy margins. Flowers head open with bell-shape scarcely evident, 1.5cm across, darker in centre, borne singly. Native of Cape Province, South Africa.

GENTIANACEAE - Gentians

Centaurium erythraea Pink Sep-Nov
Common Centaury Damp places Common
Erect annual, 15cm, smooth. Leaves 20x7mm, rounded. Flowers 3x7mm.

STACKHOUSIACEAE - Candles

Stackhousia monogyna Creamy-white Aug-Dec
White candles Woodlands and slopes Very common
Upright, unbranched stems to 50cm, with scattered leaves, 25x1.5mm. Flowers 5mm across,

triangular lobes spreading, tubes nearly 1cm clustered around upper part of stem. Sometimes regarded as two species which appear quite distinct in the Hills. A hairless, earlier-flowering form was known as Stackhousia huegelii. About one to two months later, a shortly-hairy form begins flowering and was known as S. pubescens. Both are fragrantly-scented in the late afternoon or if placed in the dark.   Page 203

Tripterococcus brunonis   Golden to greenish yellow   Aug-Dec
Yellow candles   Woodlands and slopes   Very common
   Similar to Stackhousia but with stem branched and petal lobes slender and bent backwards; translucent-winged seeds sometimes obvious; flowers can vary in colour through to almost black.   Page 207

| 4D | Petals four, regular, separate

BRASSICACEAE: *Brassica Raphanus*
HALORAGACEAE: *Glischrocaryon*
RUTACEAE: *Boronia*

BRASSICACEAE - Wild turnip, radish

Brassica tournefortii*   Pale yellow to white   Jul-Oct
Mediterranean turnip   Waste places   Uncommon
   Erect, branching stems to 40cm, stiffly-hairy at base. Basal rossette of leaves, 15x3cm, stalked and divided, stiffly-hairy underneath. Stem leaves smaller. Flowers 1cm across, scattered on stalks. Native of the Mediterranean region.

Raphanus raphanistrum*   Yellow or white   Aug-Nov
Wild radish   Waste places   Common
   Erect, stiffly-hairy, branching stems to 70cm. Lower leaves stiffly-hairy, stalked, lobed with large lobe at the end of the leaf, 20x10cm. Flowers 2cm across, in loose heads, petals usually with a network of dark veins. Beaded seed pods to 5cm. Native of Europe.

HALORAGACEAE - Pop flowers

Glischrocaryon aureum   Lemon yellow   Sep-Oct
Common popflower   Open woodland and slopes   Common
   Erect, smooth, stems 70cm, sparsely-branched, fleshy, green. Stem leaves, 3x1cm, with hooded petals. Few flowers 6mm closely clustered at the ends of branches. In colonies several square metres across.   Page 201

RUTACEAE - Boronias (For fuller description see Chapter 9, Page 226)

All are four petalled and at times can appear herbaceous, particularly the thin-stemmed Boronia tenuis. All are described in Chapter 3, Medium to Small Shrubs.   page 64

GROUP 5
Flowers inconspicuous, clustered in greenish, blackish, straw-coloured or yellow heads or borne singly OR NONE (FERNS). Includes tiny plants with minute flowers

---

5A Flowers in composite heads. DAISIES

ASTERACEAE: *Angianthus Chthonocephalus Dittrichia Gnaphalium Millotia Podotheca Siloxerus Vellereophyton Waitzia*

Described in Group 2A page 172

5B Flowers clustered in domed, spherical, cylindrical or umbrella-shaped heads. NOT DAISIES

AMARANTHACEAE:	*Alternanthera*
APIACEAE:	*Xanthosia*
EUPHORBIACEAE:	*Poranthera*
PLANTAGINACEAE:	*Plantago*
ROSACEAE:	*Acaena*
RUBIACEAE:	*Opercularia*
STYLIDIACEAE:	*Levenhookia*

AMARANTHACEAE - Mulla Mulla Family

Alternanthera nodiflora	Greenish to straw-coloured	Year-round
Common joyweed	Streamsides and valley floors	Uncommon

    Weakly upright, hairless, green stems to 20cm but with nodes hairy. Leaves 20x5mm, smooth, pointed. Flowers in spherical heads at the leaf axils, to 2cm across.

APIACEAE - Parsley Family (For fuller description see Chapter 9, Page 222)

Xanthosia huegelii	Green	Aug-Nov
	Widespread	Common

    Perennial herb to 30cm. Leaves 20x7mm, hairy, divided into three. Umbels compound, each ending in one to four flowers. Bracts to 8mm long.

EUPHORBIACEAE - Spurges (For fuller description see Chapter 9, Page 223)

Poranthera microphylla	White	Sep-Oct
	Open woodlands and slopes	Uncommon

    Straggling to erect, smooth stems to 15cm. Leaves 15x2mm. Flowers 1.5mm in leafy heads, 1cm across, the sepals, petalloid.

PLANTAGINACEAE - Plantain

    The flowers are inconspicuous although their cylindrical heads topping the ribbed, leafless flowering stalk, at least attract attention. The grasslike leaves, much longer than broad, with their lengthwise, ribs or veins, complete identification. For the full description see Chapter 5, Plants with Grasslike Leaves,   page 121

ROSACEAE - Roses

| Acaena echinata | Pinky-green | Oct-Nov |
| Sheep's Burr | Woodlands | Rare |

Weakly erect, mostly smooth stems to 15cm, leaves in basal rosette and on stems, 7x2cm, divided into about 10 paired leaflets with crinkly margins. Flowers clustered into spherical or cylindrical head 2cm across at the top of a leafless stem.

RUBIACEAE - Gardenias, Coprosmas

The family is characterised by opposite leaves with a flap of tissue across the stem where the leaves join (an inter-petiolar stipule).

Opercularia vaginata — Green — Aug-Oct
Woodlands — Common

Much branched, smooth, shiny-green, slightly ribbed, erect stems to 30cm, the leaves long and narrow, 20x1mm. Flowers clustered on shortly-stalked, spherical heads, not noticeably spiky, 1cm across.

Opercularia echinocephala — Purple and green — Aug-Nov
Woodlands — Very common

Bristly-hairy, much-branched stems often forming a domed-shaped plant to 15cm, the leaves 15x5mm, triangular with edges curled under, roughly hairy. Flowers clustered on shortly-stalked, spiky, spherical heads (echinocephala) 1cm across in the leaf axils towards the ends of the branches. Page 205

Opercularia hispidula — Purplish-green — Sep-Nov
Hispid stinkweed — Woodlands — Uncommon

Rank, weedy, upright, slightly roughly-hairy, branched stems to 1m. Leaves with stalk, about 5mm, 3x1cm, pointed. Flowers clustered on shortly-stalked, spherical heads, not noticeably spiky, 1cm across.

Galium divaricatum — White — Oct-Nov
Slope seepage areas — Uncommon

Straggling, four-ribbed, weak, green stems to 15cm with leaves apparently in whorls of six to eight, 4x0.5mm, some, the actual leaves, others, a leafy-expression of the inter-petiolar stipules. Few-flowers clustered on short stalks at leaf axils, the clusters 5mm across.

STYLIDIACEAE - Styleworts

Both Styleworts, Levenhookias, are small, but the Common Stylewort has sufficiently large flowers for the keenly-observant to notice. Levenhookia pusilla, the smallest member of the genus, has small flowers clustered in a dark-red, leafy domed head. Both are described in Group 1, page 168.

5C Flowers borne singly or, if clustered, in loose heads

APIACEAE:	*Daucus Homalosciadium Hydrocotyle Trachymene*
CARYOPHYLLACEAE:	*Stellaria*
CRASSULACEAE:	*Crassula*
EUPHORBIACEAE:	*Monotaxis*

GENTIANACEAE:	*Cicendia*
HALORAGACEAE:	*Haloragis Gonocarpus Myriophyllum*
LAMIACEAE:	*Stachys*
LOBELIACEAE:	*Grammatotheca Monopsis*
POLYGONACEAE:	*Rumex*
PORTULACACEAE:	*Calandrinia*
SCROPHULARIACEAE:	*Dischisma Gratiola*
URTICACEAE:	*Parietaria*

APIACEAE - Carrot Family (For fuller description see Chapter 9, Page 222)

Several members of this Family were described in Sub-group 2B. But there are many which are both insignificant in flower and small. These are dealt with here.

Daucus glochidiatus	Pinkish or white	Aug-Oct
Native carrot	Woodlands and slopes	Uncommon

Erect, stem to 10cm with short coarse hairs. Parsley-like leaves to 5cm. Flowers 2mm, few in cluster at end of flower-stalk. Fruit elongated in outline, to 3mm, lightly prickly.

Hydrocotyle callicarpa	Green	Aug-Oct
Small pennywort	Streamsides and valley floors, muddy, moist places	Common

Straggling, hairless, weak stems to 3cm. Leaves on stalks to 1cm, ivy-shaped, 5x5mm. Fruit, ear-shaped with a very prominent rib. Other Hydrocotyle spp. are to be found in the same habitat.

Trachymene pilosa	White	Aug-Oct
Native parsnip	Woodlands	Very common

Erect, slightly hairy stems to 10cm with divided leaves, each to 2cm. Flowers few in cluster at end of flower stalk. Notable because of two seeds produced for each flower, the outward-pointing one in the head of seeds is bristly, the inner-pointing one, smooth.

Homalosciadium homalocarpum	Green	Oct-Nov
	Woodlands and slopes	Very common

Erect, smooth, branched stems to 4cm. Leaves three-lobed, about 5mm. Flowers few in cluster at end of flower-stalk, 5mm. Fruit 1mm across, rounded, symmetrical. A long name for one of the smallest species!

CARYOPHYLLACEAE - Carnation Family

Stellaria media*	White to greeny white	Jul-Sep
Chickweed	Woodlands in disturbed places	Uncommon

See this Chapter, page 188

CRASSULACEAE - Stonecrops

Crassula colorata	Fawn to pink	Sep-Oct
Dense stonecrop	Rock outcrops	Very common

Erect stems to 5cm scarcely visible because of crowded, succulent leaves, 3x2mm, and flowers clustered in the leaf joints.

EUPHORBIACEAE - Spurges (For fuller description see Chapter 9, Page 223)

Monotaxis grandiflora	White	Sep-Nov
Diamond of the desert	Woodlands	Uncommon

(See Chapter 3, Medium to Small Shrubs, page 75).

GENTIANACEAE - Gentian Family

Cicendia filiformis*	Yellow	Nov-Dec
Slender cicendia	Open woodlands and slopes	Common

Erect, smooth, wiry stems to 10cm, sparingly-branched. Leaves few, soon withering, 3x1mm. Flowers 2mm across, four petalled, borne singly on long slender flower-stalk to 3cm. Native of the Mediterranean region.

HALORAGACEAE - Popflowers

Gonocarpus nodulosus	Deep red to brown	Aug-Oct
	Damp places	Uncommon

Partly upright, red or green, somewhat fleshy stems to 8cm. Leaves opposite, stalkless, 3x1.5mm. Flowers on short spikes in leaf axils, each about 1mm across.

Haloragis brownii	Yellow-green to reddish	Oct-Dec
	Streamsides; broad drainage lines	Rare

Straggling, somewhat fleshy, stout stems to 30cm with toothed leaves 3x2cm. Flowers clustered on short stalks at leaf axils; flower parts in twos, 2mm across.

Myriophyllum crispatum	Deep red	Oct-Feb
	Pools in Helena River	Rare

Erect stems in water with whorls of feathery leaves below the surface grading to simple cylindrical leaves on the aerial parts of the stem. Flowers stalkless in the leaf axils.

LAMIACEAE - Mint Family

Stachys arvensis*	Pink	Aug-Dec
Stagger weed	Slopes	Common

See this chapter, page 185

LOBELIACEAE - Lobelias

Grammatotheca bergiana*	Blue with white centre	Mar-Apr
	Moist stream banks	Uncommon

See this chapter, page 182

Monopsis debilis*	Deep blue to purple	Oct-Dec
	Slopes on winter wet disturbed areas	Uncommon

See this chapter, page 183

LOGANIACEAE - Loganias

Phylliangium paradoxum — White — Oct-Nov
Wiry mitrewort — Open woodland — Common
  Erect, wiry stems to 5cm with basal leaves, 2x0.5mm. Two to three flowers on thin stalks, each flower about 2mm across. Fruit distinctive: flattened, broader at tip, narrowing towards base, with a central point - like a mitre.

POLYGONACEAE - Dock (For fuller description see Chapter 9)

Acetosella vulgaris* — Reddish — Aug-Dec
Sorrel — Slopes and rock outcrops — Common
  In patches some square metres across, a suckering plant with erect, hairless stems to 10cm and blue-green, arrow-head shaped leaves, 5x1cm. Flowers crowded along upper parts of stems, individually about 2mm across. Leaves sharply sour to taste - oxalic acid. Native of Europe and south-western Asia.

Rumex crispus* — Reddish-green — Sep
Curled dock — Disturbed damper areas — Uncommon
  Erect, hairless stems to 70cm, basal leaves stalked to 5cm, shiny-green on upper surface of blade, 10x4cm, wavy surface. Flowers many, crowded on upper part of stem. Leaves used to relieve stings. Native of Europe and south-western Asia.

Polygonum aviculare* — White or pink-white — Nov-Mar
Knotweed — Disturbed places — Uncommon
  Straggling stems with blue-green leaves, 25x8mm, spreading to either side of stem. Flowers few, stalkless, in the leaf axils. Native of Europe.

PORTULACACEAE - Portulacas

Calandrinia granulifera — White — Aug-Oct
— Rock outcrops — Uncommon
  Weakly upright, fleshy stems to 3cm. Basal leaves 4x2mm. Flowers 1mm across, in small groups.

SCROPHULARIACEAE - Snapdragon Family

Dischisma arenarium* — White — Oct-Nov
  See this chapter, page 185 — Open damp places — Uncommon

Gratiola pubescens* — Purple — Dec-Jan
  See this chapter, page 185 — Slopes, damper areas — Uncommon

URTICACEAE - Nettle Family

Parietaria debilis — Greeny-white — Aug-Oct
Pellitory — Rock outcrops — Uncommon
  Weakly upright, somewhat hairy stem to 20cm. Leaves with slender stalks to 2cm and rounded, thin blades, 3x2cm. Flowers, usually three in leaf axils, each 2mm across.

5D Flowers NONE. FERNS
The ferns and closely related plants (fern-allies) are decribed in order of size from the largest, the introduced Tree fern, Sphaeropteris, up to several metres tall, to Selaginella a few centimetres tall, and the Adder's Tongue and the annual Club moss.

Cyathea cooperi*
Rough tree fern   Streamsides   Uncommon
Single trunk-forming ferns to 3m or more with fronds to 3m. Originating from New South Wales and Queensland.

Pteridium esculentum
Bracken   Woodlands   Common
Hardy plants with fronds to 2m from underground stems, usually growing in extensive patches.

Adiantum aethiopicum
Common maidenhair   Woodlands, in shaded   Uncommon
                           places and streamsides
Fronds to 30cm including wiry, shiny, dark stalks and delicate, translucent-green, rounded segments 10x7mm. The spore-producing parts evident as pale, more white-green indentations to the frond segments.

Cheilanthes austrotenuifolia
Rock fern   Rock outcrops   Very common
The commonest of three species of Cheilanthes. Fronds to 25cm from underground stems with papery, brown, triangular scales on the dark, shiny frond-stalk, sparse, small. Frond broadly triangular in outline, about as long as broad at the base. The old fronds are shed each year.
                                                                   Page 206

Lindsaea linearis
Screw fern   Woodland and streamsides   Common
Often in patches covering a square metre or more, the unbranched, erect fronds, to 12cm, come up from underground stems. The shorter, vegetative fronds have a black stalk and rounded, often bent-over segments scattered along the frond. The spore-bearing fronds are taller, with the appearance of long, brown wood screws, giving the fern its name.   Page 205

Pleurosorus rutifolius
                           Rock outcrops   Common
A tuft of fronds from a short underground stem, the fronds to 8cm with rounded segments and densely hairy. To be found in the deeper shade of rock ledges and clefts.   Page 204

Ophioglossum lusitanicum
Adder's tongue   Mossy carpets over rocks   Uncommon
A fern-ally. Tiny plants, often scattered in a group, to 5cm with a single, lance-shaped frond 20x5mm with a spore-producing spike extending above, 10x2mm.   Page 205

Herblike Plants & Annuals   199

Selaginella gracillima
Annual club moss   Overhanging stream banks   Rare
   A fern-ally. Weakly erect, sparingly-branched stems to 3cm with hairless, overlapping, scale-like, leaves, 2x0.5mm.

Cheilanthes sieberi
Mulga fern   Rock outcrops   Common
   Fronds to 15cm from underground stems, with thin, dark, wiry stalks without papery scales. The frond outline near-parallel sided.

Cheilanthes distans
Bristly cloak fern   Rock outcrops   Common
   Fronds to 12cm from underground stems, densely covered with papery, pale-brown, triangular scales on the young frond stalks, the scales persisting on the under surface of the fronds. The frond outline is near parallel-sided. Some of the fronds behave as resurrection plants (see Borya sphaerocephala), reviving after rain.   Page 206

Helena Valley

Lesmurdie Falls
National Park

Pithocarpa corymbulosa

Stylidium schoenoides
Cowkicks

Rhodanthe corymbosa

Stylidium junceum
Reed triggerplant

Stylidium calcaratum
Book triggerplant

Herblike Plants & Annuals 201

Stylidium bulbiferum
Circus triggerplant

Glischrocaryon aureum
Common popflower

Craspedia variabilis

Dampiera alata
Winged-stem dampiera

Goodenia caerulea

Goodenia caerulea

Dampiera alata
Winged-stem dampiera

Stylidium amoenum
Lovely triggerplant

Helichrysum macranthum

Herblike Plants & Annuals   203

Dampiera linearis
Common dampiera

Stackhousia monogyna
White candles

Stylidium breviscapum
Boomerang triggerplant

Comesperma virgatum

Asteridea pulverulenta

Pentapeltis peltigera

Ursinia anthemoides

Pleurosorus rutifolius

Podolepis lessonii

Stylidium petiolare
Horn triggerplant

Herblike Plants & Annuals 205

Lindsaea linearis
Screw fern

Drosera glanduligera

Drosera erythrorhiza — Red ink sundew

Opercularia echinocephala

Ophioglossum lusitanicum
Adder's tongue

Drosera bulbosa

Cheilanthes distans
Bristly cloak fern

Drosera microphylla

Drosera menziesii

Cheilanthes austrotenuifolia
Rock fern

Herblike Plants & Annuals 207

Utricularia multifida
Pink petticoats

Stylidium canaliculatum
Delicate triggerplant

Actinotus leucocephalus — Flannel flower

Tripterococcus brunonis
Yellow candles

Drosera stolonifera

Drosera menziesii

Eryngium rostratum

Levenhookia pusilla
Midget stylewort

Ptilotus manglesii
Rose-tipped mulla mulla

Ptilotis esquamatus

CHAPTER 8

Flowering Calendar

This flowering calendar lists by month those species in flower and are further separated in the flower colour - white, yellow, red, blue and other. The calendar has been compiled from records over several years. However, the user is urged not to take the information too literally. The month of flowering corresponds with the predominant flowering time of the species but occasional flowers can be found on many species outside that time. Colour can also be interpreted varingly.

Most flowers have parts of many different colours but they are listed under the predominant colour. In order to restrict the range of colours given, the colour categorised should be interpreted as:

>   White: White, off-white, cream
>   Yellow: Yellow, off-yellow, orange
>   Red: Red, pink, lilac
>   Blue: Blue, Purple
>   Other: Mixed colours, bronze, brown, greeny-brown, green, grey-white

JANUARY

White
Agonis linearifolia
Cassytha glabella
Cassytha racemosa
Convolvulus arvensis
Gomphocarpus fruticous
Hakea ruscifolia
Hemiandra pungens
Kingia australis
Leucopogon cymbiformis
Leucopogon tenuis
Logania campanulata
Pentapeltis peltigera
Platysace compressa
Polygonum aviculare
Santalum acuminatum
Schoenolaena juncea
Solanum nigrum
Trichocline spathulata
Trifolium repens

Yellow
Acacia barbinervis
Cassytha flava
Cotula coronopifolia
Foeniculum vulgare
Hibbertia pachyrrhiza
Jacksonia sternbergiana
Lotus angustissimus
Persoonia angustiflora
Persoonia elliptica
Persoonia longifolia
Platsace juncea

Red
Adenanthos barbiger
Baeckea camphorosmae
Baekea species
Comesperma virgatum
Convolvulus erubescens
Grevillea bipinnatifida
Grevillea wilsonii
Myriophyllum crispatum
Pilostyles hamiltonii
Ptilotus manglesii
Stachystemon vermicularis
Stylidium repens
Verticordia densiflora

Blue
Beaufortia purpurea
Dampiera incana
Dichopogon capillipes
Gratiola pubescens
Lobelia alata
Lobelia gibbosa
Lobelia heterophylla
Pronaya fraseri
Scaevola glandulifera
Scaevola platyphylla
Sollya heterophylla
Thysanotus anceps
Thysanotus sparteus

Other
Alternathera nodiflora
Daviesia longifolia
Daviesia preissii
Gonocarpus cordiger
Mentha spicata
Oxylobium lineare
Spiculaea ciliata

FEBRUARY

White
Agonis linearifolia
Billardiera bicolor
Convolvulus arvensis
Cortaderia selloana
Eucalyptus calophylla
Eucalyptus patens
Eucalyptus wandoo
Hakea ruscifolia
Kingia australis
Leucopogon cymbiformis
Leucopogon tenuis
Pentapeltis peltigera
Pithocarpa corymbulosa
Platysace compressa
Polygonum aviculare
Santalum acuminatum
Schoenolaena juncea
Solanum nigrum
Xanthosia atkinsoniana

Yellow
Acacia barbinervis
Cotula coronopifolia
Jacksonia sternbergiana

Red
Adenanthos barbiger
Amyema preissii
Baeckea camphorosmae
Baekea species
Comesperma virgatum
Convolvulus erubescens
Grevillea bipinnatifida
Pilostyles hamiltonii
Myriopnyllum crispatum
Stachystemon vermicularis
Stylidium repens

Blue
Dichopogon capillipes
Lobelia alata
Lobelia gibbosa
Pronaya fraseri
Scaevola glandulifera
Sollya heterophylla

Other
Alternanthera modiflora
Dodonaea ericoides
Mentha spicata
Spiculea ciliata

Flowering Calendar 211

MARCH

White
Agonis linearifolia
Astroloma pallidum
Billardiera bicolor
Convolvulus arvensis
Cortaderia sellana
Eriochilus dilatatus
Eucalyptus calophylla
Eucalyptus patens
Eucalyptus wandoo
Hakea ruscifolia
Kingia australis
Leucopogon propinquus
Pentapeltis peltigera
Pithocarpa corymbulosa
Platysace compressa
Polygonum aviculare
Schoenolaena juncea
Solanum nigrum
Xanthosia atkinsoniana

Yellow
Cotula coronopifolia
Dittrichia graveolens
Dryandra sessilis
Jacksonia sternbergiana
Senecio species

Red
Adenanthos barbiger
Amyema miquelii
Amyema preissii
Baeckea camphorosmae
Baekea species
Calothamnus sanguineus
Comesperma virgatum
Grevillea bipinnatifida
Pilostyles hamiltonii
Stachystemon vermivularis
Stylidium repens

Blue
Dichopogon capillipes
Grammatotheca bergiana
Lobelia alata
Lobelia gibbosa
Pronaya fraseri
Scaevola glandulifera

Other
Alternanthera nodiflora
Dodonaea ericoides

APRIL

White
Acacia obovata
Acacia stenoptera
Agonis linearifolia
Arundo donax
Astroloma pallidum
Eriochilus dilatatus
Eucalyptus calophylla
Leucopogon propinquus
Olearia paucidentata
Pentapeltis peltigera
Pithocarpa corymbulosa
Platysace compressa
Schoenolaena juncea
Solanum nigrum
Styphelia tenuiflora

Yellow
Cotula coronopifolia
Dittrichia graveolens
Dryandra sessilis
Jacksonia sternbergiana
Senecio species

Red
Adenanthos barbiger
Amyema miquelii
Andersonia lehmanniana
Baeckea camphorosmae
Baeckea species
Boronia crenulata
Calothamnus sanguineus
Comesperma virgatum
Drosera pulchella
Grevillea bipinnatifida
Melinis repens
Pilostyles hamiltonii
Stachystemon vermicularis
Stylidium repens

Blue
Grammatotheca barbiger
Lobelia alata
Marianthus coeruleo-punctatus

Other
Alternanthera nodiflora
Dodonaea ericoides
Leporella fimbriata

MAY

White
Acacia obovata
Acacia stenoptera
Agonis linearifolia
Arundo donax
Astroloma pallidum
Conospermum stoechadis
Drosera bulbosa
Drosera erythrorhiza

Yellow
Acacia horridula
Acacia teretifolia
Cotula coronopifolia
Daviesia angulata
Dioscorea hastifolia
Dittrichia graveolens
Dryandra sessilis
Hibbertia hypericoides

Red
Adenanthos barbiger
Amyema miquelii
Andersonia lehmanniana
Astroloma ciliatum
Astroloma foliosum
Baeckea camphorosmae
Baeckea species
Boronia crenulata

Blue
Billardiera coerulea-punctata
Hovea chorizemifolia
Hybanthus floribundus
Lobelia alata

Other
Alternanthera nodiflora
Leporella fimbriata
Lomandra drummondii
Lomandra hermaphrodita

May (continued)

White
Eriochilus dilatatus
Grevillea pilulifera
Hakea cristata
Laxmannia sessiliflora
Leucopogon nutans
Leucopogon oxycedrus
Leucopogon propinquus
Olearia paucidentata
Solanum nigrum
Styphelia tenuiflora
Thomasia foliosa
Trymalium ledifolium

Yellow
Jacksonia sternbergiana
Lomandra preissii
Oxalis pes-caprae
Senecio species
Templetonia biloba

Red
Calothamnus sanguineus
Drosera pulchella
Grevillea bipinnatifida
Hakea petiolaris
Oxalis glabra
Oxalia purpurea
Rhynchelytrum repens
Stachystemon vermicularis
Stylidium repens
Tetratheca hirsuta

JUNE

White
Acacia obovata
Acacia urophylla
Actinotus glomeratus
Agonis linearifolia
Arundo donax
Astroloma pallidum
Conospermum stoechadis
Conostylis androstemma
Cryptandra arbutiflora
Cryptandra glabriflora
Drosera bulbosa
Drosera erythrorhiza
Drosera heterophylla
Drosera macrantha
Eriochilus dilatatus
Grevillea diversifolia
Grevillea endlicheriana
Grevillea manglesii
Grevillea pilulifea
Grevillea synapheae
Hakea cristata
Hakea erinacea
Hakea incrassata
Hakea lissocarpha
Laxmannia ramosa
Laxmannia sessiliflora
Laxmannia squarrosa
Leucopogon nutans
Leucopogon oxycedrus
Leucopogon pulchellus
Lomandra caespitosa
Lomandra nigricans
Lomandra suaveolens
Olearia paucidentata
Solanum nigrum
Styphelia tenuiflora
Thomasia foliosa
Trymalium ledifolium

Yellow

Acacia horridula

Acacia nervosa
Acacia sessilis
Acacia teretifolia
Cotula coronopifolia
Daviesia angulata
Dittrichia graveolens
Dryandra armata
Dryandra sessilis
Hibbertia commutata
Hibbertia hypericoides
Hibbertia ovata
Hibbertia serrata
Jacksonia sternbergiana
Lomandra preissii
Oxalis pes-caprae
Pimelea suaveolens
Senecio species
Synaphea acutiloba
Synaphea gracillma
Templetonia biloba
Tripterococcus brunonis
Verbascum virgatum

Red
Adenanthos barbiger
Amyema miquelii
Andersonia lehmanniana
Astroloma ciliatum
Astroloma foliosum
Boronia crenulata
Boronia cymosa
Calothamnus sanguineus
Darwinia citriodora
Grevillea bipinnatifida
Hakea myrtoides
Hakea petiolaris
Hemigenia incana
Lasiopetalum glabratum
Melinis repens
Oligochaetochilus sanguineus
Oxalis glabra
Oxalis purpurea
Philotheca spicata
Stylidium repens
Tetratheca hirsuta

Blue
Hemigenia ramosissima
Hovea chorizemifolia
Hybanthus florbundus
Lobelia alata

Other
Alternanthera nodiflora
Daviesia decurrens
Daviesia hakeoides
Dryandra nivea
Leporella fimbriata
Lomandra drummondii
Oligochaetochilus vittatus
Prasophyllum parviflorum

JULY

White
Actinotus glomeratus
Agonis linearifolia
Asterolasia pallida
Astroloma pallidum
Burchardia multiflora
Caladenia denticulata
Conospermum stoechadis
Conostylis androstemma
Cryptandra arbutiflora
Cryptandra glabriflora
Drosera heterophylla
Drosera macrantha
Drosera stolonifera
Fumaria capreolata
Grevillea diversifolia
Grevillea endlicheriana
Grevillea manglesii
Grevillea pilulifera
Grevillea synapheae
Hakea amplexicaulis
Hakea cristata
Hakea erinacea
Hakea incrassata
Hakea lissocarpha
Hakea trifurcata
Hakea varia
Hypocalymma angustifolium
Laxmannia sessiliflora
Laxmannia squarrosa
Leucopogon capitellatus
Leucopogon pulchellus
Leucopogon sprengelioides
Lomandra caespitosa
Lomandra nigricans
Lomandra spartea
Olearia paucidentata
Petrophile biloba
Phyllanthus calycinus
Rinzia crassifolia
Silene gallica
Solanum nigrum
Stellaria media
Thomasia foliosa
Tribonanthes brachypetala
Tribonanthes longipetala
Tribonanthes violacea
Trymalium ledifolium
Wurmbea dioica
Xanthorrhoea preissii

Yellow
Acacia aphylla
Acacia drummondii
Acacia horridula
Acacia nervosa
Acacia pulchella
Acacia sessilis
Acacia teretifolia
Acacia willdenowiana
Arctotheca calendula
Cotula coronopifolia
Craspedia variabilis
Dandelion
Dittrichia graveolens
Diuris corymbosa
Dryandra armata
Dryandra sessilis
Foeniculum vulgare
Hedypnois rhagadioloides
Hibbertia aurea
Hibbertia commutata
Hibbertia hypericoides
Hibbertia ovata
Hibbertia serrata
Hypochaeris glabra
Hypoxis occidentalis
Isopogon sphaerocephalus
Jacksonia sternbergiana
Labichea punctata
Lambertia multiflora
Medicago polymorpha
Nemcia capitata
Oxalis pes-caprae
Paraserianthes lophantha
Pimelea suaveolens
Ranunculus colonorum
Senecio species
Synaphea acutiloba
Synaphea gracillima
Taraxacum officinale
Templetonia biloba
Thelymitra antennifera
Verbascum virgatum

Red
Adenanthos barbiger
Allocasuarina fraseriana
Allocasuarina huegeliana
Amyema miquelii
Andersonia lehmanniana
Astroloma ciliatum
Astroloma foliosum
Boronia crenulata
Boronia cymosa
Caladenia reptans
Calothamnus sanguineus
Chorizema ilicifolium
Darwinia citriodora
Diplolaena drummondii
Eriochilus scaber
Fumaria muralis
Grevillea bipinnatifida
Grevillea wilsonii
Hakea myrtoides
Hakea petiolaris
Hemigenia incana
Hybanthus floribundus
Isopogon asper
Isopogon dubius
Lasiopetalum glabratum
Lavandula stoechas
Misopates orontium
Oligochaetochilus sanguineus
Oxalis glabra
Petrophile biloba
Philotheca spicata
Stylidium repens
Tetratheca hirsuta

Blue
Boronia ramosa
Boronia tenuis
Cyanicula deformis
Dampiera linearis
Dampiera coronata
Hardenbergia comptoniana
Hemigenia ramosissima
Hemigenia sericea
Hovea chorizemifolia
Hovea pungens
Hovea trisperma
Lechenaultia biloba
Lobelia alata

Other
Alternanthera nodiflora
Bossiaea spinescens
Daviesia decurrens
Daviesia hakeoides
Daviesia horrida
Daviesia rhombifolia
Dodonaea ceratocarpa
Dryandra nivea
Lomandra micrantha
Lomandra sericea
Oligochaetochilus vittatus
Prasophyllum parvifolium
Prasophyllum fimbria

AUGUST

White
Actinotus glomeratus
Agonis linearifolia
Asterolasia pallida
Astroloma pallidum
Borya sphaerocephala
Brassica tournefortii
Burchardia multiflora
Burchardia umbellata
Caladenia denticulata
Caladenia hirta
Caladenia longiclavata
Calandrinia granulifera
Cerastium glomeratum
Conostylis aculeata
Cryptandra arbutiflora
Cryptandra glabriflora
Chamaecytisus palmensis
Daucus glochidiatus
Drosera gigantea
Drosera heterophylla
Drosera macrantha
Drosera pallida
Drosera stolonifera
Eucalyptus rudis
Freesia species
Fumaria capreolata
Goodenia fasciculata
Grevillea diversifolia
Grevillea endlicheriana
Grevillea manglesii
Grevillea pilulifera
Grevillea synapheae
Hakea amplexicaulis
Hakea cyclocarpa
Hakea erinacea
Hakea incrassata
Hakea lissocarpha
Hakea trifurcata
Hakea undulata
Hakea varia
Hypocalymma angustifolium
Laxmannia squarrosa
Leptospermum erubescens
Leucopogon capitellatus
Leucopogon pulchellus
Leucopogon sprengelioides
Lomandra integra
Lomandra odora
Parietaria debilis
Petrophile biloba
Phyllanthus calycinus
 Senecio species
August (continued)

Yellow
Acacia anomala
Acacia aphylla
Acacia drummondii
Acacia extensa
Acacia nervosa
Acacia pulchella
Acacia saligna
Acacia willdenowiana
Arctotheca calendula
Bossiaea pulchella
Conostylis caricina
Conostylis setigera
Cotula coronopifolia
Craspedia variabilis
Dandelion
Dittrichia graveolens
Diuris corymbosa
Dryandra armata
Dryandra squarrosa
Dryandra sessilis
Foeniculum vulgare
Gompholobium marginatum
Hedypnois rhagadioloides
Hibbertia amplexicaulis
Hibbertia aurea
Hibbertia commutata
Hibbertia glomerata
Hibbertia hypericoides
Hibbertia ovata
Hibbertia serrata
Hibbertia spicata
Homeria species
Hypochaeris glabra
Hypoxis occidentalis
Isopogon sphaerocephalus
Jacksonia sternbergiana
Labichea punctata
Lambertia multiflora
Medicago polymorpha
Mirbelia spinosa
Nemcia capitata
Nemcia reticulata
Oxalis corniculata
Oxalis pes-caprae
Paraserianthes lophantha
Petrophile seminuda
Pimelea suaveolens
Ranunculus colonorum
Raphanus raphanistrum
Stachys arvensis

Red
Acetosella vulgaris
Adenanthos barbigera
Allocasuarina fraseriana
Allocasuarina huegeliana
Anagallis arvensis
Andersonia lehmanniana
Anigozanthos bicolor
Anigozanthos manglesii
Boronia crenulata
Boronia cymosa
Boronia ovata
Caladenia macrostylis
Caladenia reptans
Calothamnus torulosus
Chorizema dicksonii
Chorizema ilicifolium
Darwinia citriodora
Diplolaena drummondii
Diplopeltis huegelii
Drosera neesii
Eriochilus scaber
Erodium cicutarium
Fumaria muralis
Gompholobium knightianum
Gonocarpus nodulosus
Grevillea bipinnatifida
Grevillea quercifolia
Grevillea wilsonii
Hakea myrtoides
Hakea petiolaris
Hemigenia incana
Homeria species
Hypocalymma robustum
Isopogon asper
Isopogon divergens
Isopogon dubius
Kennedia coccinea
Kennedia prostrata
Kennedia stirlingii
Kunzea recurva
Lasiopetalum bracteatum
Lasiopetalum glabratum
Lavandula stoechas
Oligochaetochilus sanguineus
Oxalis glabra
Oxalis purpurea
Pelargonium littorale
Petrophile biloba
Philotheca spicata
Romulea rosea
Sowerbaea laxiflora

Blue
Anagallis arvensis
Billardiera drummondiana
Boronia ramosa
Boronia tenuis
Chamaescilla corymbosa
Conospermum huegelii
Cyanicula deformis
Cyanicula sericea
Dampiera alata
Dampiera coronata
Dampiera linearis
Dampiera trigona
Erodium botrys
Halgania corymbosa
Hardenbergia comptoniana
Hemigenia ramosissima
Hemigenia sericea
Hovea pungens
Hovea trisperma
Hybanthus floribundus
Lechenaultia biloba
Lobelia alata
Orthrosanthus laxus
Patersonia occidentalis
Sowerbaea laxiflora
Stypandra glauca
Thysanotus patersonii
Thysanotus thyrsoideus

Other
Allocasuarina fraseriana
Allocasuarina humilis
Alternanthera nodiflora
Bossiaea aquifolium
Bossiaea spinescens
Darwinia apiculata
Daviesia hakeoides
Daviesia horrida
Daviesia polyphylla
Daviesia rhombifolia
Dillwynia species
Dodonaea ceratocarpa
Drakaea species
Dryandra nivea
Hydrocotyle callicarpa
Leptomeria cunninghamii
Lomandra micrantha
Lomandra sericea
Nemcia dilata
Oligochaetochilus vittatus
Opercularia echinocephala
Opercularia vaginata
Paracaleana nigrita
Plumatichilos barbartus
Prasophyllum fimbria
Prasophyllum parvifolium
Prasophyllum gracile
Pterostylis pyramidalis
Pterostylis recurva
Pultenea ericifolia
Xanthosia huegelii

White
Plantago lanceolata
Prasophyllum fimbria
Raphanus raphanistrum
Ricinocarpos glaucus
Rinzia crassifolia
Silene gallica
Solanum nigrum
Stackhousia monogyna
Stellaria media
Thomasia foliosa
Trachymene pilosa
Tribonanthes australis
Trymalium floribundum
Trymalium ledifolium
Trifolium repens
Trifolium subterraneum
Wurmea dioica
Xanthorrhoea preissii

Yellow
Sonchus oleraceus
Stirlingia latifolia
Synaphea acutiloba
Synaphea gracillima
Taraxacum officinale
Templetonia drummondii
Thelymitra antennifera
Thelymitra flexuosa
Tolpis barbata
Trifolium campestre
Tripterococcus brunonis
Verbascum virgatum
Verticordia acerosa

Red
Stylidium repens
Tetratheca hirsuta

SEPTEMBER

White
Acacia drummondii
Agonis linearifolia
Andersonia aristata
Asteridea pulverulenta
Astroloma pallidum
Borya sphaerocephala
Brassica tournefortii
Burchardia umbellata
Caladenia hirta
Caladenia longicauda
Caladenia longiclavata
Clematis pubescens
Conostylis setosa
Criptandra arbutiflora
Drosera gigantea
Drosera macrantha
Drosera pallida
Goodenia fassiculata
Grevillea endlicheriana
Grevillea manglesii
Grevillea pilulifera
Grevillea synapheae
Hakea amplexicaulis
Hakea cyclocarpa
Hakea prostrata
Hakea stenocarpa
Hakea trifurcata
Hakea undulata
Hemiandra pungens
Hesperantha falcata
Homeria flaccida
Homeria miniata
September (continued)

Yellow
Acacia dentifera
Acacia drummondii
Acacia extensa
Acacia horridula
Acacia nervosa
Acacia oncinophylla
Acacia pulchella
Acacia saligna
Acacia willdenowiana
Arctotheca calendula
Bossiaea pulchella
Caladenia flava
Chamaexercs serra
Conostylis caricina
Conostylis setigera
Daviesia cordata
Diuris laxiflora
Diuris longifolia
Drosera glanduligera
Drosera leucoblasta
Dryandra armata
Dryandra sessilis
Glischrocaryon aureum
Gompholobium marginatum
Hedypnois rhagadioloides
Hibbertia amplexicaulis
Hibbertia aurea
Hibbertia commutata
Hibbertia hypericoides
Hibbertia pachyrrhiza
Hibbertia spicata
Hibbertia subvaginata

Red
Allocasuarina microstachya
Anagallis arvensis
Andersonia lehmanniana
Anigozanthos bicolor
Anigozanthos manglesii
Beaufortia macrostemon
Boronia ovata
Caladenia macrostylis
Calothamnus quadrifidus
Calothamnus torulosus
Crassula colorata
Darwinia citriodora
Darwinia thymoides
Diplolaena drummondii
Drosera menziesii
Drosera neesii
Eriochilus scaber
Erodium cicutarium
Geranium retrorsum
Gladiolus caryophyllaceus
Kennedia coccinea
Kennedia prostrata
Kennedia stirlingii
Kunzea recurva
Lomandra purpurea
Melaleuca radula
Misopates orontium
Melaleuca parviceps
Parentucellia latifolia
Petrorhagia velutina
Pimelea preissii
Rhodanthe manglesii

Blue
Agrostocrinum scabrum
Billardiera drummondiana
Boronia ramosa
Boronia tenuis
Brachyscome iberidifolia
Comesperma ciliatum
Conospermum huegelii
Dampiera alata
Dampiera hederacea
Dampiera lavandulacea
Dampiera linearis
Dampiera trigona
Eryngium rostratum
Halgania corymbosa
Hemigenia incana
Hemigenia ramosissima
Hemigenia sericea
Hovea trisperma
Lechenaultia biloba
Lobelia rhombifolia
Lobelia tenuior
Lupinus species
Orthrosanthus laxus
Patersonia babianoides
Patersonia occidentalis
Patersonia rudis
Scaevola glandulifera
Scaevola platyphylla
Stypandra glauca
Thelymitra crinita
Thysanotus dichotomus
Thysanotus multiflorus

Other
Banksia littoralis
Bossiaea aquifolium
Bossiaea eriocarpa
Bossiaea ornata
Darwinia apiculata
Daviesia horrida
Daviesia polyphylla
Dillwynia species
Dodonaea ceratocarpa
Drakaea species
Dryandra nivea
Gompholobium polymorphum
Isotropis cuneifolia
Jacksonia restioides
Leptomeria cunninghamii
Leucopogon verticillatus
Lomandra micrantha
Lyperanthus serratus
Mirbelia ramulosa
Muehlenbeckia adpressa
Opercularia echinocephala
Opercularia hispidula
Opercularia vaginata
Plumatichilos barbartus
Prasophyllum giganteum
Pterostylis pyramidalis
Pterostylis recurva
Pultenea ericifolia

White	Yellow	Red	Blue
Hypocalymma angustifolium	Hypochaeris glabra	Romulea rosea	Thysanotus patersonii
Lupinus species	Hypoxis occidentalis	Sowerbaea laxiflora	Thysanotus tenellus
Lagenophora huegelii	Isopogon sphaerocephalus	Stachys arvensis	Thysanotus thyrsoideus
Leptospermum erubescens	Jacksonia alata	Stylidium affine	Wahlenbergia stricta
Leptospermum laevigatum	Jacksonia sternbergiana	Stylidium brunonianum	
Leucopogon capitellatus	Labichea lanceolata	Stylidium repens	
Leucopogon pulchellus	Labichea punctata	Tetratheca hirsuta	
Leucopogon sprengelioides	Lambertia multiflora	Thomasia glutinosa	
Lomandra brittanii	Linum trigynum	Thomasia macrocarpa	
Monotaxis grandiflora	Lupinus species	Utricularia multifida	
Pericalymma ellipticum	Mirbelia spinosa	Verticordia insignis	
Petrophile biloba	Oxalis corniculata	Verticordia pennigera	
Phyllanthus calycinus	Patersonia umbrosa	Verticordia plumosa	
Pimelea brevistyla	Petrophile seminuda		
Pimelea ciliata	Petrophile striata		
Pimelea imbricata	Pimelea argentea		
Pimelea spectabilis	Pimelea suaveolens		
Poranthera microphylla	Podolepis lessonii		
Prasophyllum elatum	Ranunculus colonorum		
Prasophyllum fimbria	Senecio ramosissimus		
Prasophyllum hians	Sonchus oleraceus		
Ricinocarpos glaucus	Sphaerolobium medium		
Rinzia crassifolia	Stirlingia latifolia		
Rulingia cygnorum	Stylidium pubigerum		
Silene gallica	Synaphea acutiloba		
Solanum nigrum	Synaphea gracillima		
Stackhousia monogyna	Synaphea pinnata		
Stylidium calcaratum	Thelymitra antennifera		
Stylidium hispidum	Thelymitra flexuosa		
Stylidium petiolare	Tricoryne elatior		
Stylidium piliferum	Tripterococcus brunonis		
Stylidium schoenoides	Ursinia anthemoides		
Trachymene pilosa	Verticordia acerosa		
Trymalium floribundum	Waitzia citrina		
Trymalium ledifolium			
Verticordia huegelii			
Xanthorrhoea gracilis			
Xanthorrhoea preissii			

OCTOBER

White	Yellow	Red	Blue	Other
Acacia drummondii	Acacia dentifera	Allocasuarina microstachya	Agrostocrinum scabrum	Bossiaea eriocarpa
Agonis linearifolia	Acacia pulchella	Anagallis arvensis	Boronia tenuis	Bossiaea ornata
Andersonia aristata	Acacia willdenowiana	Andersonia lehmanniana	Brachyscome iberidifolia	Disa bracteata
Asteridea pulverulenta	Aotus cordifolia	Anigozanthos bicolor	Comesperma calymega	Dryandra bipinnatifida
Astroloma pallidum	Banksia grandis	Anigozanthos manglesii	Comesperma ciliatum	Dodonaea cerotocarpa
Bartsia trixago	Caladenia flava	Beaufortia macrostemon	Conospermum huegelii	Euchilopsis linearis
Brassica tournefortii	Calytrix aurea	Boronia ovata	Dampiera alata	Gompholobium polymorphum
Caesia micrantha	Chamaexeros serra	Calothamnus quadrifidus	Dampiera hederacea	Gonocarpus nodulosus
Caladenia longicauda	Chthonocephalus pseudevax	Calothamnus torulosus	Dampiera lavandulacea	Hydrocotyle callicarpa
Caladenia marginata	Conostylis aurea	Convolvulus erubescens	Dampiera trigona	Isotropis cuneifolia
Calytrix acutifolia	Conostylis caricina	Crassula colorata	Echium plantagineum	Jacksonia restioides

October (continued)

White
Cassytha racemosa
Clematis pubescens
Conostylis setosa
Drosera gigantea
Eucalyptus laeliae
Euchiton sphaericus
Goodenia fasciculata
Grevillea endlicheriana
Grevillea manglesii
Grevillea pilulifera
Grevillea synapheae
Hakea amplexicaulis
Hakea prostrata
Hakea stenocarpa
Hakea trifurcata
Hemiandra pungens
Hesperantha falcata
Hyalosperma cotula
Hypocalymma angustifolium
Isotoma hypocrateriformis
Lagenophora huegelii
Leptospermum erubescens
Leptospermum laevigatum
Leucopogon capitellatus
Logania serpyllifolia
Lomandra brittanii
Lupinus species
Microtis alba
Monotaxis grandiflora
Pericalymma ellipticum
Phyllangium paradoxum
Phyllanthus calycinus
Pimelea brevistyla
Pimelea ciliata
Pimelea imbricata
Pimelea spectabilis
Poranthera microphylla
Prasophyllum elatum
Prasophyllum fimbria
Prasophyllum hians
Ptilotus esquamatus
Ptilotus spathulatus
Rinzia crassifolia
Rulingia cygnorum
Silene gallica
Solanum nigrum
Stackhousia monogyna
Stylidium calcaratum
Stylidium carnosum
Stylidium ciliatum
Stylidium crassifolium
Stylidium hispidum
Stylidium junceum
Stylidium petiolare

Yellow
Conostylis setigera
Daviesia cordata
Diuris laxiflora
Diuris longifolia
Diuris setacea
Drosera glanduligera
Drosera leucoblasta
Drosera platystigma
Dryandra sessilis
Glischrocaryon aureum
Gompholobium marginatum
Gompholobium tomentosum
Goodenia claytoniacea
Hedypnois rhagadioloides
Hibbertia amplexicaulis
Hibbertia aurea
Hibbertia commutata
Hibbertia glomerata
Hibbertia hypericoides
Hibbertia pachyrrhiza
Hibbertia spicata
Hibbertia subvaginata
Hypochaeris glabra
Hypoxis occidentalis
Isopogon sphaerocephalus
Jacksonia alata
Jacksonia sternbergiana
Labichea punctata
Lambertia multiflora
Linum trigynum
Lupinus species
Mirbelia spinosa
Patersonia umbrosa
Petrophile seminuda
Petrophile striata
Pimelea argentea
Pimelea suaveolens
Podolepis lessonii
Podotheca angustifolia
Senecio ramosissimus
Sonchus oleraceus
Sphaerolobium medium
Stirlingia simplex
Stylidium canaliculatum
Stylidium diuroides
Stylidium pubigerum
Stylidium rigidifolium
Synaphea gracillima
Synaphea pinnata
Tricoryne elatior
Tripterococcus brunonis
Ursinia anthemoides
Velleia trinervis
Verticordia acerosa

Red
Darwinia citriodora
Darwinia thymoides
Drosera menziesii
Elythranthera brunonis
Elythranthera emarginata
Geranium retrorsum
Gladiolus caryophyllaceus
Hemigenia incana
Kunzea recurva
Levenhookia pusilla
Lomandra purpurea
Melaleuca radula
Melaleuca parviceps
Misopates orontium
Parentucellia latifolia
Petrorhagia velutina
Pimelea preissii
Ptilotus drummondii
Ptilotus manglesii
Rhodanthe manglesii
Romulea rosea
Stachys arvensis
Stylidium affine
Stylidium brunonianum
Stylidium bulbiferum
Tetratheca hirsuta
Tetratheca nuda
Thomasia glutinosa
Thomasia macrocarpa
Thomasia pauciflora
Utricularia multifida
Verticordia insignis
Verticordia pennigera
Verticordia plumosa
Watsonia species

Blue
Eryngium rostratum
Gompholobium shuttleworthii
Halgania corymbosa
Hemigenia incana
Hemigenia ramosissima
Hemigenia sericea
Hovea trisperma
Leschenaultia biloba
Lobelia rhombifolia
Lobelia rhytidosperma
Lobelia tenuior
Lupinus species
Patersonia babianoides
Patersonia rudis
Scaevola calliptera
Scaevola glandulifera
Scaevola platyphylla
Sollya heterophylla
Thelymitra crinita
Thelymitra mucida
Thysanotus dichotomus
Thysanotus multiflorus
Thysanotus patersonii
Thysanotus tenellus
Thysanotus triandrus
Trachymene coerulea

Other
Leptomeria cunninghamii
Leucopogon verticillatus
Lomandra sonderi
Lyperanthus serratus
Microtis atrata
Millotia myosotidifolia
Millotia tenuifolia
Mirbelia ramulosa
Muehlenbeckia adpressa
Opercularia echinocephala
Opercularia hispidula
Opercularia vaginata
Prasophyllum giganteum
Pultenea ericifolia

October (continued)

White
Stylidium piliferum
Stylidium pycnostachyum
Stylidium schoenoides
Trachymene pilosa
Vellereophyton dealbatum
Verticordia huegelii
Villarsia albiflora
Xanthorrhoea gracilis
Xanthosia candida
Xanthosia ciliata
Xanthosia huegelii
Xanthosia pusilla

Yellow
Viminaria juncea
Waitzia aurea
Waitzia citrina

NOVEMBER

White
Actinotus leucocephalus
Agonis linearifolia
Andersonia aristata
Astroloma pallidum
Bartsia trixago
Caesia micrantha
Calytrix acutifolia
Cassytha glabella
Cassytha racemosa
Eucalyptus laeliae
Eucalyptus marginata
Euchiton sphaericus
Goodenia fasciculata
Grevillea endlicheriana
Hakea stenocarpa
Helichrysum macranthum
Hyalosperma cotula
Hemiandra pungens
Isotoma hypocrateriformis
Kingia australis
Lagenofera huegelii
Logania serpyllifolia
Lupinus species
Marianthus candidus
Melaleuca preissiana
Melaleuca rhaphiophylla
Microtis alba
Phyllangium paradoxum
Monotaxis grandiflora
Pimelea ciliata
Pimelea brevistyla
Pimelea imbricata
Pimelea spectabilis
Prasophyllum elatum
Ptilotus declinatus
Ptilotus esquamatus
Ptilotus spathulatus
November (continued)

Yellow
Aotus cordifolia
Banksia grandis
Calytrix aurea
Chthenocephalus pseudevax
Cicendia filiformis
Conostylis aurea
Drosera platystigma
Dryandra sessilis
Gompholobium preissii
Gompholobium tomentosum
Goodenia claytoniacea
Hibbertia amplexicaulis
Hibbertia glomerata
Hibbertia pachyrrhiza
Hibbertia spicata
Hibbertia subvaginata
Hypochaeris glabra
Jacksonia alata
Lambertia multiflora
Linum trigynum
Lupinus species
Nuytsia floribunda
Parentucellia viscosa
Persoonia angustiflora
Petrophile seminuda
Petrophile striata
Philydrella pygmaea
Pimelea argentea
Podolepis lessonii
Podotheca angustifolia
Senecio lautus
Sonchus oleraceus
Stirlingia simplex
Stylidium canaliculatum
Stylidium dichotomum
Stylidium diuroides
Stylidium lineatum

Red
Adenanthos barbigera
Anagallis arvensis
Baeckea camphorosmae
Beaufortia macrostemon
Boronia cymosa
Boronia ovata
Calothamnus quadrifidus
Calytrix variabilis
Centaurium erythraea
Chorizema dicksonii
Convolvulus erubescens
Darwinia citriodora
Darwinia thymoides
Diplopeltis huegelii
Drosera pulchella
Elythranthera emarginata
Gompholobium knightianum
Grevillea bipinnatifida
Grevillea quercifolia
Grevillea wilsonii
Hemigenia incana
Isopogon divergens
Kunzea recurva
Lasiopetalum bracteatum
Lavandula stoechas
Levenhookia pusilla
Levenhookia stipitata
Melaleuca radula
Melaleuca parviceps
Microcorys longifolia
Mirbelia dilatata
Misopates orontium
Parentucellia latifolia
Philotheca spicata
Pimelea preissii
Ptilotus drummondii
Ptilotus manglesii

Blue
Boronia tenuis
Comesperma calymega
Comesperma ciliatum
Dampiera alata
Dianella revoluta
Echium plantagineum
Eryngium rostratum
Gompholobium shuttleworthii
Goodenia caerulea
Halgania corymbosa
Leschenaultia biloba
Lobelia rhytidosperma
Lupinus species
Scaevola calliptera
Scaevola glandulifera
Scaevola platyphylla
Sollya heterophylla
Thelymitra crinita
Thomasia grandiflora
Thysanotus patersonii
Thysanotus sparteus
Thysanotus triandrus
Trachymene coerulea

Other
Daviesia longifolia
Daviesia preissii
Disa bracteata
Dryandra bipinnatifida
Euchilopsis linearis
Gastrolobium spinosum
Gompholobium polymorphum
Gonocarpus cordiger
Hemigenia incana
Jacksonia restioides
Microtis atrata
Muehlenbeckia adpressa
Opercularia echinocephala
Orobanche minor
Oxylobium lineare
Spiculaea ciliata

White
Rhodanthe corymbosa
Rinzia crassifolia
Rulingia cygnorum
Silene gallica
Solanum nigrum
Stackhousia monogyna
Stylidium carnosum
Stylidium crassifolium
Stylidium inundatum
Stylidium junceum
Stylidium perpusillum
Stylidium rhyncocarpum
Trachymene pilosa
Trichocline spathulata
Vellereophyton dealbatum
Verticordia huegelii
Villarsia albiflora
Xanthosia atkinsoniana
Xanthosia candida
Xanthosia ciliata
Xanthosia huegelii
Xanthosia pusilla

Yellow
Stylidium pycnostachyum
Stylidium rigidifolium
Synaphea gracillima
Tricoryne elatior
Tripterococcus brunonis
Ursinia anthemoides
Velleia trinervis
Verticordia acerosa
Viminaria juncea
Waitzia citrina
Waitzia suaveolens

Red
Rhodanthe manglesii
Samolus junceus
Scaevola pilosa
Stachys arvensis
Stachystemon vermicularis
Stylidium breviscapum
Stylidium brunonianum
Stylidium bulbiferum
Tetratheca hirsuta
Tetratheca nuda
Thomasia glutinosa
Thomasia grandiflora
Thomasia pauciflora
Verticordia densiflora
Verticordia insignis
Verticordia pennigera
Verticordia plumosa
Watsonia species

DECEMBER

White
Actinotus leucocephalus
Agonis linearifolia
Astartea fascicularis
Cassytha glabella
Cassytha racemosa
Convolvulus arvensis
Eucalyptus marginata
Euchiton sphaericus
Goodenia fasciculata
Helichrysum macranthum
Hemiandra pungens
Isotoma hypocrateriformis
Kingia australis
Leucopogon cymbiformis
Leucopogon tenuis
Logania campanulata
Logania serpyllifolia
Melaleuca incana
Melaleuca preissiana
Rinzia crassifolia
Rubus aff.selmeri
Pericalymma ellipticum
Pimelea ciliata
Pimelea imbricata
Pithocarpa corymbulosa

Yellow
Acacia barbinervis
Calytrix angulata
Calytrix depressa
Cassytha flava
Cicendia filiformis
Cotula coronopifolia
Dandelion
Dittrichia graveolens
Foeniculum vulgare
Gastrolobium spinosum
Gompholobium polymorphum
Haloragis brownii
Hedypnois rhagadioloides
Hibbertia cicerosa
Hibbertia glomerata
Hibbertia pachyrrhiza
Hypochaeris glabra
Jacksonia sternbergiana
Linum trigynum
Lotus angustissimus
Nuytsia floribunda
Parentucellia viscosa
Persoonia angustiflora
Persoonia elliptica
Platysace juncea

Red
Anagallis arvensis
Adenanthos barbigera
Baeckea camphorosmae
Baeckea species
Beaufortia macrostemon
Callistemon phoeniceus
Comesperma virgatum
Convolvulus erubescens
Drosera pulchella
Gompholobium knightianum
Grevillea bipinnatifida
Grevillea quercifolia
Grevillea wilsonii
Gompholobium polymorphum
Hibbertia cicerosa
Levenhookia stipitata
Melaleuca species
Mirbelia dilatata
Myriophyllum crispatum
Ptilotus manglesii
Acetosella vulgaris
Scaevola pilosa
Stachys arvensis
Stachystemon vermicularis
Stylidium breviscapum

Blue
Anagallis arvensis
Beaufortia purpurea
Comesperma calymega
Comesperma ciliatum
Dampiera incana
Dianella revoluta
Dichopogon capillipes
Gompholobium shuttleworthii
Goodenia caerulea
Gratiola pubescens
Lobelia alata
Lobelia gibbosa
Lobelia heterophylla
Monopsis debilis
Pronaya fraseri
Scaevola calliptera
Scaevola glandulifera
Scaevola platyphylla
Sollya heterophylla
Thysanotus anceps
Thysanotus fastigiatus
Thysanotus patersonii
Thysanotus sparteus

Other
Alternathera species
Daviesia longifolia
Daviesia preissii
Gastrolobium spinosum
Gompholobium polymorphum
Gonocarpus cordiger
Haemodorum
Mentha spicata
Muehlenbeckia adpressa
Orobanche minor
Oxylobium lineare
Spiculaea ciliata
Stylidium leptophyllum

December (continued)

White
Polygonum aviculare
Ptilotus declinatus
Rhodanthe corymbosa
Schoenolaena juncea
Silene gallica
Solanum nigrum
Stackhousia monogyna
Stylidium perpusillum
Stylidium rhyncocarpum
Trichocline spathulata
Trifolium repens
Vellereophyton dealbatum
Waitzia suaveolens
Xanthosia atkinsoniana

Yellow
Senecia lautus
Senecio species
Stylidium dichotomum
Taraxacum officinale
Tolpis barbata
Tricoryne elatior
Tripterococcus brunonis
Ursinia anthemoides
Verticordia acerosa
Velleia trinervis
Viminaria juncea
Waitzia suaveolens
Watsonia Mariana var. bulbillifera

Red
Stylidium repens
Tetratheca hirsuta
Tetratheca nuda
Thomasia glutinosa
Trifolium angustifolium
Pilostyles hamiltonii
Verticordia densiflora
Verticordia pennigera
Verticordia plumosa

CLIMATE of the DARLING RANGE

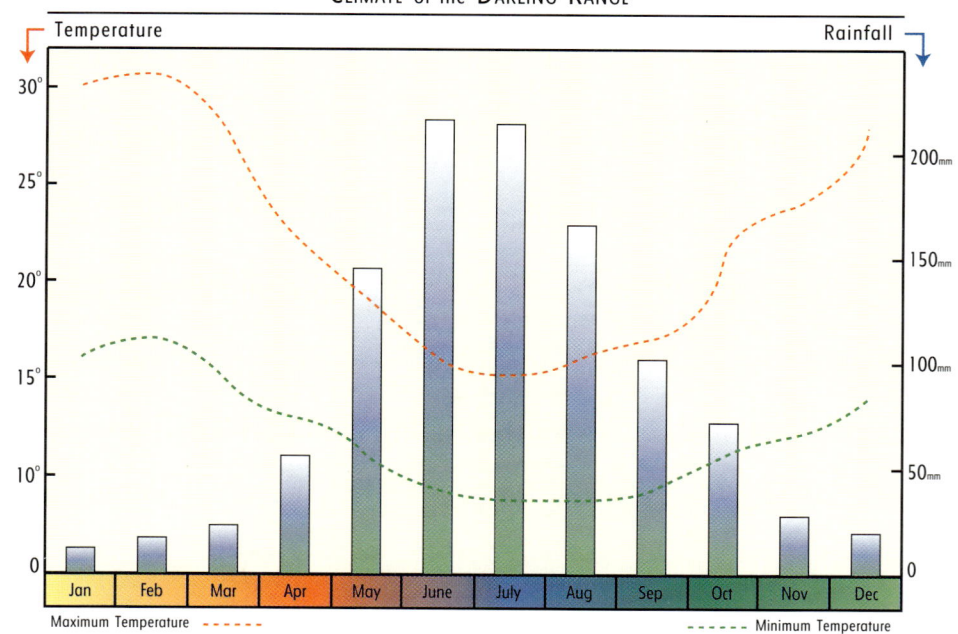

CHAPTER 9

Interesting Snippets

This chapter covers many interesting discussions which relate directly back to the main text. In the planning of this publication it was decided to make this a separate chapter and not to include these interesting snippets throughout the text of the book.

There are many interesting features about plants which are a story within themselves. The simple "leaved" wattles have an interesting germination and foliage development; how close are *Kingia* species and *Xanthorrhoea* species; why do Sundews have sticky hairs on their leaves; what is characteristic about gum trees? All these and more are explained.

Also the distinguishing features of many plant families and genera are given, the meaning of scientific names is discussed and where a name commemorates a person, the significance of that person is given.

APIACEAE - Carrot Family

There are some 20 species belonging to this Family in the Hills, many of which appear weedy and which have their flowers in heads, the heads composed of single flowers on individual stalks radiating like the spokes of an umbrella in an arrangement called "umbels" (the Family used to be named Umbelliferae). All species have a carrot smell when crushed. Carrots, Celery, Dill, Parsley, Fennel and other vegetables and herbs belong to this Family.

The fruits are small, mostly ribbed, paired seeds. Many species are common, and many, inconspicuous.

ASTERACEAE - Daisies

With over 20,000 species Worldwide, 450 in Western Australia about 40 in the Hills, this is one of the largest Plant Families. Many of the species are not prominent in the Hills because the plants are small, weedy or with inconspicuous flowers. Exceptions include the Everlastings. The Family brings together species in which each 'flower' is a compact head of flowers. What appear to be petals are either irregular flowers round the edge of the head with their five petals joined forming a strap-shape (ray florets) or coloured bracts around the head of flowers. The centres of the heads are often yellow, and comprise many, tightly-packed, regular, tubular flowers (disk florets). Apart from the small shrub, Olearia paucidentata, Daisybush (Chapter 3, Medium to Small Shrubs page 70), the remaining members of this Family are all herbaceous (i.e. non-woody).

Papery-Bracted Everlastings

While not in the masses of inland Western Australia, these plants usually occur in moderately large colonies in suitable habitats. Like the Everlastings of the Inland, some, such as Waitzia aurea and Waitzia citrina appear when the season suits them. Many flourish on open ground, after a fire, in gravel pits, on rock outcrops, or spaces between established shrubs. The fluffy, light, wind-dispersed seeds favour this opportunistic way of life.

CASUARINACEAE - Sheoaks

A small family of plants with uncertain relations, the Casuarinaceae has four representatives in the Hills, two of which are trees. All have green, minutely-grooved, branches giving a superficial appearance to pine trees. The leaves of Sheoaks are reduced to tiny, brown, triangular scales at the joints in the green branches, the number of scale leaves corresponding to the grooves on the branch.

DROSERACEAE - Sundews

Sundews are carnivorous plants with obvious, long, hairs at the tip of each is a sticky drop - a condition referred to as glandular-hairy. Any insect unfortunate enough to become stuck will find the neighbouring hairs reaching over to trap it more firmly. The sticky drops also contain digestive chemicals which enable the plant to use the insect to augment its nitrogen supply.

As for Triggerplants, south-west Western Australia is a special place for Sundews (Drosera spp.) with an exceptionally large number occurring here. The Hills' bushland has its share with about 13 species; some large and will become familiar early; others, very small, will await more detailed searching. None are in evidence all year round because the delicate aboveground parts shrivel in early summer and aestivate below ground or as tiny bud clusters at the ground surface.

EUPHORBIACEAE - Spurges

This family seems an odd collection of species with little in common except that the sexes are separated into male and female plants, a condition known as dioecious - having two homes. It is the less common condition in flowering plants. They have berry-shaped fruits splitting into separate segments. It is a cosmopolitan family with four shrubs in the Hills. Several members of the Euphorbiaceae overseas and elsewhere in Australia have a milky sap observable when a leaf is broken off.

FERNS

Unlike flowering plants, ferns do not have flowers but instead produce spores which are borne in special structures appearing as brown spots or streaks on the underside of the fronds. The actual function of flowers, however, to allow the recombining of genetic material and involving half the complement present in the flowering plant is carried out in ferns in a completely different stage of the life-cycle. Tiny, pale-green, plates of cells, scarcely-known because of their size, develop from the fern spores. It is in this 'prothallus' stage of the fern life-cycle that the equivalent function of flowers takes place. Because that function requires a thin film of water, ferns tend to be more abundant in moist, humid climates. Consequently, there are relatively few ferns in south-west Western Australia compared with the Dandenongs north of Melbourne or the rainforests of Queensland. Though only ten can be listed, they cover a considerable size-range and are to be found in most habitats.

IRIDACEAE - Patersonia - Native Iris

These native members of the Iris family (Iridaceae) have three-part flowers. The petals delicate, soon shrivel emerging one after the other from an enclosed, brown-bracted "purse" of flowers. The petals appear separate.

LENTIBULARIACEAE - Bladderworts

Small plants of wet swampy areas, less obviously insectivorous until uprooted and looked at with a hand lens. Then, tiny translucent bladders become apparent. At still smaller scale, usually requiring greater magnification to observe, the bladders have a hinged 'door'. When tripped, the unwary, small insect is swept into the bladder by the inflowing water and is there digested.

MIMOSACEAE - Acacia - Wattles

The fluffy yellow pompoms or sausage-shaped blossoms of wattles are a familiar sight in spring. Less well-appreciated is that these "flowers" are, in fact, heads of much smaller flowers. This becomes obvious on closer observation and the presence of more than one developing fruit - pods - on a "single" wattle "flower".

Leaves of wattles appear to be of two kinds: divided or simple. The true leaves are divided and are possessed by all wattles. In those wattles that appear to have simple "leaves", the divided leaves only occur on the seedling or after lopping (so-called juvenile leaves). In the transition from the divided seedling leaves to adult, simple "leaves", the origin of the stalk of the divided leaves becomes more developed, and often flattens. Eventually, no divided part appears at the end of these leaf stalks: they are the simple "leaves" of many adult wattles. Because they are derived from leaf stalks, technically they are given a different name: phyllodes instead of leaves.

Their phyllodes may be flattened, with one or more obvious nerves, or they may be like fat needles, roughly circular in cross-section. Their flower clusters may be pompom-like (spherical) or sausage-shaped (cylindrical).

ORCHIDACEAE - Orchids

The orchids deserve special attention because as a family, of all the wildflowers, they are the most easily threatened, and endangered. Usually they occur in low numbers, though sometimes they appear locally abundant. The life cycle of orchids includes many unusual facets such as the specialisation of their pollination mechanism in pre-packaging the pollen in pollinia, the reliance on particular insects, and the production of minute, dust-like size seeds unable to produce a new plant without first establishing an association with a fungus in the soil. And even then, that new plant, as evidenced by an orchid leaf at the ground surface for the first time, is often the result of several years of development below ground: up to ten years for many species. Flowering is usually a further several years on from the first appearance of that leaf.

It is the combination of this specialised life cycle and lengthy growth period with the inherent attractiveness of many orchids, which makes them particularly threatened, and their tendency to be endangered by picking is evident.

PAPILIONACEAE - Peas

This is the best represented family in the Hills with over eighty species ranging from small trees to herbs. All have the typical 'pea' flower made up of five petals. The most obvious is the upright rounded 'standard' petal at the back of the flower. The two 'wing' petals project forward enclosing the pair of fused petals called the 'keel'. These, in turn, enclose a tubular structure of ten anthers and the style and ovary. The petals emerge from a five-lobed calyx representing five sepals partly joined together.

Peas, like the other legumes - Wattles and Cassias - can extract nitrogen from the air and convert it to nitrate, useable by the plant as a 'fertiliser'. This ability depends on the activities of bacteria which live in colonies in nodules on the roots. This 'nitrogen fixation' eventually benefits all the plants in the bush. The fixed nitrogen can be used by other plants as the pea plants decay.

The hard seeds within the characteristic pea pods explain their quick appearance after fire. While some peas resprout from underground rootstocks, many also germinate from seeds after a fire. Peas possess a hard seed coat, so that each year as the seed is shed, it is added to the seed-bank in the topsoil. The seed coat must be broken for the seed to absorb water and begin to germinate. In a forest fire while many seeds are killed others are heated just enough to crack the seed-coat. Without fire, seeds 'softened' by abrasion and other accidents, germinate each year. Pea seeds left undisturbed have a lifetime measured in decades.

POACEAE - Grasses

The majority of the grasses are introduced species. There is no overall distinguishing feature between native and introduced grasses except that the latter are mainly annuals and are usually found where there is some disturbance along roadsides or bush-tracks. Their spread is favoured by increased frequency of fires and increased soil fertility.

All grasses have leaves in two distinct parts: a section free from the stem, the leaf blade, which is usually flattened although may curl inwards from the edges, attached to a sheathing part which encircles the stem joined at the next lowermost joint or node. At the junction of leaf blade and sheath there is a papery part, or ring of hairs (1mm or so) projecting upwards beyond the junction are called ligules and are often used as features to distinguish grasses.

An especially helpful feature in distinguishing species is the presence of a pointed extension (awn) to some of the bracts. It varies in length from 1mm to 30mm.

POLYGALACEAE - Milkworts

Plants with pea-like flowers but with the large, dominating, uppermost, standard petal absent, and so dominated by two wing petals which are actually petal-like sepals. The flowers crowded on long, erect spikes. Called Milkworts because of milky sap which appears at the ends of broken surfaces although this characteristic is shared by plants of a few other families (e.g. Asclepiadaceae; some Asteraceae; Campanulaceae; some Euphorbiaceae).

PROTEACEAE - Banksia family

As a general characteristic, the Proteaceae, as with Myrtaceae, are all woody. Their petal-like sepals are united into a tube which more or less distinctly splits into four parts each with an anther closely-fixed, sometimes in a small hollow, near the tip.

The flowers may be tightly packed on cones, clustered in heads or borne singly. The individual flower is more or less tubular with four "petal" lobes radiating in regular fashion or curled back with the stamens in pouches near the lobe tips. The style often protrudes well out of the flower.

The seeds are carried in persistent woody fruits like Banksia (cones) and Hakea (nuts) or in less substantial seed pods which soon fall off, like Grevilleas.

PERSOONIA - Snottygobbles

Two trees of the jarrah forest, of similar height of about 6m, go by the uncomplimentary common name of Snottygobbles, a reference to the appearance of the ripe fruit. Which is the more prominent varies with locality.

RUTACEAE - Boronias

The perfumed brown boronia (B. megastigma) though well known, is unrepresentative of those in the Hills. Boronias generally have four-petalled regular flowers with eight stamens, are coloured pink or blue and lack a distinctive perfume. The leaves are opposite or whorled. They are in the same family as citrus (orange, lemon, grapefruit etc.) with which they share the characteristic of leaves dotted with small oil glands giving an aromatic scent when crushed but usually less noticeable than members of the eucalypt and myrtle family (Myrtaceae).

STYLIDIACEAE - Triggerplants

Triggerplants get their name from their vigorous activity during pollination. Between and behind the four petals is set a long, strap-shaped column with the anthers and stigma at its tip. When the right kind of insect lands on the flower seeking nectar from its centre, it triggers the column which moves rapidly up and round to deposit pollen on the insect, usually on its back. At the next flower, the insect again receives the same treatment, and if the stigma has emerged on the column (the anthers are usually in readiness first), it picks up some of the pollen.

Triggering columns by touching their base near the centre of the flower with a small twig or grass stalk is great fun and a source of fascination. The columns generally reset within an hour.

The pollination mechanism of styleworts is similar to Triggerplants but is not active.

There are 30 species of Triggerplant in the Hills, a family which is better represented in Western Australia than anywhere else in the World with over 100 species.

XANTHORRHOEA - Grass trees

The ideal tree should have a single stem or trunk. Given this, there are some other fascinating contenders: the grass trees.

Grasslike plants have anatomical limitations which mean they do not form wood of the familiar consistency of broad-leaved plants. Two very different grass trees are found, both commonly in the Hills, Balga and Grasstree, excluding the flower stalks, Balga do not attain the heights of the Grasstree, with 4m being quite tall for a Balga.

The growth rate of Balgas is similar to that of Grasstrees, about 3cm a year. A commonly-held view is that Balgas need to be burnt to flower. This is not only incorrect but, with the increased frequency of burning losses of Balga are likely. In a large population of Balgas, occasional flowering occurs in most years in the absence of fire. After a fire, flowering is almost invariable. However, the massive flowering stalk of Balgas takes a lot out of them, and where frequent burning has induced frequent flowering, the reserves of the plant are rapidly depleted and premature death occurs in these otherwise well-adapted, very long-lived grass trees. Young Balgas are common in the bush and may be confused for some other grasslike plants. They take 10-15 years to develop a trunk.

ZAMIACEAE - Macrozamia - Zamia

Zamia is of ancient stock in the lineage of plants, remotely related to the conifers - pines and cypress - and may be pictured more at home in swamp margins of the Cretaceous, 120 million years ago, amongst its fellow-Cycads, than today, a relict in strange new company. It is not a Palm which belongs to a more recently evolved group.

To be certain of seeing Macrozamia reproducing, make a note of when an area is burnt and return two years later. (Conversely, an estimate when an area was burnt can be made from the flowering of Balgas (fire one season ago) and the fruiting of the Zamia (fire two seasons ago)). When you return, the centre of each plant will have, if male, up to three cones, 25x12cm in November and maturing in May-June. By then the bracts (microsporophylls) of the cones will have separated, revealing on their upper surface, masses of tiny enclosures from which the equivalent of pollen emerges. If female there will be one cone, 40x25cm, again taking several months to ripen. The bracts (megasporophylls) are much stouter than in the male cones with a large (4cm), upward-pointing, central spike. Nestling in these bracts are two large megaspores (seeds), each 3.5x6cm. When first exposed and maturing in June they are covered with a thin, bright-red, outer fleshy part. Beneath this is the somewhat woody, straw-coloured casing of the "seed".

Emus eat the fleshy red covering, and pass the seed without ill-effect. To humans, both are poisonous without thorough washing, as was the aboriginal custom.

The woody seed cases of the Zamia are a common sight on the forest floor and near female plants there are usually groves of tiny Zamia "seedlings" as well.

Welshpool Road
Scarp

FEATURES OF MONOCOTS AND DICOTS

	Leaves	Flowers
Monocotyledons	Long, narrow, grasslike with parallel veins but some with heart-shaped leaves and with cross-veining. Margins entire, continuous, not toothed, or indented. Leaf blade never divided into lobes, segments or leaflets.	Parts in threes, often inconspicuous. Rarely in twos.
Dicotyledons	Broad leaves with criss-cross veins but some with cylindrical leaves, or with long, narrow leaves and appearing to have parallel veins. Margins can be notched, toothed, wavy. Leaf blade can be divided into lobes, segments or leaflets.	Parts in fours, fives or several.

Lesmurdie Falls National Park

CHAPTER 10

Parks, Reserves and Walk Trails

All the Parks and Reserves dealt within this Chapter were proposed as such in "The Darling System - System 6", Report 13 of the Department of Conservation and Environment.

These Parks and Reserves have been divided up here on the basis of natural access points so that each of the segments would make an appropriate objective for an excursion. Walk Trails, especially those along the Scarp, often link adjoining segments, and are dealt with under Official Walk Trails (page 240).

The Parks and Reserves referred to are open to the public for recreational walking and study.

The Parks and Reserves are grouped according to the major landscape elements they represent: the VALLEY of the Helena River; the SCARP; and the Darling RANGE. The Reserve reference numbers are those published in the System 6 Report. Tracks, either official or informal, are found leading from the access points listed for the different areas. For locations see map inside the back cover.

The VALLEY of the Helena River.

1. Adopted Name: **Helena Valley**
   Reserve: Part M34   Area: 433.5ha
   Location: South bank Helena River nearest the Scarp and the Coastal Plain.
   Access Points: Helena Valley Road, HELENA VALLEY
   Terrain: Sweeping, rugged, at times steep, north-facing valley slopes.
   Habitats: Mainly slope shrublands, rock outcrops and streamsides/seepage with some woodland.
   Restrictions: No unauthorised vehicle access beyond Parking area.
   No fires. No camping.

2. Adopted Name: **Paulls Valley**
   Reserve: Part M34   Area: 175ha
   Location: South bank Helena River adjoining and to the east of No.1
   Access Points: Fern Road off Humerston Road, PAULLS VALLEY
   Paulls Valley Road PAULLS VALLEY
   Asher Road, PAULLS VALLEY
   Terrain: Rugged, at times steep, north-facing valley slopes
   Habitats: Mainly slope shrublands, rock outcrops and streamside/seepage with some woodland.
   Restrictions: No unauthorised vehicle access beyond Parking area.
   No fires. No camping.

3. Adopted Name: **Kalamunda National Park**
   Reserve: Part M34   Area: 375ha
   Location: Piesse Brook catchment adjoining 1, to north
   Access Points: Tregenna Place or Hill Street or Ledger Road, GOOSEBERRY HILL
   Spring Road, KALAMUNDA,
   Schipp Road off Humerston Road, PIESSE BROOK
   Terrain: Rugged valley slopes but with good walking trails
   Habitats: Forest/woodland, streamside/seepage, some slope shrublands and rock outcrops.
   Restrictions: No unauthorised vehicle access beyond Parking area.
   No fires. No camping. Additional restrictions apply because of National Park status.

Helena Valley

Paulls Valley

Kalamunda
National Park

The SCARP

4. **Adopted Name:** **Gooseberry Hill National Park**
   Reserve: Part M34   Area: 33ha
   Location: Scarp adjoining 1, the Helena Valley reserve.
   Access Points: Zig Zag Scenic Drive, GOOSEBERRY HILL/HELENA VALLEY.
   Terrain: Scarp slope, rugged in places but with tracks along the contours.
   Habitats: Mainly slope shrublands and some rock outcrops.
   Restrictions: No unauthorised vehicle access beyond Parking area.
   No fires. No camping. Additional restrictions apply because of National Park status.

5. **Adopted Name:** **Kalamunda Scarp**
   Reserve: Part M80   Area: 37ha
   Location: Scarp south of Kalamunda Road (Poison Gully)
   Access Points: West Terrace, KALAMUNDA (beginning of Darling Scarp Walk Trail)
   Brine Road, KALAMUNDA.
   Terrain: Scarp slope, rugged in places, but with tracks along the contours.
   Habitats: Mainly slope shrublands, some rock outcrops, woodland and streamside/seepage
   Restrictions: No unauthorised vehicle access beyond Parking area.
   No fires. No camping.

6. **Adopted Name:** **Lesmurdie Scarp**
   Reserve: Part M80   Area: 99ha
   Location: Scarp and Whistlepipe Gully to south of 5.
   Access Points: Lewis Road, FORRESTFIELD
   Ozone Terrace, KALAMUNDA
   Orange Valley Road, KALAMUNDA
   Connor Road, LESMURDIE
   Ashurst Drive, LESMURDIE
   Terrain: Steep slopes to gully stream; scarp slope, rugged in places, but with tracks along contours.
   Habitats: Mainly slope shrublands and streamside/seepage with some rock outcrops and woodland
   Restrictions: No unauthorised vehicle access beyond Parking area.
   No fires. No camping.

Parks, Reserves & Walk Trails 233

Gooseberry Hill
National Park

Kalamunda Scarp

Lesmurdie Scarp

7. | Adopted Name: | **Lesmurdie Falls National Park** |
   | --- | --- |
   | Reserve: | Part M80   Area: 55.5ha |
   | Location: | Scarp and Lesmurdie Brook Gully extending north and south. beyond the National Park. To the south of 6. |
   | Access Points: | Palm Terrace, FORRESTFIELD |
   | | Honey Road, FORRESTFIELD |
   | | Falls Road, LESMURDIE |
   | | Ford Road, LESMURDIE |
   | Terrain: | Steep slopes to streamsides; scarp slope, rugged in places, but with tracks along the contours. |
   | Habitats: | Mainly slope shrublands and streamside/seepage with some rock outcrops and woodland. |
   | Restrictions: | No unauthorised vehicle access beyond Parking area. No fires. No camping. Additional restrictions apply because of National Park status. |

8. | Adopted Name: | **Welshpool Road Scarp** |
   | --- | --- |
   | Reserve: | Part M80   Area: 29.2ha |
   | Location: | Scarp to south of Welshpool Road. |
   | Access Points: | Welshpool Road opposite Gladys Road, LESMURDIE |
   | | Gilchrist Road, LESMURDIE. |
   | Terrain: | Scarp slopes, rugged in places but includes good tracks from both access points. |
   | Habitats: | Mainly slope shrublands, some streamside/seepage, rock outcrops, and woodland. Woodland at Gilchrist Road access point. |
   | Restrictions: | No unauthorised vehicle access beyond Parking area. No fires. No camping. |

9. | Adopted Name: | **Bickley Scarp** |
   | --- | --- |
   | Reserve: | Part M80   Area: 134.8ha |
   | Location: | Scarp to south of 8 and continuing on south, facing slope down to Bickley Reservoir and Brook. |
   | Access Points: | Gilchrist Road, LESMURDIE |
   | | Hardinge Road, ORANGE GROVE |
   | Terrain: | Scarp slopes, rugged in places with steep gully side north from Bickley Reservoir. Good tracks from both access points. |

Parks, Reserves & Walk Trails 235

Lesmurdie Falls
National Park

Welshpool Road Scarp

Bickley Scarp

	Habitats:	Mainly slope shrublands streamside/seepage and rock outcrops with some woodland. Woodland at Gilchrist Road access point.
	Restrictions:	No unauthorised vehicle access beyond Parking area. No fires. No camping.

THE DARLING RANGE

10.
Adopted Name:	**Mundaring Weir Road Reserve**	
Reserve:	Part M77	Area: 36.4ha
Location:	Alongside Mundaring Weir Road, KALAMUNDA, opposite Croxton Road	
Access Points:	Mundaring Weir Road opposite Croxton Road, KALAMUNDA	
Terrain:	Rough going on laterite on woodland slope. Small tracks.	
Habitats:	Mainly forest.	
Restrictions:	No unauthorised vehicle access beyond Parking area. No fires. No camping.	

11.
Adopted Name:	**Mitchell Road Reserve**	
Reserve:	Part M77	Area: 59.7ha
Location:	To south of 10 on broad laterite ridge either side of Mitchell Road, BICKLEY	
Access Points:	Mitchell Road, BICKLEY.	
Terrain:	Moderate going on forested ridge. Few tracks.	
Habitats:	Mainly forest.	
Restrictions:	No unauthorised vehicle access beyond Parking area. No fires. No camping.	

12.
Adopted Name:	**TV Towers Reserve**	
Reserve:	Part M80	Area: 4.6ha
Location:	South-west of 11. Bounded by Lawnbrook and Pomeroy Roads, WALLISTON.	
Access Points:	Lawnbrook Road, near junction with Pomeroy Road, WALLISTON Pomeroy Road, WALLISTON.	
Terrain:	Gently sloping forested laterite with good tracks.	
Habitats:	Mainly forest.	
Restrictions:	No unauthorised vehicle access beyond Parking area. No fires. No camping.	

Parks, Reserves & Walk Trails 237

Mundaring Weir Road Reserve

Mitchell Road Reserve

TV Towers Reserve

13. | Adopted Name: | **Lesmurdie High School Reserve**
    | Reserve | Part M80   Area 98ha
    | Location: | South-west of 12. Bounded by Canning Road, Pomeroy Road near Welshpool Road, CARMEL/LESMURDIE
    | Acces Points: | Pomeroy Road near Canning Road, CARMEL
    | | Pomeroy Road near Welshpool Road, CARMEL/LESMURDIE
    | | Albert Road/Welshpool Road Junction, LESMURDIE
    | Terrain: | Gently Sloping forest laterite with good tracks
    | Habitat | Forest and woodland
    | Restrictions: | No unauthorised vehicle access beyond Parking area
    | | No fires. No camping.
    | Comments: | The Reserve is divided by major roads. The section of Pomeroy Road is the larger part. The smaller, largely trackless part west of Pomeroy Road and north of Welshpool Road is dense and rich.

14. | Adopted Name | **Carmel Reserve**
    | Reserve: | M78   Area: 20ha
    | Location: | South of 12 and 13 with a small section between Masonmill Road and Canning Road and extending eastwards
    | Acces Points: | Masonmill Road, CARMEL
    | | Canning Road in vicinity of Masonmill Road, CARMEL
    | Terrain: | Rough in places on forested laterite with a track
    | Habitat | Forest
    | Restrictions: | No unauthorised vehicle access beyond Parking area
    | | No fires. No camping.

14. | Adopted Name | **Munday Brook Reserve**
    | Reserve: | M79   Area: 40ha
    | Location: | East of Canning Road opposite Douglas Road, CANNING MILLS
    | Acces Points: | As for location
    | Terrain: | Wet in winter but gently sloping valley floor and sides with good tracks
    | Habitat | Exceptional streamside and forest including W.A. Blackbutt, Eucalyptus patens
    | Restrictions: | No unauthorised vehicle access beyond Parking area
    | | No fires. No camping.

Parks, Reserves & Walk Trails 239

Lesmurdie High School Reserve

Carmel Reserve

Munday Brook Reserve

OFFICIAL WALK TRAILS

Official Walk Trails pass through Reserves Nos. 1 (Kalamunda Shire Trails), 2 (Bibbulmen Track), 3 (Kalamunda Shire Trails), 4 (Kalamunda Shire Trails), 5 (Darling Scarp Walk Trail begins at West Terrace), 6 (Darling Scarp Walk Trail continues), 7 (Darling Scarp Walk Trail and Western Australian Department of Conservation and Land Management Trails), 8 (Darling Scarp Walk Trail continues), 9 (Darling Scarp Walk Trail continues), 15 (Western Australian Department of Youth, Sport and Recreation Trail passes through this Reserve).

DO'S and DON'TS

- Care of bush reserves is easily practised. Much is common sense and thoughtfulness.
- Do take a good map or other means of knowing where you are going.
- Do take a compass but recognise its limited use in the presence of ironstone.
- Do take a whistle to help others locate you if you get lost.
- Do wear stout footwear with good ankle protection because it is easy to turn an ankle on some of the rough bush tracks.
- Do take an elementary First-Aid Kit including provision for treating a snake bite.
- Do take food both to enjoy and in case an emergency means staying out longer than planned.
- Do take a hat and water, especially if walking in the hotter weather.
- Some of the do's are more important if going for a walk in the more rugged areas such as the Scarp face and the Helena Valley, and less important if going to one of the reserves on the wooded, upland, Range country. Don't treat the latter lightly though, it is very easy to lose sense of direction in the wooded reserves where trees limit visibility and there is a sameness to the surroundings.
- Don't expect reserves to lack evidence of desecration. Should the spirit move you to tidy up the messes of others, then please do so. The reward will be the enhanced enjoyment of all.
- Don't take vehicles further than properly made tracks. Never drive them through the bush. A single pass of a vehicle breaks stems which lasts for several years to come.
- Don't leave any refuse in the bush. If you have the energy to carry these things into the bush, respect it and carry them out again.
- Don't bush-bash, even on foot, indiscriminately. When walking, by all means leave the paths to view some plant or scene of interest, but tread carefully. Watch where you put your feet.
- Don't light fires.
- Additional restrictions may apply in National Parks or Water Catchment Areas such as NO DOGS ALLOWED. Notices at the access points to such areas, will indicate any restrictions.

CHAPTER 11

Illustrated Glossary

Very few technical terms have been used throughout this book. In this chapter labelled illustrations name the parts of flowers, shapes and margins of leaves and several other technical terms.

As Hakeas are readily identified by their woody fruits which persist on the plants all year, the fruits of all fifteen described in the book are illustrated in this chapter. These illustrations enable the quick identification of the fifteen species by comparing the illustrations with the fruit collected.

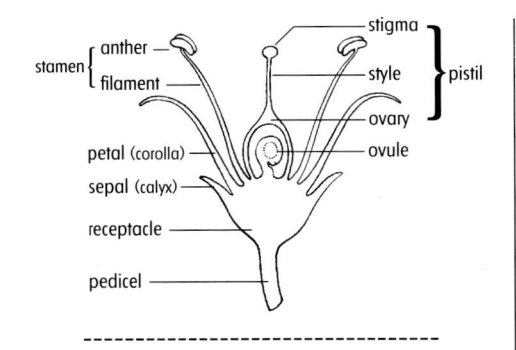

stamen { anther, filament }
pistil } stigma, style, ovary
stigma
style
ovary
ovule
petal (corolla)
sepal (calyx)
receptacle
pedicel

Regular flower   Irregular flower

A compound leaf:
- leaflet
- rachis
- petiole
- axilliary bud

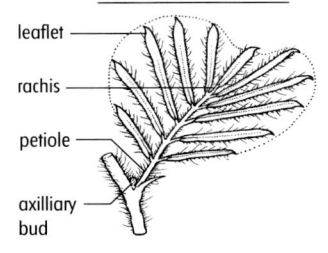

Lobed   Entire   Serrate
Dentate
Palmate   Undulate   Parted

Simple leaves on a small branch:
- leaf { blade, petiole }
- stem
- terminal bud
- axilliary bud
- old leaf (subtending branch in its axil)

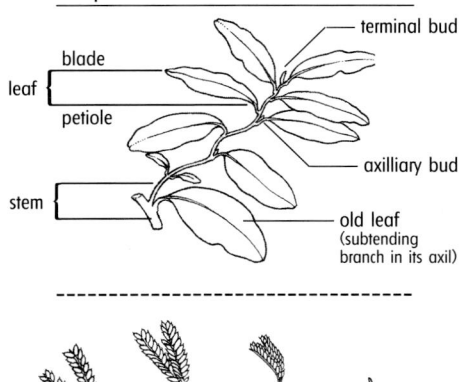

Oblong   Needle-shaped   Linear (flat)

Lanceolate   Ovate

Stages in development of phyllode in Australian Acacia
  A. A pinnately compound leaf
  B. Petiole and part of rachis developing
  C. into phyllode
  D. Phyllode

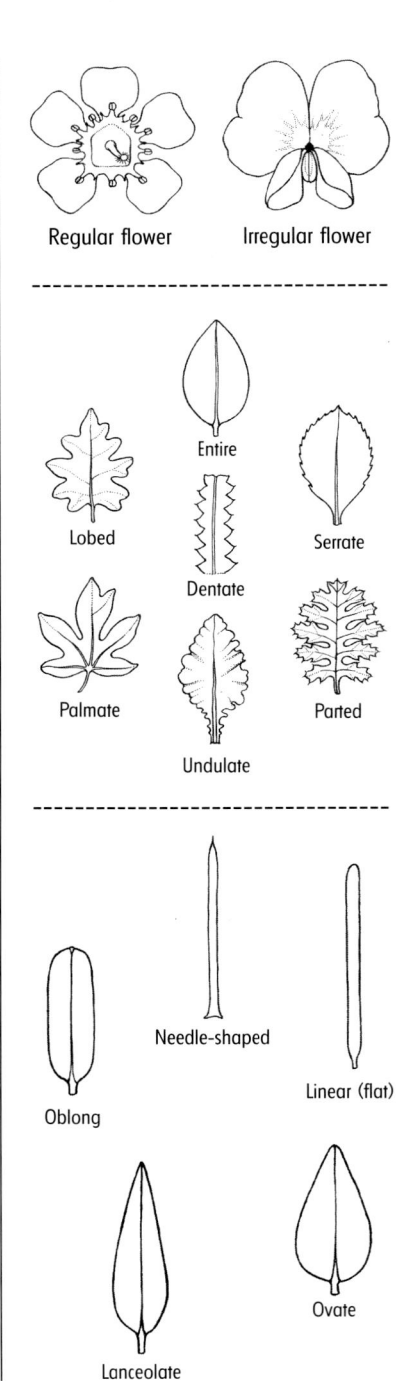

HAKEA FRUITS

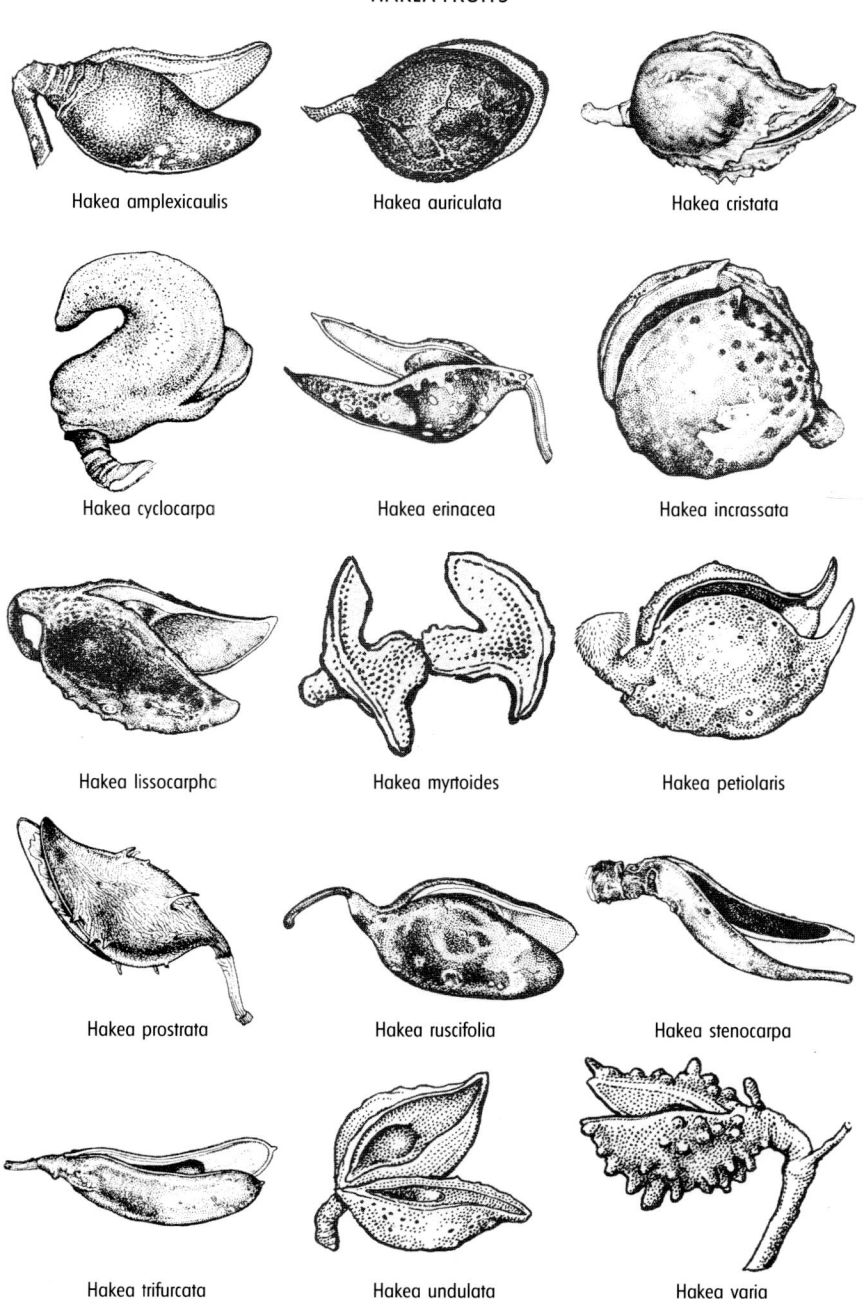

Hakea amplexicaulis

Hakea auriculata

Hakea cristata

Hakea cyclocarpa

Hakea erinacea

Hakea incrassata

Hakea lissocarpha

Hakea myrtoides

Hakea petiolaris

Hakea prostrata

Hakea ruscifolia

Hakea stenocarpa

Hakea trifurcata

Hakea undulata

Hakea varia

CREDITS AND ACKNOWLEDGEMENTS

There are all kinds of credits and acknowledgements in a book of this sort.

It arose as a project of the Darling Range Branch of the Wildflower Society of Western Australia following a suggestion by John Imison. Members, both of that Branch and of the Society generally in Western Australia, have assisted in many ways.

Most of the text was written by Dr John Marshall, with the photographs by Brian Tullis and the illustrations by Margaret Wilson. Aileen Marshall kept the herbarium records. Members of the Marshall, Martin, Reynolds and Tullis families paticipated in the floral surveys of Parks and Reserves which provided the basis for this book.

Dr Philip Reynolds assisted in the early stages. Further assistance and editing was undertaken by Dr Eleanor Bennett, Wendy Hearn, Mavis Holdcroft, Jean Kemp, Rae Papenfus, Elizabeth Sarfaty, Mary Smith, Bernard Thomason, Jean Thomason, Peter Traynor, Rodney van Proctor, Myra Hamilton (dec.), Ross Hamilton, Elizabeth George, Joanna Seabrook and other members of the Darling Range Branch.

Michael Brooker of C.S.I.R.O. made available his records for Gooseberry Hill National Park.

Fauna photography by Derk Mead Hunter. The botanical nomenclature was checked by Paul Wilson and the Orchid chapter by Andrew Brown. Diana Carr is thanked for her computer editing of this publication.

The following are acknowledged for their financial assistance:

- Wildflower Society of W.A.
- Wilflower Society of W.A. (Eastern Hills Branch)
- Wildflower Society of W.A. (Darling Range Branch)

Index

A groundsel 174
Acacia alata 13, 71
Acacia anomala 71, 214
Acacia aphylla 71, 213, 214
Acacia barbinervis 71, 210, 219
Acacia dentifera 14, 72, 215, 216
Acacia divergeus 14, 73
Acacia drummondii 70, 213, 214, 215, 216
Acacia extensa 13, 72, 214, 215
Acacia horridula 13, 71, 211, 212, 213, 215
Acacia incrossata 72
Acacia nervosa 72, 212, 213, 214, 215
Acacia obovata 72, 211, 212
Acacia oncinophylla 14, 72, 215
Acacia pukhella 14, 70, 213, 214, 215, 216
Acacia saligna 14, 72, 214, 215
Acacia sessilis 13, 72, 212, 213
Acacia stenoptera 71, 211
Acacia teretifolia 72, 211, 212, 213
Acacia urophylla 13, 72, 212
Acacia varia 71
Acacia wildenowiana 71, 213, 214, 214, 216
Acaena echinata 194
Acetosella vulgaris 197, 214, 219
Actinotus glomeratus 177, 212, 213, 214
Actinotus leucocephalus 178, 218, 219
Adenanthos barbiger 57, 210, 211, 212, 213, 214, 218, 219
African love grass 116
Agonis linearifolla 22, 210, 212, 213, 214, 215, 216, 218, 219
Agrostocrinum scabrum 127, 215, 216
Albizia 14
Allocasuarina frasenana 29, 213, 214
Allocasuarina huegeliana 29, 213, 214
Allocasuarina humilis 29, 74, 214
Allocasuarina microstachya 74, 215, 216
Alternanthera nodiflora 193, 210, 211, 212, 213, 214
Amyema miquelil 105, 211, 212, 213
Amyema preissii 104, 105, 210, 211
Anagallis arvensis 190, 214, 215, 216, 218, 219
Andersonia aristata 68
Andersonia lehmanniana 68, 211, 212, 213, 214, 215, 216
Anigozanthos bicolor 133, 214, 215, 216
Anigozanthos humilis 133
Anigozanthos manglesii 133, 214, 215, 216
Aniseed boronia 64
Annual club mass 198, 199
Aotus cordifolia 18, 50, 216, 218
Aphelia cyperoides 119
Aphelia brizula 119

Aphelia drummondii 119
Aphelia spp. 119
Arctotheca calendula 175, 213, 214, 215
Aristida spa. 116
Arrhenatherum bulbosum 116
Arundo donax 114, 211, 212
Astartea fascicularis 23, 219
Asteridea pulyerulenia 173, 215, 216
Asterolasia pallida 63, 213, 214
Astroloma ciliatum 68, 211, 212, 213
Astroloma foliosum 68, 211, 212, 213
Astroloma pallidum 68, 211, 212, 213, 214, 215, 216, 218
Australian bluebell 24, 103
Austrodanthonia caespitosa 115
Austrostipa compressa 115
Austrostipa elegantissima 117
Autumn leek orchid 151
Autumn scrub daisy 70
Avena barbata 116
Avena fatua 116

Babiana angustifolia 127
Baboon flower 127
Bacon and eggs 49
Baeckea comphorosmae 60, 210, 211, 218, 219
Banded greenhood 19
Banksia 15, 16, 26, 28, 54, 65, 215, 216, 218, 215
Banksia family 28, 54, 65, 225
Banksia grandis 16, 26, 64, 216, 218
Banksia littoralis 16
Barley grass 117
Bartsia 165
Bartsia trixago 185, 216, 218
Beard-heath 69
Bearded oats 116
Beaufortia macrostemon 73, 215, 216
Beaufortia purpurea 15, 73, 210, 219
Bee orchid 152
Beyeria lechenaultii 29
Billardiera bicolor 102, 210, 211
Billardiera drummondiana 103, 214, 215
Billardiera floribunda 103
Billardiera variifolia 103
Bird hakea 54
Bird orchid 150
Black beaked triggerplant 169
Black berry nightshade 191
Black-eyed Susan 63
Blackberry 24, 104
Blackboy 27, 128, 226
Blackgin 28, 226

Bladderworts 184, 223
Blind grass 127
Blowfly grass 116
Blue beard 147
Blue boronia 65
Blue china orchid 149
Blue lace flower 177
Blue lady orchid 146
Blue leschenaultia 52
Blue-spike milkwort 184
Blue squill 126
Blueboy 28
Book-leaf 17, 48
Book triggerplant 168
Boomerang triggerplant 169
Boronia crenulata 64, 211, 212, 213, 214
Boronia cymosa 64, 212, 213, 214, 218
Boronia ovata 65, 214, 215, 216, 218
Boronia ramosa 64, 213, 214, 215
Boronias 64, 192, 226
Borya sphaeracephala 126, 214, 215
Bossiaea aquifolium 17, 49, 214, 215
Bossiaea eriocarpa 48, 215, 216
Bossiaea ornata 48, 215, 216
Bossiaea pulchella 49, 214, 215
Bossiaea spinescens 17, 49, 213, 214
Brachyscome iberidifolia 173, 215, 216
Bracken 198
Branching fringed lily 129
Branching lily 125
Brassica tournefortii 192, 214, 215, 216
Bridal sundew 102
Bristly cloak fern 199
Bristly cottonhead 131
Bristly donkey orchid 153
Bristly scaevola 52
Briza maxima 116
Briza minor 116
Broad-leafed brown pea 48
Broad-leaved fan flower 52
Broad-leaved haemodorum 124
Broad-leaved mistletoe 105
Brome 116
Bromus sp. 116
Bronze leek orchid 151
Brown finger orchid 151
Bugle lily 132
Bull banksia 16, 66
Bunjong 26, 67
Burchardia multiflora 125, 213, 214
Burchardia umbellata 126, 214, 215
Burr medic 178
Buttercup 23, 58, 189

Butterfly plant 133
Caesia micrantha 126, 216, 218
Caladenia denticulata 147, 213, 214
Caladenia discoidea 148
Caladenia falcata 148
Caladenia flava 148, 215, 216
Caladenia hirta 148, 214, 215
Caladenia longiclavata 148, 214, 215
Caladenia macrostylis 148, 214, 215
Caladenia marginata 149, 216
Caladenia reptans 147, 213, 214
Calandrinia granulifera 197, 214
Callistemon phoeniceus 15, 219
Calothamnus quadritidus 15, 73, 215, 216, 218
Calothamnus sanguineus 15, 73, 211, 212, 213
Calothamnus torulosus 73, 214, 215, 216
Calytrix acutifolia 23, 216, 218
Calytrix angulata 61, 219
Calytrix aurea 61, 216, 218
Calytrix depressa 61, 219
Calytrix glutinosa 61
Calytrix variabilis 61, 218
Camphor myrtle 60
Candle cranberry 68
Candle hakea 20, 55
Cape bluebell 191
Cape tulips 126
Capeweed 174
Carrot Family 177, 195, 222
Cassutha flava 100, 210, 219
Cassytha glabella 100, 210, 218, 219
Cassytha racemosa 100, 210, 216, 218, 219
Catkin grevillea 56
Centaurium erythaea 191, 218
Centrolepis aristata 119
Centrolepis drummondiana 119
Centrolepis spp. 119
Cerastium glomeratum 188, 214
Chaetanthus aristatus 119
Chamaecytisus palmensis 17, 214
Chamaescilla corymbosa 126, 214, 215
Chamaexeros serra 129, 215, 216
Cheilanthes austrotenuifolia 198, 206
Cheilanthes distans 199, 206
Cheilanthes sieberi 199
Cheiranthera preissiana 103
Chickweed 188, 195
Chorizema dicksonii 49, 214, 218
Chorizema ilicifolium 47, 213, 214
Christmas Tree 11, 22, 23, 29
Chthonocephalus pseudevax 175, 216
Cicendia filiformis 196, 218, 219
Cinnamon sun orchid 147
Circus triggerplant 169
Clematis pubescens 100, 215, 217
Climbing fringed lily 100
Climbing lignum 104

Club Rush 121
Clubbed spider orchid 148
Clustered heath 69
Coast teatree 23
Comesperma calymega 184, 216, 218, 219
Comesperma ciliatum 102, 184, 215, 216, 218, 219
Comesperma virgatum 184, 210, 211, 219
Common bartsia 185
Common brown pea 48
Common centaury 191
Common crowfoot 180
Common dampiera 182
Common donkey orchid 152
Common forest heath 69
Common hovea 48
Common joyweed 193
Common maidenhair 198
Common mignonette 150
Common pin-heath 68
Common popflower 192
Common smokebush 28, 57
Common sowthistle 173
Common spurry 188
Common stylewort 194
Common wallaby grass 115
Compact needlegrass 115
Compacted featherflower 62
Conospermum huegelii 54, 57, 214, 215, 216
Conospermum stoechadis 28, 57, 211, 212, 213
Conostylis aculeata 131, 214
Conostylis androstemma 131, 212, 213
Conostylis aurea 132, 216, 218
Conostylis caricina 131, 214, 215, 216
Conostylis setigera 131, 214, 215, 216
Conostylis setosa 131, 215, 217
Convolvulus arvensis 104, 210, 211, 219
Convolvulus erubescens 104, 210, 216, 218, 219
Coral pea 101
Cortaderia selloana 114, 210
Cotula coronopifolia 175, 210, 211, 212, 213, 214, 219
Couch grass 118
Couch honeypot 77
Cowkicks 133, 170
Cowslip orchid 148
Craspedia variabilis 175, 213, 214
Crassula colorata 195, 215, 216
Creeping oxalis 190
Cudweeds 178
Curled dock 197
Curly-leaved mat rush 122
Curved mulla mulla 177
Cyrtostylis huegelii 146, 155
Cryptandra arbutiflora 70, 212, 213, 214, 215
Cryptandra glabriflora 70, 212, 213, 214
Cyanicula deformis 147, 213, 214
Cyanicula sericea 148, 214
Cyathea cooperi 198

Cyathochaeta avenacea 120
Cymbopogon obtectus 114
Cynodon dactylon 118
Cynosurus echinatus 114
Cyperus alterniflorus 120

Daisies 45, 70, 164, 166, 167, 172, 175, 176, 186, 193, 222
Dampiera alata 181, 214, 215, 216, 218
Dampiera coronata 182, 213, 214
Dampiera hederacea 182, 215, 216
Dampiera incana 182, 210, 219
Dampiera lavandulacea 181, 215, 216
Dampiera linearis 182, 213, 214, 215
Dampiera trigona 181, 214, 215, 216
Dancing orchid 148
Dandelion 174, 213, 214, 219
Dark banded greenhood 149
Darling Range Ghost Gum 12
Darwinia apiculata 75, 214, 215
Darwinia citriodora 29, 75, 212, 213, 214, 215, 216, 218
Darwinia thymoides 75, 215, 217, 218
Daucus glochidiatus 195, 214
Daviesia angulata 46, 21, 212
Daviesia cordata 16, 48, 215, 217
Daviesia decurrens 46, 212, 213
Daviesia hakeoides 47, 212, 213, 214
Daviesia horrida 16, 48, 213, 214
Daviesia longifolia 47, 210, 218, 219
Daviesia polyphylla 47, 214, 215
Davesia preissii 47, 210, 218, 219
Daviesia rhombifolia 48, 213, 214
Dawny triggerplant 171
Delicate triggerplant 170
Dense stonecrop 195
Desmocladus fasciculatus 118
Desmocladus flexuosus 118, 139
Diamond of the desert 75, 196
Dianella revoluta 128, 141, 218, 219
Dichopogon capillipes 128, 141, 210, 211, 219
Dillwynia species 47, 214, 215
Dioscorea hastifolia 100, 211
Diplaena drummondii 76, 213, 214, 215
Diplopeltis huegelii 21, 53, 214, 218
Disa bracteata 151, 217, 218
Dischisma arenarium 185, 197
Dittrichia graveolens 175, 211, 212, 213, 214, 219
Diuris brumalis 152
Diuris laxiflora 152, 215, 217
Diuris longifolia 152, 215, 217
Diuris magnifica 153
Diuris setacea 217
Dodonaea ceratocarpa 76, 213, 214, 215, 216
Dodonaea ericoides 76, 210, 211
Donkey triggerplant 171
Drakaea gracilis 153
Drakaea livida 154, 158
Drakaea species 214, 215

Drooping heath 69
Drosera bullosa 186, 211, 212
Drosera erythrorhiza 186, 211, 212
Drosera gigantea 188, 214, 215, 217
Drosera glanduligera 187, 215, 217
Drosera heterophylla 187, 212, 213, 214
Drosera leucoblasta 187, 215, 217
Drosera macrantha 102, 212, 213, 214, 215
Drosera menziesii 188, 215, 217
Drosera microphylla 188
Drosera neesii 187, 214, 215
Drosera pallida 102, 214, 215
Drosera platystigma 187, 217, 218
Drosera pulchella 187, 211, 212, 218, 219
Drosera stolonifera 187, 213, 214
Drumstick isopogon 25, 66
Dwarf burchardia 125
Dwarf fringed lily 129
Dwarf greenhood 150
Dwarf leek fringed lily 129
Dwarf patersonia 130
Dwarf pink fairy 147
Dwarf sheoak 74
Dwarf yellow autumn lily 127
Dryandra armata 27, 77, 212, 213, 214, 215
Dryandra bipinnatifida 77, 216, 218
Dryandra lindleyana 77, 212, 213, 214, 215
Dryandra sessilis 26, 77, 211
Dryandra squarrosa 26, 41, 77, 214

Echium plantagineum 191, 216, 218
Ehrharta calycina 115
Eight-anthered sedge 121
Elbow orchid 153, 154
Elegant pronaya 103
Elythranthera brunonis 149, 217
Elythranthera emarginata 149, 217, 218
Eragrostis curvula 116
Eriochilus dilatatus 153, 211, 212
Eriochilus scaber 153, 213, 214, 215
Erodium botrys 180, 214
Erodium cicutarium 180, 214, 215
Eryngium pinnatifidum 177, 215, 216, 218
Eucalyptus calophylla 12, 210, 211
Eucalyptus laeliae 12, 217, 218
Eucalyptus marginata 13, 218, 219
Eucalyptus patens 12, 210, 211
Eucalyptus rudis 12, 214
Eucalyptus wandoo 12, 210, 211
Euchilopsis linearis 47, 216, 218
Euchiton sphaericus 176, 217, 218, 219
Evening Iris 127

False blind grass 127
False boronia 64, 125
False oat grass 116
Feather-spear 117

Feathertop 115
Felt-leaved thomasia 24
Fennel 177, 222
Few flowered thomasia 24, 62
Field bindweed 104
Field woodrush 121
Fingerbrush 75
Fireweeds 175
Flannel flower 178
Flat-topped coneflower 65
Flying Duck Orchid 153, 154
Foeniculum vulgare 177, 210, 213, 214, 219
Forest ricegrass 117
Foxtail mulga grass 115
Freesia 113, 132, 214
Freesia species 214
French catchfly 188
French flax 189
French lavender 53
Fringed leek orchid 151
Fringed lily 128, 129
Fringed mantis orchid 148
Fumaria capreolata 184, 213, 214
Fumaria muralis 184, 213, 214

Gahnia decomposita 120, 138
Galium divaricatum 194
Gastrolobium bilobum 17, 50
Gastrolobium spinosum 17, 50, 218, 219
Geranium retrorsum 180, 215, 217
Giant reed 114
Gladiolus caryophyllacus 132, 215, 217
Glischrocaryon aureum 192, 215, 217
Golden conostylis 132
Golden hibbertia 58
Golden triggerplant 170
Gomphocarpus fruticosus 23, 210
Gompholobium knightianum 50, 214, 218,. 219
Gompholobium marginatum 50, 214, 215, 217
Gompholobium polymorphum 50, 102, 214, 216, 218, 219
Gompholobium preissii 50, 218
Gompholobium shuttleworthii 51, 217, 218, 219
Gompholobium tomentosum 51, 217, 218
Gonocarpus cordiger 75, 210, 218, 219
Gonocarpus nodulosus 196, 214, 216
Goodenia caerulea 181, 218, 219
Goodenia claytoniacea 183, 217, 218
Graceful honeymyrtle 23, 73
Grammatotheca bergiana 182, 196, 211
Granite boronia 64
Granite featherflower 62
Granite petrophile 25, 65
Granite synaphea 57
Grass mat rush 123
Grass sedge 120
Grass tetratheca 63

Index 249

Grass trees 27, 226
Grass wattle 71
Grasses 100, 110, 114, 115, 116, 117, 225
Gratiola pubescens 185, 197, 210, 219
Grevillea 10, 18, 19, 44, 54, 56, 57, 210, 211, 212, 213, 214, 215, 217, 218, 219, 225
Grevillea bipinnatifida 57, 210, 211, 212, 213, 214, 218, 219
Grevillea diversifolia 18, 57, 212, 213, 214
Grevillea endlicheriana 19, 56, 212, 213, 214, 215, 217, 218
Grevillea manglesii 19, 32, 56, 212, 213, 214, 215, 217
Grevillea pilulifera 56, 212, 213, 214, 215, 217
Grevillea quercifolia 56, 214, 218, 219
Grevillea synapheae 56, 212, 213, 214, 215, 217
Grevillea wilsonii 19, 57, 210, 213, 214, 218, 219
Grey honeymyrtle 74
Grey stinkwood 18
Ground dryandra 77
Guildford grass 127

Haemodorum brevisepalum 124
Haemodorum laxum 124
Haemodorum paniculatum 123
Haemodorum simulans 124, 219
Haemodorum spicatum 124
Hairbrush hakea 55
Hairy flag 130
Hairy fringed lily 129
Hairy jugflower 57
Hakea 18, 19, 20, 21, 44, 54, 55, 210, 211, 212, 213, 214, 215, 217, 218, 225
Hakea amplexicaulis 20, 55, 213, 214, 215
Hakea auriculata 55
Hakea cristata 20, 55, 212, 213
Hakea cyclocarpa 21, 214
Hakea erinacea 21, 55, 212, 213, 214
Hakea incrassata 55, 212, 213, 214
Hakea lissocarpha 20, 55, 212, 213, 214
Hakea myrtoides 54, 212, 213, 214
Hakea petiolaris 20, 54, 212, 213
Hakea prostrata 20, 55, 215, 217
Hakea ruscifolia 20, 55, 210, 211
Hakea stenocarpa 54, 215, 217, 218
Hakea trifurcata 21, 55, 213, 214, 215, 217
Hakea undulata 19, 54, 214, 215
Hakea varia 19, 54, 213, 214
Halgania corymbosa 63, 214, 215, 217, 21
Haloragis brownii 196, 219
Hammer orchid 153, 154
Hardenbergia comptonina 101, 213, 214
Hare orchid 152
Harsh hakea 20, 55
Heart leaf poison 18, 50

Heart-leaved boronia 65
Hedgehog hakea 21, 55
Hedypnois rhagadioloides 174, 213, 214, 215, 217, 219
Helena synaphea 58
Helena velvet bush 24, 62
Helichrysum macranthum 173, 218, 219
Hemiandra pungens 53, 210, 215, 217, 218, 219
Hemigenia incana 21, 53, 212, 213, 214, 215, 217, 218
Hemigenia ramosissima 52, 212, 213, 214, 215, 217
Hemigenia sericea 53, 213, 214, 215, 217
Hesperantha falcata 127, 215, 217
Hibbertia acerosa 58, 219
Hibbertia amplexicaulis 59, 214, 215, 217, 218
Hibbertia aurea 58, 213, 214, 215, 217
Hibbertia commutata 59, 212, 213, 214, 215, 217
Hibbertia glomerata 59, 214, 217, 218, 219
Hibbertia hypenicoides 58, 211, 212, 213, 214, 215, 217
Hibbertia lasiopus 59
Hibbertia ovata 59, 212, 213, 214
Hibbertia pachyrrhiza 59, 210, 215, 217, 218, 219
Hibbertia serrata 23, 59, 212, 213, 214
Hibbertia spicata 58, 214, 215, 217, 218
Hibbertia subvaginata 23, 59, 215, 217, 218
Hispid stinkweed 194
Holcus lanatus 115
Holly flame pea 47
Holly-leaved hovea 47
Holly-leaved mirelia 18
Homalosciadium homalocarpum 195
Homeria flaccida 215
Homeria miniata 126, 215
Honey bush 20, 55
Hooked-leaf wattle 14, 72
Hop clover 179
Hordeum leporinum 117
Hordeum marinum 117
Hordeum spp. 117
Horn-leaved bossiaea 49
Horn triggerplant 168
Hovea chorizemifolia 47, 211, 212, 213
Hovea pungens 16, 213, 214
Hairy fringed lily 129
Hyalosperma cotula 172, 217, 218
Hyalosperma demissum 176
Hybanthus floribundus 52, 211, 213, 214
Hydrocotyle callicarpa 195, 214, 216
Hyparrhenia hirta 118
Hypocalymma angustifolium 60, 213, 214, 215, 217
Hypocalymma robustum 60, 214
Hypochaeris globra 174, 213, 214, 216, 217, 218, 219
Hypoxis accidentalis 133, 213, 214, 216, 217

Isolepis sp. 121
Isolepis marginata 121

Isopogon asper 65, 213, 214
Isopogon divergens 25, 66, 214, 218
Isopogon dubius 25, 66, 213, 214
Isopogon sphaerocephalus 25, 66, 213, 214, 216, 217
Isotoma hypocrateriformis 183, 217, 218, 219
Isotropis cuneifolia 52, 179, 215, 216

Jacksonia alata 51, 216, 217, 218
Jacksonia furcellata 18, 51
Jacksonia restioides 51, 215, 216, 218
Jacksonia sternbergiana 18, 51, 210, 211, 212, 213, 214, 216, 217, 219
Jarrah 13, 147, 225
Jug orchid 150
Juncus effusus 121
Juncus holoschoenus 121
Juncus pallidus 121

Kangaroo grass 117
Kangaroo paw 132, 133
Karri dampiera 182
Karri hazel 28, 76
Kennedia coccinea 101, 214, 215
Kennedia prostrata 101, 214, 215
Kennedia stirlingii 101, 214, 215
Kick bush 68
Kingia australis 27, 210, 211, 218, 219
Knotweed 197
Kunzea recurva 22, 214, 215, 217, 218

Labichea lanceolata 21, 53, 216
Labichea punctata 53, 213, 214, 216, 217
Lagenophora huegelii 174, 216, 217, 218
Lagurus ovatus 115
Lamb poison 52, 179
Lambertia 18, 21, 44, 54, 56, 213, 214, 216, 217, 218
Lambertia multiflora 21, 56, 213, 214, 216, 217, 218
Lanced leaf labichea 53
Large flowered hibbertia 59
Large fruited thomasia 62
Largeflower wood sorrel 190
Lasiopetalum bracteatum 24, 62, 214, 218
Lasiopetalum glabratum 62, 212, 213, 214
Lathyrus tingitanus 179
Laughing leek orchid 151
Lavandula stoechas 53, 213, 214, 218
Lawrencella rosea 172
Laxmannia ramosa 125, 212
Laxmannia sessiliflora 125, 212, 213
Laxmannia squarrosa 125, 212, 213, 214
Leaf sedge 120
Leafless globe pea 51
Leafless rock wattle 71
Leaping spider orchid 148
Lechenaultia biloba 52, 213, 96, 214, 215,
Lemon-scented darwinia 75
Leopard orchid 146
Lepidobolus chaetocephalus 119
Lepidobolus preissianus 119
Lepidobolus spp. 119
Lepidosperma spp. 120

Lepidosperma drummondii 120
Lepidosperma squamatum 120
Lepidosperma tenue 120
Lepidosperma tetraquetrum 120
Lepidosperma tuberculatum 120
Leporella fimbriata 152, 211, 212
Leptocarpus spp. 119
Leptocarpus tenax 119
Leptoceras menziesii 153
Leptomeria cunninghamii 75, 214, 215, 216
Leptospemum erubescens 22, 214, 216, 217
Leptospemum laevigatum 22, 216
Lesser broomrape 185
Lesser snapdragon 185
Lesser waxflower 70
Leucopogon capitellatus 69, 213, 214, 216, 217
Leucopogon cymbiformis 69, 210, 219
Leucopogon nutans 69, 212
Leucopogon oxycedrus 69, 212
Leucopogon propinquus 69, 211, 212
Leucopogon pulchellus 69, 212, 213, 214, 216
Leucopogon sprengelioides 69, 213, 214, 216
Leucopogon tenuis 69, 210, 219
Leucopogon verticillatus 28, 215, 216
Levenhookia pusilla 168, 194, 217, 218
Levenhookia stipitata 169, 218, 219
Linum marginale 189
Lindsaea linearis 198
Linum marginale 189
Linum trigynum 189, 216, 217, 218, 219
Little Kangaroo paw 133
Little leek orchid 152
Lobelia alata 182, 210, 211, 212, 213, 214, 219
Lobelia gibbosa 183, 210, 211, 219
Lobelia heterophylla 183, 210, 219
Lobelia rhombifolia 182, 183, 215, 217
Lobelia rhytidosperma 183, 217, 218
Lobelia tenuir 183, 215, 217
Logania campanulata 189, 210, 219
Logania serpyllifoalia 189, 217, 218, 219
Lolium perenne 117
Lolium rigidum 117
Lolium spp. 117
Lomandra brittanii 123, 216, 217
Lomandra caespitosa 122, 212, 213
Lomandra drummondii 122, 211, 212
Lomandra hermaphrodita 122, 211
Lomandra integra 123, 214
Lomandra micrantha 123, 213, 214, 215
Lomandra nigricans 122, 212, 213
Lomandra odora 123, 214
Lomandra preissii 122, 212
Lomandra purpurea 123, 128, 215, 217
Lomandra senicea 122, 213, 214
Lomandra sonderi 123, 217
Lomandra spartea 122, 213
Lomandra suaveolens 212
Long Storksbill 180
Lotus angustissimus 180, 210

Index 251

Love creeper 102
Lovely triggerplant 171
Loxocarya cinerea 118
Loxocaryra spp. 118
Lupinus albus 179
Lupinus angustifolius 179
Lupinus luteus 179
Lupins species 179, 215, 216, 217, 218
Luzula meridonalis 121
Lyperanthus serratus 150, 215, 217

Macrozamia riedlei 27
Many-flowered lambertia 56
Many-flowered honeysuckle 21
Marble hakea 55
Marianthus candidus 103, 218
Marianthus coerulea-punctatus 103, 211
Marri 12
Matted triggerplant 101, 169
Medicago polymorpha 178, 213, 214
Mediterranean turnip 192
Melaleuca incana 74, 219
Melaleuca preissiana 15, 218, 219
Melaleuca radula 23, 73, 215, 217, 218
Melaleuca rhaphiophylla 15, 218
Melaleuca parviceps 74, 82, 215, 217, 218
Melaleuca species 74, 219
Melinis repens 115, 211, 212
Mentha spicata 178, 210, 219
Microcorys longifolia 53, 218
Microtis alba 150, 217, 218
Microtis atrata 151, 217, 218
Microtis media 150
Midget stylewort 168
Milk maid 126
Milkworts 184, 225
Millotia myosotidifolia 175, 217
Millotia tenuifolia 175, 217
Mirbelia dilatata 18, 49, 218, 219
Mirbelia ramulosa 51, 215, 217
Mirbelia spinosa 17, 49, 214, 216, 217
Misopates orontium 185, 213, 215, 217, 218
Monopsis debilis 183, 196, 219
Monotaxis grandiflora 75, 196, 216, 217, 218
Moonah 16
Morning iris 126
Mosquito orchid 146
Moss-leaved heath 68
Mouse-ear chickweed 188
Muehlenbeckia adpressa 104, 215, 217, 218, 219
Mulga fern 199
Myriophyllum crispatum 196, 210, 219
Myrtyle hakea 54
Myrtles 15, 60

Narrow fruited hakea 54
Narrow-leaved oxylobium 17
Narrow winged wattle 71
Narrow-leaved mistletoe 104
Narrowleaf clover 179
Narrowleaf cottonbush 24
Narrowleaf trefoil 180
Native broom 52
Native carrot 195
Native fuchsia 19, 57
Native gerbera 174
Native Iris 130, 223
Native parsnip 177, 195
Native pelargonium 180
Native wisteria 101
Native yam 100
Needle-leaved mat rush 122
Nemcia acuta 50
Nemcia capitata 49, 213, 214
Nemcia dilata 50, 214
Nemcia reticulata 48, 214
Nemcia spathulata 49
Neurachne alopecuroidea 115
Noddying lily 125, 128
Nuytsia floribunda 23, 218, 219

Oak-leaved grevillea 56
Olearia paucidentata 70, 211, 212, 213, 222
Opercularia echinocephala 194, 214, 215, 217, 218
Opercularia hispidula 194, 215, 217
Opercularia vaginata 194, 214, 215, 217
Ophioglossum lusitanicum 198
Oligochaetochilus sanguineus 149, 212, 213, 214
Oligochaetochilus vittatus 149, 212, 213, 214
Orange wattle 14, 72
Orchids 143, 144, 145, 146, 147, 151, 153, 224, 229
Orobanche minor 185, 218, 219
Orthrosanthus laxus 126, 214, 215
Oxalis corniculata 190, 214, 216
Oxalis glabra 190, 212, 213, 214
Oxalis pes-caprae 190, 212, 213, 214
Oxalis purpurea 190, 212, 214
Oxylobium lineare 17, 48, 210, 218, 219

Painted billardiera 102
Pale fawn 114, 175, 176
Pale grass lily 123
Pale rush 120
Pale sundew 102
Pale turpentine bush 29
Pampas grass 114
Pansy orchid 152, 153
Papery-Bracted Everlastings 222
Paracalaena nigrita 154, 214
Paraserianthes lophantha 14, 213, 214
Parentucrllia latifolia 185, 215, 217, 218
Parentucellia viscosa 185, 218, 219

Parietaria devilis 197, 214
Parrot bush 26, 77
Paspalum 118
Paspalum dilatatum 118
Patersonia babianoides 130, 215, 217
Patersonia juncea 131
Patersonia accidentalis 130, 214, 215
Patersonia pygmaea 130
Patersonia rudis 130, 215, 217
Patersonia umbrosa 130, 216, 217
Peas 16, 46, 101, 224
Pelargonium littorale 180, 214
Pellitory 197
Pennisetum villosum 115
Pentapeltis petigera 177, 210, 211
Pepper and salt 64
Pericalymma ellipticum 23, 216, 217, 219
Persoonia angustiflora 67, 210, 218, 219
Persoonia elliptica 26, 210, 219
Persoonia longifolia 26, 210
Petrophile biloba 25, 213, 214, 216
Petrophile seminuda 66, 214, 216, 217, 218
Petrophile striata 66, 216, 217, 218
Petrorhagia velutina 189, 215, 217
Philydrella pygmaea 133, 218
Philotheca spicata 64, 95, 212, 213, 214, 218
Phyllanthus calycinus 64, 213, 214, 216, 217
Phyllangium paradoxum 197, 217, 218
Pilostyles hamiltonii 46, 48, 105, 210, 211, 220
Pimelea argentea 26, 67, 216, 217
Pimelea brevistyla 66, 216, 217, 218
Pimelea ciliata 67, 216, 217, 218
Pimelea imbricata 67, 216, 217, 218, 219
Pimelea lehmanniana 67
Pimelea preissii 67, 216, 217, 218
Pimelea spectabilis 26, 67, 216, 217,. 218
Pimelea suaveolens 66, 212, 213, 214, 216, 217
Pincushions 126
Pindak 15
Pingle 27, 77
Pink bindweed 104
Pink bunny orchid 153
Pink enamel orchid 149
Pink petticoats 184
Pins-and-needles 169
Pithocarpa corymbulosa 173, 210, 211, 219
Plantago lanceolata 121, 214
Platysace juncea 210
Platysace compressa 177, 210, 211
Pleurosorus rutifolius 198
Plum orchid 147
Poa sp. 116
Podolepis gracilis 173
Podolepis lessonii 175, 216, 217, 218
Podotheca amgustifolia 175, 217, 218
Poison bush 50
Polygonum aviculare 197, 210, 211, 219

Poranthera microphylla 193, 216, 217
Potato lowered thomasia 63
Prasophyllum brownii 152
Prasophyllum elatum 152, 216, 217, 218
Prasophyllum fimbria 151, 213, 214, 215
Prasophyllum giganteum 151, 215, 217
Prasophyllum gracile 151, 214
Prasophyllum hians 151, 216, 217
Prasophyllum parvifolium 151, 212, 213, 214
Prasophyllum plumiforme 152
Prickly bitter-pea 16, 46
Prickly conostylis 131
Prickly dryandra 27, 77
Prickly hakea 20, 55
Prickly mirbelia 49
Prickly moses 14, 70
Prickly poison 17, 50
Prickly wattle 13
Pronaya fraseri 103, 210, 211, 219
Pteridum esculentum 198
Pterochaeta paniculata 176
Plumatichilos barbatus 150, 214, 215
Pterostylis pyramidalis 150, 158, 214, 215
Pterostylis recurva 150, 214, 215
Ptilotus declinatus 177, 218, 219
Ptilotus drummondii 176, 217, 218
Ptilotus esquamatus 176, 217, 218
Ptilotus manglesii 176, 210, 217, 218, 219
Ptilotus spathulatus 176, 217, 218
Pultenea ericifolia 214, 215, 217
Purple beaufortia 15, 73
Purple enamel orchid 149
Purple flag 130
Purple mat rush 123, 128
Purple pansy orchid 152
Purple tassels 127
Pyrorchis nigricans 150, 156

Quandong 29
Queen trigger plant 133, 170

Rabbit orchid 153
Ramshorn hakea 21, 55
Ranunculus colonorum 189, 213, 214, 216
Raphanus raphanistrum 192, 214, 215
Rattle beaks 150
Reed triggerplant 171
Red beaks 150
Red ink sundew 186
Red natal grass 114, 115
Rhodanthe 172, 215, 217, 218
Rhodanthe citrina 172, 216, 218, 219, 222
Rhodanthe corymbosa 173, 218, 219
Rib-leaved patersonia 130
Ribbed wattle 72
Ribwort plantain 121
Rice flower 26, 66, 68

Index

Ricinocarpos glaucus 62, 79, 137, 215, 216,
Rinzia crassifolia 60, 213, 215, 216, 217, 218, 219
Roadside teatree 22
Rock fern 198
Rock sheoak 29
Romulea rosea 127, 214, 216, 217
Rose coneflower 25, 66
Rose-tipped mulla mulla 176
Rough dogstail 114
Rough honeymyrtle 74
Rough tree fern 198
Royal robe 181
Rubus aff selmeri 24, 104
Rulingia cygnorum 63, 216, 217, 218
Rumex crispus 197
Running postman 102
Rush Jacksonia 51
Rush leaf patersonia 131
Rusty Kennedia 102
Rye grass 117

Sailboat wattle 14, 73
Samolus junceus 190, 218
Santalum acuminatum 29, 210
Saw false mat rush 127
Saw sedge 120
Scaevola calliptera 181, 217, 218, 219
Scaevola glandulifera 181, 211, 215, 217, 218, 219, 210
Scaevola pilosa 181, 218, 219
Scaevola platyphylla 52, 210, 215, 217, 218, 219
Scarlet or blue pimpernel 190
Scarp darwinia 75
Scented banjine 66
Scented haemodorum 124
Scented sun orchid 146
Schoenolaena juncea 178, 210, 211, 220
Schoenus benthamii 120
Schoenus globifer 120
Schoenus unispiculatus 120
Schoenus spp. 120
Screw fern 198
Scrub sheoak 29, 74
Sea urchin hakea 20
Sedge conostylis 131
Selaginella gracillima 199
Semaphore sedge 120
Senecio hispidulus 175
Senecio lautus 174, 218
Senecio quadridentatus 175
Senecio ramosissimus 175, 216, 217
Senecio species 211, 212, 213, 214, 215, 219
Sheoak 11, 27, 29, 74, 222
Shivery grass 116
Showy billardiera 103
Showy hybanthus 52

Shrub persoonia 67
Silene gallica 188, 213, 215, 216, 217, 219, 220
Silky blue orchid 148
Silky heads 114
Silky hemigenia 22, 53
Silky mat rush 122
Silver grass 116, 117
Silvery leaved pimelea 26, 67
Slender blackboy 128
Slender cicendia 196
Slender fringed lily 129
Slender smokebush 57
Slender sun orchid 146
Small flower mat rush 123
Small pennywort 195
Smooth grevillea 19, 56
Snail hakea 20, 55
Snakebush 53
Snottygobble 25, 26, 225
Solanum nigrum 191, 210, 211, 212, 213, 215, 216, 217, 219, 220
Sollya heterophylla 24, 104, 210, 217, 218, 219
Sonchus oleraceus 173, 215, 216, 217, 218
Sorrel 190, 197
Soursop 190
Sowerbaea laxiflora 127, 214, 216
Spearmint 178
Sphaerolobium medium 51, 216, 217
Sphaerolobium vimineum 51
Spiculaea ciliata 210, 218, 219
Spindly grevillea 19, 56
Spiny wattle 13, 72
Spotted billardiera 103
Spreading coneflower 25, 66
Spreading snottygobble 26
Spurges 62, 193, 196, 223
Square sedge 120
Stachys arvensis 185, 196, 214, 216, 217, 219
Stachystemon vermicularis 75, 210, 211, 212, 219
Stackhousia monogyna 191, 215, 216, 217, 219, 220
Stagger weed 185, 196
Star orchid 147
Stellaria media 188, 195, 213, 215
Stem flower 105
Sticky bartsia 185
Sticky calytrix 61
Sticky thomasia 63
Stinkwood 18
Stinkwort 75
Stirlingia latifolia 28, 215, 216
Stirlingia simplex 65, 217, 218
Storksbill 180
Stylidium affine 133, 170, 216, 217
Stylidium amoenum 171
Stylidium breviscapum 169, 219
Stylidium brunonianum 171, 216, 217, 219
Stylidium bulbiferum 169, 217, 219

Stylidium calcaratum 168, 216, 217
Stylidium canaliculatum 170, 217, 218
Stylidium carnosum 170, 190, 217, 219
Stylidium ciliatum 170, 217
Stylidium crassifolium 171, 217, 219
Stylidium dichotomum 169, 218, 219
Stylidium diuroides 171, 217, 218
Stylidium diversifolium 172
Stylidium emarginatum 168
Stylidium hispidum 170, 216, 217
Stylidium inundatum 168
Stylidium junceum 171
Stylidium leptophyllum 169, 219
Stylidium lineatum 171, 218
Stylidium perpusillum 171, 219, 220
Stylidium petiolare 168, 216, 217
Stylidium piliferum 170, 216, 217
Stylidium pubigerum 170, 216, 217
Stylidium pycnostachyum 171, 217, 218
Stylidium repens 101, 169, 210, 211, 212, 213, 215, 216, 219
Stylidium rhyncocarpum 169, 219, 220
Stylidium rigidifolium 172, 217, 218
Stylidium schoenoides 133, 170, 216, 218
Stypandra glauca 127, 214, 215
Styphelia tenuiflora 68, 211, 212
Subterraneum clover 179
Sugar candy orchid 148
Sun orchid 167, 147
Sundews 102, 186, 222, 223
Sunny triggerplant 171
Swamp banksia 16, 66
Swamp migonette 151
Swamp paperbark 15
Swamp pea 47
Swamp peppermint 22
Swamp teatree 33
Swan River blackbutt 12
Swan River daisy 173
Swan River myrtle 60
Swishbush 18
Sword sedges 120
Synaphea 44, 54, 56, 57, 58, 212, 213, 214,215, 216, 217, 218
Synaphea acutiloba 57, 58, 212, 213, 215, 216
Synaphea gracillima 58, 212, 213, 215, 216, 217, 218
Synaphea pinnata 58, 216, 217

Tagasaste 17
Tall labichea 21, 54
Tall leek orchid 152
Tambookie grass 118
Tangier pea 179
Tapeworm plant 177
Taraxacum officinale 174, 213, 215, 220
Tassel flower 28
Templetonia biloba 46, 49, 212, 213

Templetonia drummondii 48, 215
Tetraria octandra 121
Tetrarrhena laevis 117
Tetratheca hirsuta 63, 212, 213, 215, 216, 217, 219
Tetratheca nuda 63, 217, 219
Thelymitra antennifera 146, 213, 215, 216
Thelymitra benthamiana 146
Thelymitra crinita 146, 215, 217, 218
Thelymitra dedmaniarum 147
Thelymitra flexuosa 146, 215, 216
Thelymitra macrophylla 146
Thelymitra mucida 147, 217
Thelymitra pauciflora 146
Thelymitra stellata 147
Themeda triandra 117, 139
Thomasia foliosa 62, 212, 213, 215
Thomasia glutinosa 63, 216, 217, 219, 220
Thomasia grandiflora 63, 218, 219
Thomasia macrocarpa 24, 62, 216, 217
Thomasia pauciflora 24, 62, 217, 219
Three awn grass 116
Thysanotus anceps 130, 210, 219
Thysanotus arbuscula 129
Thysanotus asper 129
Thysanotus dichotomus 129, 215, 217
Thysanotus fastigiatus 130, 219
Thysanotus gracilis 129
Thysanotus multiflorus 129, 215, 217
Thysanotus patersonii 100, 128, 214, 216, 217, 218, 219
Thysanotus scaber 129
Thysanotus sparteus 130, 210, 218, 219
Thysanotus tenellus 129
Thysanotus thyrsoideus 128, 214, 216
Thysanotus triandrus 129, 217, 218
Tiered mat rush 123
Tiny triggerplant 169
Tolpis barbata 174, 215, 220
Toothed wattle 14, 72
Touch-me-not 17
Trachymene coerulea 177, 217, 218
Trachymene pilosa 195, 215, 216, 218, 219
Tree Lucerne 17
Tribonanthes australis 125, 215
Tribonanthes brachypetala 125, 213
Tribonanthes longipetala 125, 137, 213
Tribonanthes violacea 125, 213
Trichocline spathulata 174, 210, 219, 220
Tricoryne elatior 128, 216, 217, 219, 220
Tricoryne humilis 127
Trifolium angustifolium 179, 220
Trifolium arvense 179
Trifolium campestre 179, 215
Trifolium repens 179, 210, 215, 220
Trifolium subterraneum 179, 215
Triggerplants 164, 168, 223, 226, 229
Triglochin lineare 124

Index 255

Tripterococcus brunonis 192, 212, 215, 216, 217, 219, 220
Trumpets 131
Trymalium floribundum 28, 76, 215, 216
Trymalium ledifolium 76, 212, 213, 215, 216
Tuffed mat rush 122
Twiggy mullein 190
Twisted sun orchid 146
Two-leafed hakea 21
Two-sided fringed lily 130

Ursinia anthemoides 174, 216, 217, 219, 220
Utricularia multifida 184, 216, 217

Vanilla orchid 146
Variable billardiera 103
Variable gompholobium 50, 102
Variable-leafed heakea 19, 54
Variable-leaved grevillea 18, 57
Variegated featherflower 61
Veldt grass 115
Velleia trinervis 183, 217, 219, 220
Vellereophyton dealbatum 176, 218, 219, 220
Velvet pink 189
Verbascum virgatum 190, 212, 213, 215
Verticordia acerosa 61, 215, 216, 217, 219, 220
Verticordia densiflora 62, 210, 219, 220
Verticordia huegelil 61, 216, 218, 219
Verticordia insignis 61, 216, 217, 219
Verticordia pennigera 62, 216, 217, 219, 220
Verticordia plumosa 62, 216, 217, 219, 220
Villarsia albiflora 189, 218, 219
Viminaria juncea 18, 51, 217, 219, 220
Vulpia myuros 117

W.A. flooded gum 12
Wahlenbergia capensis 191
Wahlenbergia stricta 191, 216
Waitzia nitida 172
Waitzia suaveolens 173, 219, 220
Wall fumitory 184
Wandoo 12, 26, 62, 67, 101, 102, 177, 190, 210, 211
Warrine 100
Warty hammer orchid 154
Water bush 17, 49
Water ribbons 124
Waterbuttons 175
Watsonias 132
Watsonia meriana var bulbillifera 132, 220
Watsonia meriana 132
Watsonia species 217, 219
Watsonias versfeldii 132
Wattles 13, 70, 99, 104, 223, 224

Wavy-leaved hakea 19, 54
Wavy-leaved wattle 72
Waxy cryptandra 70
Wedding bush 62
Wedge-leaved oxylobium 50
White banjine 67
White bunny orchid 153
White candles 191
White clover 179
White cottonhead 131
White fairy orchid 149
White mignonette 150
White murtle 60
White spider orchid 149
White spray 103
White tribonanthes 124
Whiteflower fumitory 184
Wild flax 189
Wild gladiolus 132
Wild oats 116
Wild radish 192
Winged Jacksonia 51
Winged wattle 13, 71
Winged-stem dampiera 181
Wiry mitrewort 197
Wiry wattle 13, 72
Wood mat rush 123
Woodbridge poison 183
Woolly flowered grevillea 56
Woolly-heads 47
Wormflower 75
Wurmbea tenella 125, 213

Xanthorrhoea gracilis 128, 216, 218
Xanthorrhoea preissii 27, 213, 215, 216
Xanthosia atkinsoniana 178, 210, 211, 219, 220
Xanthosia candida 177, 218, 219
Xanthosia ciliata 177, 218, 219
Xanthosia huegelii 177, 193, 214, 218, 219
Xanthosia pusilla 178, 218, 219

Yawning leek orchid 151
Yellow autumn lily 128
Yellow buttercup 58
Yellow calytrix 61
Yellow candles 192
Yellow-eyed flame pea 49
Yellow flags 130
Yellow spider orchid 147
Yellow star 133
Yellow-eyed flame pea 49
Yorkshire fog grass 115

Zamia 11, 27, 227

A
Glimpse of
Walk Trail
Fauna